# Search Engine Optimization

## FOR

# DUMMIES®

### 2ND EDITION

# Search Engine Optimization For Dummies, 2nd Edition

*Cheat Sheet*

## The Most Important Search Sites and Feeders

Get into these systems, and you've got most of the Web's searches covered. Chapter 1 explains why.

- **Google:** www.google.com
- **Yahoo!:** www.yahoo.com
- **The Open Directory Project:** www.dmoz.org
- **MSN:** www.msn.com
- **Ask.com:** www.ask.com

## Your 1-Hour Search-Engine Friendly Web Site Makeover Checklist

In Chapter 2, you find how to quickly analyze your site for problems. Ask yourself the following questions:

- Is my site already in the Google index?
- Are some of my sites invisible to search engines?
- Have I checked my keywords with Overture's keyword tool?
- Am I using frames?
- Do I have a good page TITLE?
- Do I have a good DESCRIPTION tag?
- Is my site navigation visible to the search engines?
- Do I have a pointless Flash animation on the front page?
- Do I have real text, or is it embedded into images?
- Do I have page content with the right keywords?
- Do I have links pointing to my site?

## Finding Sites to Link to Yours

Links to your site are critical to your search engine ranking. This checklist should help jog your memory about ways to get these links:

- Search Directories — Yahoo! Directory, the Open Directory Project, and specialty directories
- Friends and family
- Employees
- Association sites
- Manufacturers' Web sites
- Companies you do business with
- Announcement sites and newsletters
- Press releases
- Pages linking to your competition
- Reciprocal link requests
- Link-building software and services
- E-mail newsletters
- Discussion groups
- Offline PR
- Award sites

In addition, you may want to try these methods:

- Respond to link-swap requests.
- Search for *keyword add url.*
- Create a blog page.
- Give away content.
- Advertise.
- Use a service or buy links.
- Ask to be a featured client.
- Promote something on your site.
- Ask other sites for links.

*For Dummies: Bestselling Book Series for Beginners*

# Search Engine Optimization For Dummies, 2nd Edition

Cheat Sheet

## Things to Do When Building Web Pages

- ✔ Use keywords that result from a full keyword analysis.
- ✔ Pick one or two phrases for each page.
- ✔ Keep other keywords in mind while building the pages.
- ✔ Use keywords in filenames and directory names.
- ✔ Keep a shallow directory tree; don't have too many levels of subdirectories.
- ✔ Create a good TITLE right below <HTML>.
- ✔ Create a KEYWORDS meta tag (but don't worry too much about the details).
- ✔ Create a good DESCRIPTION meta tag. (This is much more important than the KEYWORDS.)
- ✔ Make sure your pages contain actual text, not text embedded into images.
- ✔ Use Cascading Style Sheets if you wish, but use them in combination with <H> tags.
- ✔ Use keywords in <H> tags, bold, italics, bullets, <STRONG> tags, and title case.
- ✔ Use important keywords near the top of the page and multiple times.
- ✔ Use keywords in your link text — no more click here links!
- ✔ Don't overdo any of these techniques!

## Places to Submit Your Site's URL

The following systems accept free URL submissions; remember, though, that submitting your site may not help. You need links to your site to make sure you get picked up.

- ✔ **Google:** www.google.com/addurl. html
- ✔ **Yahoo:** http://search.yahoo.com/ info/submit.html
- ✔ **MSN:** http://search.msn.com/ docs/submit.aspx
- ✔ **The Open Directory Project:** www.dmoz.org

## Shopping Directories

If you sell a product online, you should check out these directories. A few are free, but some charge for every click they send you.

- ✔ **Google Catalogs:** catalogs.google.com
- ✔ **Froogle:** www.froogle.com
- ✔ **Yahoo! Shopping:** shopping.yahoo.com
- ✔ **Shopping.com:** www.shopping.com
- ✔ **Shop.com:** www.shop.com
- ✔ **PriceGrabber.com:** www.pricegrabber.com
- ✔ **BizRate & Shopzilla:** www.shopzilla.com
- ✔ **NexTag:** www.nextag.com
- ✔ **Price Watch:** www.pricewatch.com
- ✔ **PriceSCAN:** www.pricescan.com

**For Dummies: Bestselling Book Series for Beginners**

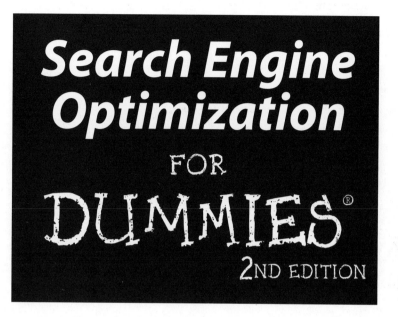

# Search Engine Optimization

## FOR

## DUMMIES®

### 2ND EDITION

**by Peter Kent**

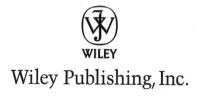

Wiley Publishing, Inc.

**Search Engine Optimization For Dummies®, 2nd Edition**

Published by
**Wiley Publishing, Inc.**
111 River Street
Hoboken, NJ 07030-5774

www.wiley.com

Copyright © 2006 by Wiley Publishing, Inc., Indianapolis, Indiana

Published by Wiley Publishing, Inc., Indianapolis, Indiana

Published simultaneously in Canada

For general information on our other products and services, please contact our Customer Care Department within the U.S. at 800-762-2974, outside the U.S. at 317-572-3993, or fax 317-572-4002.

For technical support, please visit www.wiley.com/techsupport.

Wiley also publishes its books in a variety of electronic formats. Some content that appears in print may not be available in electronic books.

Library of Congress Control Number: 2006921155

ISBN-13: 978-0-471-97998-2

ISBN-10: 0-471-97998-8

Manufactured in the United States of America

10 9 8 7 6 5 4 3 2 1

2B/RZ/QU/QW/IN

WILEY

# About the Author

**Peter Kent** is the author of numerous other books about the Internet, including *Pay Per Click Search Engine Marketing For Dummies,* the best-selling *Complete Idiot's Guide to the Internet,* and the most widely reviewed and praised title in computer-book history, *Poor Richard's Web Site: Geek Free, Commonsense Advice on Building a Low-Cost Web Site*. His work has been praised by *USA Today, BYTE,* CNN.com, *Windows Magazine, Philadelphia Inquirer,* and many others.

Peter has been online since 1984, doing business in cyberspace since 1991, and writing about the Internet since 1993. Peter's experience spans virtually all areas of doing business online, from editing and publishing an e-mail newsletter to creating e-commerce Web sites, from online marketing and PR campaigns to running a Web-design and -hosting department for a large ISP.

Peter was the founder of an e-Business Service Provider funded by one of the world's largest VC firms, Softbank/Mobius. He was VP of Web Solutions for a national ISP and VP of Marketing for a Web applications firm. He also founded a computer-book publishing company launched through a concerted online marketing campaign.

Peter now consults with businesses about their Internet strategies, helping them to avoid the pitfalls and to leap the hurdles they'll encounter online. He also gives seminars and presentations on subjects related to online marketing in general and search engine marketing in particular. He can be contacted at Consult@PeterKentConsulting.com, and more information about his background and experience is available at www.PeterKentConsulting.com.

# Dedication

*For the boys, who haven't had a book dedicated to them in awhile*

# Author's Acknowledgments

I'd like to thank all my clients, who have given me an opportunity to play with search-engine optimization in a wide variety of businesses. I'd also like to thank Acquisitions Editor Terri Varveris, who has moved on, but whose assistance was critical in getting my idea from proposal to contract, and my editors Susan Pink and Tonya Cupp, who kept me on the straight and narrow. And, of course, the multitude of Wiley staff involved in editing, proofreading, and laying out the book.

## Publisher's Acknowledgments

We're proud of this book; please send us your comments through our online registration form located at www.dummies.com/register/.

Some of the people who helped bring this book to market include the following:

*Acquisitions, Editorial, and Media Development*

**Project Editor:** Tonya Maddox Cupp

*Previous Edition: Paul Levesque*

**Acquisitions Editor:** Tiffany Franklin

**Technical Editor:** Tyler Knott Gregson

**Editorial Manager:** Jodi Jensen

**Media Development Specialists:** Angela Denny, Kate Jenkins, Steven Kudirka, Kit Malone, Travis Silvers

**Media Development Coordinator:** Laura Atkinson

**Media Project Supervisor:** Laura Moss

**Media Development Manager:** Laura VanWinkle

**Media Development Associate Producer:** Richard Graves

**Editorial Assistant:** Amanda Foxworth

**Cartoons:** Rich Tennant (www.the5thwave.com)

*Composition*

**Project Coordinator:** Erin Smith

**Layout and Graphics:** Andrea Dahl, Stephanie D. Jumper, Barbara Moore

**Proofreaders:** Jessica Kramer, Christine Pingleton, Techbooks

**Indexer:** Techbooks

**Special Help:** Susan Pink

---

*Publishing and Editorial for Technology Dummies*

> **Richard Swadley,** Vice President and Executive Group Publisher
>
> **Andy Cummings,** Vice President and Publisher
>
> **Mary Bednarek,** Executive Acquisitions Director
>
> **Mary C. Corder,** Editorial Director

*Publishing for Consumer Dummies*

> **Diane Graves Steele,** Vice President and Publisher
>
> **Joyce Pepple,** Acquisitions Director

*Composition Services*

> **Gerry Fahey,** Vice President of Production Services
>
> **Debbie Stailey,** Director of Composition Services

# Contents at a Glance

# Table of Contents

# Introduction

*W*elcome to *Search Engine Optimization For Dummies,* 2nd Edition. What on earth would you want this book for? After all, can't you just build a Web site, and then pay someone $25 to register the site with thousands of search engines? I'm sure you've seen the advertising: "We guarantee top-ten placement in a gazillion search engines!" "We'll register you in 5,000 search engines today!"

Well, unfortunately, it's not that simple. (Okay, fortunately for me, because if it were simple, Wiley wouldn't pay me to write this book.) The fact is that search engine optimization is a little complicated. Not brain surgery complicated, but not as easy as "Give us 50 bucks and we'll handle it for you."

The vast majority of Web sites don't have a chance in the search engines. Why? Because of simple mistakes. Because the people creating the sites don't have a clue what they should do to make the site easy for search engines to work with. Because they don't understand the role of links pointing to their site, and because they've never thought about keywords. Because, because, because. This book helps you deal with those becauses and gets you not just one step, but dozens of steps, ahead of the average Web-site Joe.

## About This Book

This book demystifies the world of search engines. You find out what you need to do to give your site the best possible chance to rank well in the search engines.

In this book, I show you how to

- ✔ Make sure that you're using the right keywords in your Web pages.

- ✔ Create pages that search engines can read and will index in the way *you* want them to.

- ✔ Avoid techniques that search engines hate — things that can get your Web site penalized (knocked down low in search engine rankings).

- ✔ Build pages that give your site greater visibility in search engines.

- ✔ Get search engines and directories to include your site in their indexes and lists.
- ✔ Get search engines to display your site when people search locally.
- ✔ Encourage other Web sites to link to yours.
- ✔ Keep track of how well your site is doing.
- ✔ Use pay-per-click advertising and shopping directories.
- ✔ And plenty more!

# Foolish Assumptions

I don't want to assume anything, but I have to believe that if you're reading this book, you already know a few things about the Internet and search engines. Things such as

- ✔ You have access to a computer that has access to the Internet.
- ✔ You know how to use a Web browser to get around the Internet.
- ✔ You know how to carry out searches at the Web's major search engines, such as Google and Yahoo!

Of course, for a book like this, I have to assume a little more. This is a book about how to get your Web site to rank well in the search engines. I have to assume that you know how to create and work with a site, or at least know someone who can create and work with a site. In particular, you (or the other person) know how to

- ✔ Set up a Web site.
- ✔ Create Web pages.
- ✔ Load those pages onto your Web server.
- ✔ Work with *HTML (HyperText Markup Language),* the coding used to create Web pages. In other words, you're not just using a program such as Microsoft FrontPage — you, or your geek, understand a little about HTML and feel comfortable enough with it to insert or change HTML tags.

I don't go into a lot of complicated code in this book; this isn't a primer on HTML. But in order to do search-engine work, you or someone on your team needs to know what a TITLE tag is, for instance, and how to insert it into a page; how to recognize JavaScript (though not how to create or modify it); how to open a Web page in a text editor and modify it; and so on. You have to have basic HTML skills in order to optimize a site for the search engines. If you need more information about HTML, take a look at *HTML 4 For Dummies,* 5th Edition, by Ed Tittel and Natanya Pitts (Wiley).

# How This Book Is Organized

Like all good reference tools, this book is designed to be read "as needed." It's divided into several parts: the basics, building search-engine-friendly Web sites, getting your site into the search engines, what to do after your site is indexed by the search engines, search engine advertising, and the Part of Tens. So if you just want to know how to find sites that will link to your Web site, read Chapter 15. If you need to understand the principles behind getting links to your site, read Chapter 14. If all you need today is to figure out what keywords are important to your site, Chapter 5 is for you.

However, search engine optimization is a pretty complex subject, and all the topics covered in this book are interrelated. Sure, you can register your site with the search engines, but if your pages aren't optimized for the search engines, you may be wasting your time! You can create pages the search engines can read, but if you don't pick the right keywords, it's a total waste of time. So I recommend that you read everything in this book; it will make a huge difference in how well your pages are ranked in the search engines.

## Part I: Search Engine Basics

In this part, I provide, yep, the basics — the foundation on which you can build your search-engine-optimization skills. Which search engines are important, for instance? In fact, what *is* a search engine? And what's a *search directory?* And why am I using the term *search system?* In this part, you find out the basics of sensible site creation, discover how to pick the keywords that people are using to find your business, and discover how to do a few quick fixes to your site.

## Part II: Building Search-Engine-Friendly Sites

Do you have any idea how many sites are invisible to the search engines? Or that, if they're not invisible, are built such that search engines won't see the information they need to index the site in the way the site owners would like?

Well, I don't know an exact number, but I do know it's most sites. If you read Part II, you will be way ahead of the vast majority of site owners and managers. You discover how to create techniques that search engines like and avoid the ones they hate. You also find out about tricks that some people use — and the dangers involved.

## Part III: Adding Your Site to the Indexes and Directories

After you've created your Web site and ensured that the search engines can read the pages, somehow you have to get the *search systems* — the engines and directories — to include your site. That's hard if you don't know what you're doing. In this part, you find out which search systems are important, how to register, and how to find other search engines and directories that are important to your site. You also find out why registering sometimes doesn't work, and what to do about it.

## Part IV: After You've Submitted Your Site

Your work isn't over yet. In this part of the book, you find out why links to your site are so important and how to get other sites to link to you. You discover the shopping directories, such as Froogle and Shopping.com. I also explain the multibillion-dollar search engine advertising business. You find out how to work with the hugely popular Google AdWords and Yahoo! Search Marketing pay-per-click programs . . . *and* how to buy cheaper clicks. You also discover paid placement and other forms of advertising.

## Part V: The Part of Tens

All *For Dummies* books have the Part of Tens. In this part, you find ten ways to keep up to date with the search-engine business. You also find out about ten common mistakes that make Web sites invisible to search engines, and ten services and tools that will be useful in your search engine campaign.

## Appendix

Don't forget to check out the appendix, where you find information on copyright laws.

# Icons Used in This Book

This book, like all *For Dummies* books, uses icons to highlight certain paragraphs and to alert you to particularly useful information. Here's a rundown of what those icons mean:

A Tip icon means I'm giving you an extra snippet of information that may help you on your way or provide some additional insight into the concepts being discussed.

The Remember icon points out information that is worth committing to memory.

The Technical Stuff icon indicates geeky stuff that you can skip if you really want to, though you may want to read it if you're the kind of person who likes to have the background info.

The Warning icon helps you stay out of trouble. It's intended to grab your attention to help you avoid a pitfall that may harm your Web site or business.

Don't forget to visit the Web sites associated with this book. At www.dummies.com/go/searchoptimization, you find all the links in this book (so you don't have to type them!), as well as a Bonus Chapter on how to power up your search engine skills. At www.SearchEngineBulletin.com, you find the aforementioned links along with additional useful information that didn't make it into the book.

# Part I
# Search Engine Basics

The 5th Wave   By Rich Tennant

"This is amazing! You can stop looking for Derek. According to an MSN search I did, he's hiding behind the dryer in the basement."

# In this part . . .

The basics of search engine optimization are surprisingly, um, basic. In fact, you may be able to make small changes to your Web site that make a huge difference in your site's ranking in the search results.

This part starts with the basics. I begin by explaining which search engines are important. You may have heard the names of dozens of sites and heard that, in fact, hundreds of search engines exist. You'll be happy to hear that the vast majority of search results are provided by no more than four systems, and half of all the results come from a single company.

You also discover how to make some quick and easy changes to your Web site that may fix serious search engine problems for you. On the other hand, you may discover a significant (and common) problem in your site that must be resolved before you have any chance of getting into the search engines at all, let alone ranking well.

This part of the book also includes basic information on how to create a Web site that works well for both visitors and search engines, and you find out about one of the most important first steps you can take: carrying out a detailed keyword analysis.

# Chapter 1

# Surveying the Search Engine Landscape

**In This Chapter**

▶ Discovering where people search

▶ Understanding the difference between search sites and search systems

▶ Distilling thousands of search sites down to four search systems

▶ Understanding how search engines work

▶ Gathering tools and basic knowledge

**Y**ou've got a problem. You want people to visit your Web site; that's the purpose, after all — to bring people to your site to buy your product, or learn about service, or hear about the cause you support, or for whatever other purpose you've built the site. So you've decided you need to get traffic from the search engines — not an unreasonable conclusion, as you find out in this chapter. But there are *so many* search engines! You have the obvious ones — the Googles, AOLs, Yahoo!s, and MSNs of the world — but you've probably also heard of others: HotBot, Dogpile, Ask Jeeves, Netscape, EarthLink, LookSmart . . . even Amazon provides a Web search on almost every page. There's Lycos and InfoSpace, Teoma and WiseNut, Mamma.com and WebCrawler. To top it all off, you've seen advertising asserting that, for only $49.95 (or $19.95, or $99.95, or whatever sum seems to make sense to the advertiser), you too can have your Web site listed in hundreds, nay, thousands of search engines. You may have even used some of these services, only to discover that the flood of traffic you were promised turns up missing.

Well, I've got some good news. You can forget almost all the names I just listed — well, at least you can after you've read this chapter. The point of this chapter is to take a complicated landscape of thousands of search sites and whittle it down into the small group of search systems that really matter. (Search sites? Search systems? Don't worry, I explain the distinction in a moment.)

If you really want to, you can jump to "Where Do People Search," near the end of the chapter, to the list of search systems you need to worry about and ignore the details. But I've found that, when I give this list to someone, he or she looks at me like I'm crazy because they know that some popular search sites aren't on the list. This chapter explains why.

# Investigating Search Engines and Directories

The term *search engine* has become the predominant term for *search system* or *search site,* but before reading any further, you need to understand the different types of search, um, thingies, you're going to run across. Basically, you need to know about four thingies.

## Search indexes or search engines

Search indexes or engines are the predominant type of search tools you'll run across. Originally, the term *search engine* referred to some kind of search index, a huge database containing information from individual Web sites.

Large search-index companies own thousands of computers that use software known as *spiders* or *robots* (or just plain *bots*) to grab Web pages and read the information stored in them. These systems don't always grab all the information on each page or all the pages in a Web site, but they grab a significant amount of information and use complex *algorithms* — calculations based on complicated formulae — to index that information. Google, shown in Figure 1-1, is the world's most popular search engine, closely followed by Yahoo! and MSN.

## Index envy

Late in 2005, Yahoo! (www.yahoo.com) claimed that its index contained information about almost 20 *billion* pages, along with almost 2 billion images and 50 million audio and video pages. Google (www.google.com) used to actually state on its home page how many pages it indexed — they reached 15 billion or so at one point — but decided not to play the "mine is bigger than yours" game with Yahoo!

**Figure 1-1:**
Google, the
world's most
popular
search
engine,
produced
these
results.

## *Search directories*

A *directory* is a categorized collection of information about Web sites. Rather than containing information *from* Web *pages,* it contains information *about* Web *sites.*

The most significant search directories are owned by Yahoo! (`dir.yahoo.com`) and the Open Directory Project (`www.dmoz.org`). (You can see an example of Open Directory Project information, displayed in Google — `dir.google.com` — in Figure 1-2.) Directory companies don't use spiders or bots to download and index pages on the Web sites in the directory; rather, for each Web site, the directory contains information, such as a title and description, submitted by the site owner. The two most important directories, Yahoo! and Open Directory, have staff members who examine all the sites in the directory to make sure they're placed into the correct categories and meet certain quality criteria. Smaller directories often accept sites based on the owners' submission, with little verification.

Here's how to see the difference between Yahoo!'s search results and the Yahoo! directory:

1. **Go to www.yahoo.com.**

2. **Type a word into the Search box.**

3. **Click the Search button.**

   The list of Web sites that appears is called the Yahoo! Search results, which are currently provided by Google.

4. **Notice the Directory tab at the top of the page.**

   You see a line that says something like *Category: Footwear Retailers.* You also see the line underneath some of the search results.

5. **Click either the tab or link.**

   You end up in the Yahoo! directory. (You can go directly to the directory by using `dir.yahoo.com`.)

## Non-spidered indexes

I wasn't sure what to call these things, so I made up a name: *non-spidered indexes.* A number of small indexes, less important than major indexes such as Google, don't use spiders to examine the full contents of each page in the index. Rather, the index contains background information about each page, such as titles, descriptions, and keywords. In some cases, this information comes from the meta tags pulled off the pages in the index. (I tell you about meta tags in Chapter 2.) In other cases, the person who enters the site into the index provides this information. A number of the smaller systems discussed in Chapter 13 are of this type.

**Figure 1-2:**
Google also has a search directory, but it doesn't create the directory itself; it gets it from the Open Directory Project.

## Pay-per-click systems

Some systems provide *pay-per-click* listings. Advertisers place small ads into the systems, and when users perform their searches, the results contain some of these sponsored listings, typically above and to the right of the free listings. Pay-per-click systems are discussed in more detail in Chapter 17.

## Keeping the terms straight

Here are a few additional terms that you will see scattered throughout the book:

- ✔ **Search site:** This Web site lets you search through some kind of index or directory of Web sites, or perhaps both an index and directory. (In some cases, search sites known as *meta indexes* allow you to search through multiple indices.) Google.com, AOL.com, and EarthLink.com are all search sites. DogPile.com and Mamma.com are meta-index search sites.

- ✔ **Search system:** This organization possesses a combination of software, hardware, and people that indexes or categorizes Web sites — they build the index or directory you search through at a search site. The distinction is important, because a search site may not actually own a search index or directory. For instance, Google is a search system — it displays results from the index that it creates for itself — but AOL.com and EarthLink.com aren't. In fact, if you search at AOL.com or EarthLink. com and search, you actually get Google search results.

  Google and the Open Directory Project provide search results to hundreds of search sites. In fact, most of the world's search sites get their search results from elsewhere; see Figure 1-3.

- ✔ **Search term:** This is the word, or words, that someone types into a search engine when looking for information.

- ✔ **Search results:** Results are the information returned to you (the results of your search term) when you go to a search site and search for something. As just explained, in many cases the search results you see don't come from the search site you're using, but from some other search system.

- ✔ **Natural search results:** A Web page can appear on a search-results page two ways: The search engine may place it on the page because the site owner paid to be there (pay-per-click ads), or it may pull the page out of its index because it thinks the page matches the search term well. These free placements are often known as *natural search results*; you'll also hear the term *organic* and sometimes even *algorithmic*.

- ✔ **Search engine optimization (SEO):** Search engine optimization (also known as *SEO*) refers to "optimizing" Web sites and Web pages to rank well in the search engines . . . the subject of this book, of course.

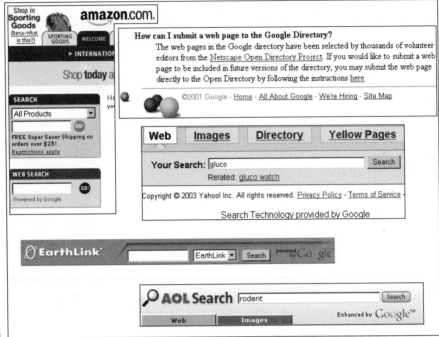

**Figure 1-3:**
Look
carefully,
and you'll
see that
many
search sites
get their
search
results from
other
search
systems.

## Why bother with search engines?

Why bother using search engines for your marketing? Because search engines represent the single most important source of new Web site visitors.

You may have heard that most Web site visits begin at a search engine. Well, this isn't true. It was true several years ago, and many people continue to use these outdated statistics because they sound good — "80 percent of all Web site visitors reach the site through a search engine," for instance. However, in 2003, that claim was finally put to rest. The number of search-originated site visits dropped below the 50-percent mark. Most Web site visitors reach their destinations by either typing a *URL* — a Web address — into their browsers and going there directly or by clicking a link on another site that takes them there. Most visitors don't reach their destinations by starting at the search engines.

However, search engines are still extremely important for a number of reasons:

✔ The proportion of visits originating at search engines is significant. Not so long ago, one survey put the number at almost 50 percent. Sure, it's not 80 percent, but it's still a lot of traffic.

✔ According to a report by eMarketer published early in 2005, 21 percent of American Internet users use a search engine four or more times each day; PEW Internet estimated that 38 million Americans use search engines every day.

✔ A study by iCrossing in the summer of 2005 found that 40 percent of people do online research prior to purchasing products.

✔ Of the visits that don't originate at a search engine, a large proportion are revisits — people who know exactly where they want to go. This isn't new business; it's repeat business. Most *new* visits come through the search engines — that is, search engines are the single most important source of new visitors to Web sites.

✔ Some studies indicate that a large number of buyers begin at the search engines. That is, of all the people who go online planning to buy something or looking for product information, perhaps over 67 percent use a search engine, according to a study in 2005 by iCrossing.

✔ The search engines represent a cheap way to reach people. In general, you get more bang for your buck going after free search-engine traffic than almost any other form of advertising or marketing.

# Where Do People Search?

You can search for Web sites at many places. Literally thousands of sites, in fact, provide the ability to search the Web. (What you may not realize, however, is that many sites search only a small subset of the World Wide Web.)

However, *most* searches are carried out at a small number of search sites. How do the world's most popular search sites rank? That depends on how you measure popularity:

✔ Percentage of site visitors *(audience reach)*

✔ Total number of visitors

✔ Total number of searches carried out at a site

✔ Total number of hours visitors spend searching at the site

Each measurement provides a slightly different ranking, though all provide a similar picture, with the same sites generally appearing on the list, though some in slightly different positions.

The following list runs down the world's most popular search sites, based on one month of searches during 2005 — 4.5 billion searches — according to a Nielsen/NetRatings study. These statistics are for U.S. Internet users:

Google.com   46.2%

Yahoo.com   22.5%

MSN.com   12.6%

AOL.com   5.4%

My Way   2.2%

Ask (AskJeeves)   1.6%

Netscape.com   1.6%

iWon   0.9%

Earthlink   0.8%

DogPile   0.9%

Others   5.3%

Remember, this is a list of search sites, not search systems. In some cases, the sites have own their own systems. Google provides its own search results, but AOL doesn't. (AOL gets its results from Google.)

The fact that some sites get results from other search systems means two things.

✔ **The numbers in the preceding list are somewhat misleading.** They suggest that Google has around 46.2 percent of all searches. But Google also feeds AOL its results — add AOL's searches to Google's, and you've got 51.6 percent of all searches. In addition, Google feeds Netscape (another 1.6 percent according to NetRatings) and EarthLink (0.8 percent ). And DogPile is a meta search engine: Search at DogPile, and you see results from Google, Yahoo!, MSN, and Ask.

✔ **You can ignore some of these systems.** At present, for example, and for the foreseeable future, you don't need to worry about AOL.com. Even though it's one of the world's top search sites, you can forget about it. Sure, keep it in the back of your mind, but as long as you remember that Google feeds AOL, you need to worry about Google only.

Now reexamine the preceding list of the world's most important search sites and see what you remove so you can get closer to a list of sites you care about. Check out Table 1-1 for the details.

| Table 1-1 | The Top Search Sites | |
|---|---|---|
| **Search Site** | **Keep It On the List?** | **Description** |
| Google.com | Yes | The big kid on the block. Lots of people search the Google index on its own search site, *and* it feeds many sites. Obviously, Google has to stay on the list. |
| Yahoo.com | Yes | Yahoo! is obviously a large, important site; keep it. |
| MSN.com | Yes | Ditto; MSN creates its own index, and gets many searches. |
| AOL.com | No | Fuggetaboutit — AOL gets search results from Google (although it manipulates their appearance) and from the Open Directory Project. |
| MyWay.com | No | MyWay uses data from Ask, so forget about it. |
| Ask.com (also known as AskJeeves.com) | Yes | It has its own search engine, and feeds some other systems — such as MyWay, Lycos, Excite, and HotBot. Keep it, though it's small. |
| Netscape.com | No | Netscape gets results from Google and the Open Directory Project. (Netscape owns the Open Directory Project.) Netscape is pretty much a Google clone, so no need to keep it on the list. |
| iWon.com | No | iWon gets its search results from Ask.com, so forget it. |
| EarthLink.com | No | Another Google clone, EarthLink gets all its results from Google and the Open Directory Project; it's out, too. |
| DogPile.com | No | DogPile simply searches through other systems' search indexes (Google, Yahoo!, MSN, and Ask). Forget it. |

Based on the information in Table 1-1, you can whittle down your list of systems to four: Google, Yahoo!, MSN, and Ask. The top three search systems are all very important, with a small follower, Ask, that provides results to many smaller search sites.

There's one more system I want to add to these four systems, though. Very few people search at the Open Directory Project (www.dmoz.org). However, this directory system feeds data to hundreds of search sites, including Google, AOL, and EarthLink.

To summarize, five important systems are left:

 ✔ Google

 ✔ Yahoo

 ✔ MSN

 ✔ Ask

 ✔ Open Directory Project

That's not so bad, is it? You've just gone from thousands of sites down to five. Note, by the way, that the top three positions may shift around a little. Google has already lost a large proportion of its share (when I wrote the first edition of this book Google had around three quarters of the market . . . now it's probably a little over one half), and a big battle's brewing between the top three; in fact 2006 is turning out to be the year of bribing people to bring them to search. Take a look at Google partner Blingo (www.blingo.com) and at MSN Search and Win (www.MSNSearchAndWin.com).

Now, some of you may be thinking, "Aren't you missing some sites? What happened to HotBot, Mamma.com, WebCrawler, Lycos, and all the other systems that were so well known a few years ago?" A lot of them have disappeared or have turned over a new leaf and are pursuing other opportunities.

For example, Northern Light, a system well known in the late 1990s, now sells search software. And in the cases in which the search sites are still running, they're generally fed by other search systems. Mamma.com, DogPile, and MetaCrawler get search results from the top four systems, for instance, and HotBot gets results from Ask. Altavista and AllTheWeb get their data from Yahoo! If the search site you remember isn't mentioned here, it's either out of business, being fed by someone else, or simply not important in the big scheme of things.

When you find a new search system, look carefully on the page near the search box, or on the search results page, and you may find where the search results are coming from. For instance, if you use Alexa (www.Alexa.com), one of Amazon.com's search engines, you see the words POWERED BY GOOGLE next to the Search button; use Amazon.com's *other* search system, A9 (www.A9.com), and at the bottom of the search results you see this:

```
Search results enhanced by Google. Results also provided
                by a9.com and Alexa.
```

The same search run at all three systems — Alexa, A9, and Google — produces very similar results. (Although a site may get its search-results feed from another one place, it may manipulate the results so they're listed in a slightly different order.)

You'll also want to work with some other search systems, as you find out in Chapters 12 and 13. In some cases, you need to check out specialty directories and indexes related to the industry in which your Web site operates. But the preceding systems are the important ones for every Web site.

Google alone provides well over 50 percent of all search results (down from 75 percent just a year or two ago). Get into *all* the systems on the preceding list, and you're in front of probably more than 95 percent of all searchers. Well, perhaps you're in front of them. You have a chance of being in front of them, anyway, if your site ranks highly (which is what this book is all about).

# Search Engine Magic

Go to Google and search for the term *personal injury lawyer*. Then look the blue bar below the Google logo, and you see something like this:

```
Results 1 - 10 of about 16,300,000 for personal injury
        lawyer
```

This means Google has found over 16M pages that contain these three words. Yet somehow it has managed to rank the pages. It's decided that one particular page should appear first, then another, then another, and so on, all the way down to page 16,300,000. (By the way, this has to be one of the wonders of the modern world: The search engines have tens of thousands of computers, evaluating 10 or 20 *billion* pages, and returning the information in a fraction of a second.)

# How do they do it?

How on earth does Google do it? How does it evaluate and compare pages? How do other search engines do the same? Well, I don't know *exactly*. The search engines don't want you to know how they work (or it would be too easy to create pages that exactly match the search system, "giving them what they want to see"). But I can explain the general concept.

When Google searches for your search term, it begins by looking for pages containing the exact phrase. Then it starts looking for pages containing the words close together. Then it looks for pages that have the pages scattered around. This isn't necessarily the order in which a search engine shows you pages; in some cases, pages with words close together (but not the exact phrase) appear higher than pages with the exact phrase, for instance. That's because search engines evaluate pages according to a variety of criteria.

The search engines look at many factors. They look for the words throughout the page, both in the visible page and in the HTML source code for the page. Each time they find the words, they are *weighted* in some way. A word in one position is "worth" more than a word in another position. A word formatted in one way is "worth" more than a word formatted in another. (You read more about this in Chapter 5.)

There's more, though. The search engines also look at links pointing to pages, and uses those links to evaluate the referenced pages: How many links are there? How many are from popular sites? What words are in the link text? You read more about this in Chapters 14 and 15.

# Stepping into the programmers' shoes

There's a lot of conflicting information out there about SEO. Some of it's good, some of it's not so good, and some of it's downright wrong. When evaluating a claim about what the search engines do, I sometimes find it useful to step into the shoes of the people building the search engines; I try to think, "what would make sense" from the perspective of the programmers who write the code that evaluates all these pages.

Consider this: Say you search for *personal injury lawyer*, and the search engine finds one page with the term in the pages title" (between the `<title>` and `</title>` tags, which you read more about in Chapters 2 and 6), and another page with the term somewhere deep in the page text. Which do you think is likely to match the search term better? If the text is in the title, doesn't that indicate that page is likely to be, in some way, related to the term? If the text is deep in the body of the page, couldn't it mean that the page isn't directly related to the term, that it is related to it in some incidental or peripheral manner?

Considering SEO from this point of view makes it easier to understand how the search engines try to evaluate and compare pages. If the keywords are in the links pointing to the page, the page must be relevant to those keywords; if the keywords are in headings on the page, that must be significant; if the keywords appear frequently throughout the page, rather than just once, that must mean something. All of sudden, it all makes sense.

By the way, in Chapter 7 I discuss things that the search engines don't like. You may hear elsewhere all sorts of warnings that may or may not be correct. Here's an example: I've read that using a refresh meta tag to automatically push a visitor from one page to another will get your site penalized, and may even get your site banned from the search engine. You've seen this situation: You land on a page on a Web site, and there's a message saying something like "We'll forward you to page *x* in five seconds, or you can click here." The theory is that search engines don't like this, and they may punish you for doing this.

Now, does this make any sense? Aren't there good reasons to sometimes use such forwarding techniques? Yes, there are. So why would a search engine punish you for doing it? They don't. They probably won't index the page that is forwarding a visitor — based on the quite reasonable theory that if the site doesn't want the visitor to read the page, they don't need to index it — but you're not going to get punished for using it.

Remember that the search-engine programmers are not interested in punishing anyone, they're just trying to make the best choices between billions of pages. In general, search engines use their "algorithms" to determine how to rank a page, and try to adjust the algorithms to make sure "tricks" are ignored. But they don't want to punish anyone for doing something for which there might be a good reason, even if the technique could also be used as a trick.

I like to use this as my "plausibility filter" when I hear someone make some unusual or even outlandish claim about how the search engines function. *What would the programmers do?*, I ask myself.

# Gathering Your Tools

You need several tools and skills to optimize and rank your Web site. I talk about a number of these in the appropriate chapters, but I want to cover a few basics before I move on. It goes without saying that you need

✔ Basic Internet knowledge.

✔ A computer connected to the Internet.

✔ A Web site.

✔ One of these two things:

   • Good working knowledge of HTML.

   • Access to a geek with a good working knowledge of HTML.

Which path should you take? If you don't know what HTML means (HyperText Markup Language), you probably need to run out and find that geek. HTML is the code used to create Web pages, and you need to understand how to use it to optimize pages. Discussing HTML and how to upload pages to a Web site is beyond the scope of this book. If you're interested in finding out more, check out *HTML For Dummies,* 4th Edition, by Ed Tittel and Natanya Pitts, and *Creating Web Pages For Dummies,* 6th Edition, by Bud Smith and Arthur Bebak (both published by Wiley).

✔ Toolbars. Install the Google toolbar in your Web browser . . . and perhaps the Yahoo!, MSN, and Ask.com toolbars, too. And, maybe, the Alexa toolbar. (Before you complain about spyware, I explain in a few moments.) You may want to use these tools even if you plan to use a geek to work on your site. They're simple to install and open up a completely new view of the Web. The next two sections spell out the details.

## Search toolbars

I definitely recommend the Google toolbar, which allows you to begin searching Google without going to the Web site first. In addition, you might want to use the Yahoo! and MSN toolbars, which do the same. (You might also try the Ask.com toolbar, but remember that Ask is far less important than Google, Yahoo!, and MSN.) In addition, these toolbars have plenty of extras: auto form fillers, tabbed browsing, desktop search, spyware blockers, translators, spell checkers, and so on. I'm not going to describe all these tools, as they aren't directly related to SEO, but they're definitely useful.

You really don't need all of them, but hey, here they are if you really want to experiment. You can find these toolbars here:

✔ `toolbar.google.com`

✔ `toolbar.yahoo.com`

✔ `toolbar.msn.com`

✔ `toolbar.ask.com`

## Geek or no geek

Many readers of this book's first edition are business people who don't plan to do the search-engine work themselves (or, in some cases, realize that it's a lot of work and need to find someone with more time or technical skills to do the work). However, having read the book, they understand far more about search engines and are in a better position to find and direct someone. As one reader-cum-client, told me, "There's a lot of snake oil in this business," so his reading helped him understand the basics and ask the right questions of search-engine optimization firms.

Unfortunately, all these toolbars require Microsoft Windows and Internet Explorer; that's most of you but, I realize, not all. You can see these toolbars, along with the Alexa toolbar, in Figure 1-4. Don't worry, you don't have to have all this clutter on your screen all the time. Right-click a blank space on any toolbar, and you can add and remove toolbars temporarily; simply open a toolbar when you need it. I leave the Google toolbar on all the time, and open the others now and then.

One thing I do find frustrating about these systems is the pop-up blockers. Yes, they can be helpful, but often they block pop-up windows that I want to see; if you find that you click a link and it doesn't open, try Ctrl+clicking (which may temporarily disable the pop-up blocker), or disable the blocker on the toolbar.

I refer to the Google toolbar here and there throughout this book because it provides you with the following useful features:

- ✔ A way to search Google without going to www.google.com first
- ✔ A quick view of the Google PageRank, an important metric that I explain in Chapter 14
- ✔ A quick way to see if a Web page is already indexed by Google
- ✔ A quick way to see some of the pages linking to a Web page

The toolbar has a number of other useful features, but the preceding features are the most useful for the purposes of this book. Turn on the Info button after installing the toolbar:

1. **Click the Options button.**
2. **Click the More tab in the Toolbar Options dialog box.**
3. **Enable the Page Info checkbox and click OK.**

**Figure 1-4:**
The toolbars
provide
useful
information
for search-
engine
campaigns;
the Google
bar's Info
button is
shown
open.

## Alexa toolbar

Alexa is a company owned by Amazon.com, and a partner with Google and Microsoft. It's been around a long time, and millions of people around the world use it. Every time someone uses the toolbar to visit a Web site, the toolbar sends the URL to Alexa, allowing the system to create an enormous database of site visits. The toolbar can provide traffic information to you; you can quickly see how popular a site is and even view a detailed traffic analysis, such as an estimate of the percentage of Internet users who visit the site each month.

Work with the Alexa toolbar for a while, and you'll quickly get a feel for site popularity. A site ranks 453? That's pretty good. 1,987,123? That's a sign that hardly anyone visits the site. In addition, it provides a quick way to find information about who owns the site on which the current page sits, and how many pages link to the current page. You can find the Alexa toolbar, shown in Figure 1-4, at download.alexa.com.

I've been criticized for recommending the Alexa toolbar in the first edition of this book: Many people claim it is spyware. Some anti-spyware programs search for the toolbar and flag it as spyware, though others don't. As I mentioned, the toolbar sends the URLs you're visiting. However, Alexa states on the site (and I believe them) that "The Alexa Toolbar contains no advertising and does not profile or target you." I know for sure that it doesn't display ads. Alexa doesn't steal your usernames and passwords, as is occasionally claimed. Alexa does gather information about where you visit, but it doesn't know who you are, so does it matter? Decide for yourself.

# Chapter 2

# Your One-Hour Search-Engine-Friendly Web Site Makeover

*In This Chapter*

▶ Finding your site in the search engines

▶ Choosing keywords

▶ Examining your pages for problems

▶ Getting search engines to read and index your pages

*A* few small changes can make a big difference in your site's position in the search engines. So rather than force you to read this entire book before you can get anything done, this chapter helps you identify problems with your site and, with a little luck, shows you how to make a significant difference through quick fixes.

It's possible that you may not make significant progress in a single hour, as the chapter title promises. You may identify serious problems with your site that can't be fixed quickly. Sorry, that's life! The purpose of this chapter is to help you identify a few obvious problems and, perhaps, make some quick fixes with the goal of really getting something done.

## Is Your Site Indexed?

It's important to find out if your site is actually in a search engine or directory. Your site doesn't come up when someone searches at Google for *rodent racing?* Can't find it in the Yahoo! Directory? Have you ever thought that perhaps it simply isn't there? In the next several sections, I explain how to find out if your site is indexed in a few different systems.

Some of the systems into which you want to place your Web site aren't household names. If I mention a search system that you don't recognize, page back to Chapter 1 to find out more about it.

# *Google*

I'll start with the behemoth: Google. Here's the quickest and easiest way to see what Google has in its index. Search Google, either at the site or through the Google toolbar (see Chapter 1) for this:

```
site:domain.com
```

Don't type the www. piece, just the domain name. For instance, say your site's domain name is *RodentRacing.com*. You'd search for this:

```
site:rodentracing.com
```

Google returns a list of pages it's found on your site; at the top, on the blue bar, you see something like this:

```
Results 1 - 10 of about 256 from rodentracing.com
```

That's it — quick and easy. You know how many pages Google has indexed on your site, and can even see which pages.

Here's another way to see what's in the index, in this case a particular page in your site. Open your browser and load a page at your site. Then follow these steps:

1. **Click the i icon on the Google toolbar.**

   I'm assuming that you're using Internet Explorer and have, as I suggest in Chapter 1, downloaded the Google toolbar — available at `toolbar.google.com` — to your computer. If you don't have the toolbar, don't worry; I explain a non-toolbar method in a moment.

2. **Select Cached Snapshot of Page from the drop-down list that appears.**

   If you're lucky, Google loads a page showing you what it has in its cache, so you know Google has indexed the page. (See Figure 2-1.) If you're unlucky, Google tells you that it has nothing in the cache for that page. That doesn't necessarily mean Google hasn't indexed the page, though.

A *cache* is a temporary storage area in which a copy of something is placed. In the context of the Web, a cache stores a Web page. Google, Yahoo!, MSN, and Ask.com keep a copy of many of the pages they index, and all but Yahoo! even tell you the date that they indexed the cached pages.

If you don't have the Google Toolbar, you can instead go to Google (`www.google.com`) and type the following into the Google search box:

```
cache:http://yourdomain.com/page.htm
```

Replace *yourdomain.com* with your actual domain name, and *page.htm* with the actual page name, of course. When you click Search, Google checks to see if it has the page in its cache.

What if Google doesn't have the page? Does that mean your page isn't in Google? No, not necessarily. Google may not have gotten around to caching it. Sometimes Google grabs a little information from a page but not the entire page.

By the way, you can see a cached page saved by Google, Yahoo!, or MSN directly from the search results; look for the Cached or Cached page link after a search result.

## Yahoo! and MSN

And now, here's a bonus. The search syntax I used to see what Google had in its index for rodentracing.com — site:rodentracing.com — not only works on Google, but also on Yahoo! and MSN. That's right, type the same thing into any of these search sites and you see how many pages on the Web site are in the index . . . with one caveat. MSN, at the time of writing at least, is a little flaky.

MSN reports a much higher number when you first run this search; but view a later page, and this number drops. For instance, MSN may show you this:

```
Page 1 of 456 results containing
          site:peterkentconsulting.com
```

At the bottom of the page you see the page-navigation numbers, like this:

```
1 2 3 4 5 Next
```

I suggest you click the number 5, to move to Page 5 in the results. Then you see this:

```
Previous 1 2 3 4 5 6 7 8 9 Next
```

Click page 9, and continue this way until you get to the last page or until the Page *x* of *xxx* line at the top changes. You then see the actual number of pages that MSN has in its index. Why is this? Just a bug; by the time you read this, in fact, it may not be necessary to do this, MSN may have fixed the problem, but it's been there for some time now.

You can search for a Web site at Google another way, too. Simply type the domain name into the Google search box and click Search. Google returns just that site's home page. If you want to use the search box on the Google toolbar to do this, type the domain name and then click the binoculars button. (If you type the domain name and press Enter, Google simply redirects your browser to the specified domain name.)

# Yahoo! Directory

You must check whether your site is listed in the Yahoo! Directory. You have to pay to get a commercial site into the Yahoo! Directory, so you may already know if you're listed there. Perhaps you work in a large company and suspect that another employee may have registered the site with Yahoo! Here's how to find out:

1. **Point your browser to** dir.yahoo.com.

   This takes you directly to the Yahoo! Directory search page.

2. **Type your site's domain name into the Search text box.**

   All you need is *yourdomain.com*, not http://www. or anything else.

3. **Make sure that the Directory option button is selected, then click Search.**

   If your site is in the Yahoo! Directory, your site's information appears on the results page. You may see several pages, one for each category in which the site has been placed (though in most cases a site is placed into only one category).

## Open Directory Project

You must also know if your site is listed in the Open Directory Project (`www.dmoz.org`). If it isn't, it should be. Just type the domain name, without the `www.` piece. If your site is in the index, the Open Directory Project will tell you. If it isn't, you'd better register it; see Chapter 12.

# Taking Action if You're Not Listed

First, if your site isn't in Yahoo! Directory or the Open Directory Project, you have to go to those systems and register your site. See Chapter 12 for information. What if you search for your site in the search engines and can't find it? If the site isn't in Google, Yahoo!, and MSN, you have a huge problem.

Here are two possible reasons your site isn't being indexed in the search engines:

- The search engines haven't found your site yet. The solution is relatively easy, though you won't get it done in an hour.

- The search engines have found your site, but can't index it. This is a serious problem, though in some cases you can fix it quickly.

For the lowdown on getting your pages indexed in the search engines — to ensure that the search engines can find your site — see the section "Getting Your Site Indexed," later in this chapter. To find out how to make your pages search-engine-friendly — to ensure that once found, your site will be indexed well — check out the section "Examining Your Pages," later in this chapter. But first, let's see how to check to see if your site *can* be indexed.

## Is your site invisible?

Some Web sites are virtually invisible. A search engine might be able to find the site (by following a link, for instance). But when it gets to the site, can't read it or, perhaps, can read only parts of it. A client (before he was a client) built a Web site that had only three visible pages; all the other pages, including those with product information, were invisible.

How does a Web site become invisible? I talk about this subject in more detail in Chapter 7, but here's a brief explanation:

- The site is using some kind of navigation structure that the search engines can't read, so they can't find their way through the site.

- The site is creating dynamic pages that the search engines choose not to read.

## Unreadable navigation

Many sites have perfectly readable pages, with the exception that the *search-bots* — the programs the search engines use to index Web sites — can't nego-tiate the site navigation. The searchbots can reach the home page, index it, and read it, but they can't go any further. If, when you search Google for your pages, you find only the home page, this is likely the problem.

Why can't the searchbots find their way through? The navigation system may have been created using JavaScript, and because search engines ignore JavaScript, they don't find the links in the script. Look at this example:

```
<SCRIPT TYPE="javascript" SRC="/menu/menu.js"></SCRIPT>
```

In one site I reviewed, this was how the navigation bar was placed into each page: The page called an external JavaScript, held in menu.js in the menu subdirectory. The search engines won't read menu.js, so they'll never read the links in the script.

Try these simple ways to help search engines find their way around your site, whether or not your navigation structure is hidden:

✔ **Create more text links throughout the site.** Many Web sites have a main navigation structure and then duplicate the structure by using simple text links at the bottom of the page. You should do the same.

✔ **Add a sitemap page to your site.** This page contains links to most or all of the pages on your Web site. Of course, you also want to link to the sitemap page from those little links at the bottom of the home page.

## Dealing with dynamic pages

In many cases, the problem is that the site is *dynamic* — that is, a page is cre-ated on the fly when a browser requests it. The data is pulled out of a data-base, pasted into a Web page template, and sent to the user's browser. Search engines often won't read such pages, for a variety of reasons explained in detail in Chapter 7.

How can you tell if this is a problem? Take a look at the URL in the browser's location bar. Suppose that you see something like this:

```
http://www.yourdomain.edu/rodent-racing-scores/march/
          index.php
```

This address is okay. It's a simple URL path made up of a domain name, two directory names, and a filename. Now look at this one:

```
http://www.yourdomain.edu/rodent-racing/scores.php?prg=1
```

The filename ends with `?prg=1`. This *parameter* is being sent to the server to let it know what information is needed for the Web page. If you have URLs like this, with just a single parameter, they're probably okay, especially for Google; however, a few smaller search engines may not like them. Here's another example:

```
http://yourdomain.com/products/index.html?&DID=18&CATID=13
        &ObjectGroup_ID=79
```

This one may be a real problem, depending on the search engine. This URL has too much weird stuff after the filename: `?&DID=18&CATID=13&ObjectGroup_ID=79`. That's three parameters — `DID=18`, `CATID=13`, and `ObjectGroup_ID=79` — which are too many. Some systems *cannot* or *will not* index this page. (My feeling is that Google tends to index "deeper" into dynamic sites than, for instance, Yahoo!)

Another problem is caused by *session IDs* — URLs that are different every time the page is displayed. Look at this example:

```
http://yourdomain.com/buyAHome.do;jsessionid=07D3CCD4D9A6A
        9F3CF9CAD4F9A728F44
```

Each time someone visits this site, the server assigns a special ID number to the visitor. That means the URL is never the same, so Google won't index it.

Search engines may choose not to index pages with session IDs. If the search engine sees links to a page that appears to have a session ID, it doesn't know whether the URL will change between sessions or whether many different URLs point to the same page. Search engines don't want to overload the site's server and don't want garbage in their indexes.

If you have a clean URL with no parameters, the search engines should be able to get to it. If you have a single parameter in the URL, it's probably fine. Two parameters may not be a problem, although they're more likely to be a problem than a single parameter. Three parameters are almost certainly a problem with some search engines. If you think you have a problem, I suggest reading Chapter 7.

# Picking Good Keywords

Getting search engines to recognize and index your Web site can be a problem, as the first part of this chapter makes clear. Another huge problem — one that has little or nothing to do with the technological limitations of search engines — is that many companies have no idea what *keywords* (the words people are using to search for Web sites at the search engines) they should be using. They try to *guess* the appropriate keywords, without knowing what people are really using in the search engines.

In Chapter 5, I explain keywords in detail, but here's how to do a quick keyword analysis:

1. **Point your browser to** `http://searchmarketing.yahoo.com/rc/srch/`.

   You see the Yahoo! Search Marketing Resource Center; Search Marketing is Yahoo!'s PPC (pay-per-click) division. See Chapter 17 for more about PPC.

2. **Click the Advertiser Keyword Selector Tool link on the right side of the page.**

   A small window opens with a search box.

3. **In the search box, type a keyword you think people may use to search for your products or services.**

4. **Press Enter.**

   The tool returns a list of keywords, showing you how often that term and related terms are used by people searching on Yahoo! and partner sites. See Figure 2-2.

I'm tired of looking for the Yahoo! keyword tool, and having to explain to people how to find it. It keeps moving! So I've placed a link on my site; go to `http://searchenginebulletin.com/yahoo-keywords.html`.

You may find that the keyword you guessed is perfect. Or you may discover better words, or, even if your guess was good, find several other great keywords. A detailed keyword analysis almost always turns up keywords or keyword phrases you need to know about.

Don't spend a lot of time on this task. See if you can come up with some useful keywords in a few minutes and then move on; see Chapter 5 for details about this process.

**Figure 2-2:**
The Yahoo!
Search
Marketing
Keyword
Selector
Tool
provides a
quick way
to check
keywords.

# Examining Your Pages

Making your Web pages "search-engine-friendly" was probably not uppermost in your mind when you sat down to design your Web site. That means your Web pages — and the Web pages of millions of others — probably have a few problems in the search-engine-friendly category. Fortunately, such problems are pretty easy to spot; you can fix some of them quickly, but others are more troublesome.

## Using frames

In order to examine your pages for problems, you need to read the pages' source code; remember, I said you'd need to be able to understand HTML! In order to see the source code, choose View➪Source in your browser.

When you first peek at the source code for your site, you may discover that your site is using frames. (Of course, if you built the site yourself, you already know whether it uses frames. However, you may be examining a site built by someone else.) You may see something like this in the page:

```
<HTML>
<HEAD>
</HEAD>
    <FRAMESET ROWS="20%,80%">
        <FRAME SRC="navbar.html">
        <FRAME SRC="content.html">
    </FRAMESET>
<BODY>
</BODY>
</HTML>
```

When you choose View⇨Source in Internet Explorer, you're viewing the source of the *frame-definition document,* which tells the browser how to set up the frames. In the preceding example, the browser creates two frame rows, one taking up the top 20 percent of the browser and the other taking up the bottom 80 percent. In the top frame, the browser places content taken from the `navbar.html` file; content from `content.html` goes into the bottom frame.

Framed sites don't index well. The pages in the internal frames get *orphaned* in the search engines; each page ends up in search results alone, without the navigation frames with which they were intended to be displayed.

Framed sites are bad news for many reasons. I discuss frames in more detail in Chapter 7, but here are a few quick fixes:

✔ Add `TITLE` and `DESCRIPTION` tags between the `<HEAD>` and `</HEAD>` tags. (To see what these tags are and how they can help with your frame issues, check out the next two sections.)

✔ Add `<NOFRAMES>` and `</NOFRAMES>` tags between the `<BODY>` and `</BODY>` tags, and place 200 to 300 words of keyword-rich content between the tags. The `NOFRAMES` text is designed to be displayed by browsers that can't work with frames, and search engines will read this text, although they won't rate it as high as normal text (because many designers have used `NOFRAMES` tags as a trick to get more keywords into a Web site).

✔ Include a number of links, in the text between the `NOFRAMES` tags, to other pages in your site to help the search engines find their way through.

## Looking at the TITLE tags

`TITLE` tags tell a browser what text to display in the browser's title bar, and they're very important to search engines. Quite reasonably, search engines figure that the TITLE tags may indicate the page's title — and therefore its subject.

Open your site's home page and then choose View➪Source (in Internet Explorer) to view the page source. A text editor opens, showing you what the page's HTML looks like. Here's what you should see at the top of the page:

```
<HTML>
<HEAD>
<TITLE>Your title text is here</TITLE>
```

Here are a few problems you may have with your TITLE tags:

- ✔ **They're not there.** Many pages simply don't have TITLE tags. If not, you're not giving the search engines one of the most important pieces of information about the page's subject matter.

- ✔ **They're in the wrong position.** Sometimes you find the TITLE tags, but they're way down in the page. If they're too low in the page, search engines may not find them.

- ✔ **They're there, but they're poor.** The TITLE tags don't contain the proper keywords.

Your TITLE tags should be immediately below the <HEAD> tag and should contain useful keywords. Have around 40 to 60 characters between the <TITLE> and </TITLE> tags (including spaces) and, perhaps, repeat the primary keywords once. If you're working on your Rodent Racing Web site, for example, you might have something like this. Find out more about keywords in Chapter 5:

```
<TITLE>Rodent Racing Info. Rats, Mice, Gerbils, Stoats,
        all kinds of Rodent Racing</TITLE>
```

## Examining the DESCRIPTION tag

The DESCRIPTION tag is important because search engines often index it (under the reasonable assumption that the description describes the contents of the page) and, in some cases, may use the DESCRIPTION tag to provide the site description on the search-results page.

In most cases these days, the major search engines usually *don't* use the DESCRIPTION tag to provide the description in the search results. Instead, they typically find the search words in the page, grab a snippet of information from around the words, and use that as the description. (In some cases, Google and MSN may grab the description from the Open Directory project, while Yahoo! may use the description from the Yahoo! Directory.)

In some cases, though, if the search engine can't find the keywords in the page (if it finds the page based on its TITLE tag, for example, or links pointing at the page rather than page content), it may use the DESCRIPTION tag.

Open a Web page, then open the HTML "source" (select View➪Source from your browser's menu), and take a quick look at the DESCRIPTION tag. It should look something like this:

```
<META NAME="description" CONTENT="your description goes
            here">
```

Sites often have the same problems with DESCRIPTION tags as they do with TITLE tags. The tags aren't there, are hidden away deep down in the page, or simply aren't very good.

Place the DESCRIPTION tag immediately below the TITLE tags (see Figure 2-3) and create a keyworded description of up to 250 characters (again, including spaces). Here's an example:

```
<META NAME="description" CONTENT="Rodent Racing - Scores,
            Schedules, everything Rodent Racing. Whether
            you're into mouse racing, stoat racing, rats,
            or gerbils, our site provides everything you'll
            ever need to know about Rodent Racing and
            caring for your racers.">
```

**Figure 2-3:**
A clean
start to your
Web page,
showing the
TITLE and
DESCRIP
TION tags.

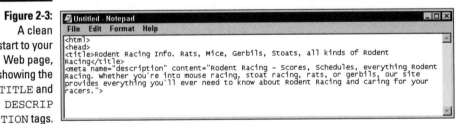

Sometimes Web developers switch the attributes in the tag, putting the CONTENT= first and then the NAME=, like this:

```
<META CONTENT="your description goes here"
            NAME="description">
```

Make sure that your tags do *not* switch the tag attributes. I don't know if the order of the attributes causes a problem for Google or the other big search engines, but it does confuse some smaller systems. There's no reason to do it, so don't.

# Giving search engines something to read

You don't necessarily have to pick through the HTML code for your Web page to evaluate how search-engine-friendly it is. You can find out a lot just by looking at the Web page in the browser. Determine whether you have any text on the page. Page *content* — text that the search engines can read — is essential, but many Web sites don't have any page content on the front page and often have little or any on interior pages. Here are some potential problems:

✔ Having a (usually pointless) Flash intro on your site

✔ Embedding much of the text on your site into images, rather than relying on readable text

✔ Banking on flashy visuals to hide the fact that your site is light on content

✔ Using the wrong keywords; Chapter 5 explains how to pick keywords

If you have these types of problems, they can often be time consuming to fix. (Sorry, you may run over the one-hour timetable by several weeks.) The next several sections detail ways you might overcome the problems.

### Eliminating Flash

Huh? What's Flash? You've seen those silly animations when you arrive at a Web site, with a little *Skip Intro* link hidden away in the page. Words and pictures appear and disappear, scroll across the pages, and so on. You create these animations with a product called Macromedia Flash.

I suggest that you kill the Flash intro on your site. I have very rarely seen a Flash intro that actually served any purpose. In most cases, they are nothing but an irritation to site visitors. (The majority of Flash intros are created because the Web designer likes playing with Flash.)

### Replacing images with real text

If you have an image-heavy Web site, in which all or most of the text is embedded onto images, you need to get rid of the images and replace them with real text. If the search engine can't read the text, it can't index it.

It may not be immediately clear whether text on the page is real text or images. You can quickly figure it out a couple of ways:

✔ Try to select the text in the browser with your mouse. If it's real text, you can select it character by character. If it's not real text, you simply can't select it — you'll probably end up selecting an image.

✔ Use your browser's View➪Source command to look at the HTML for the page and then see if you can find the actual words in the text.

### Using more keywords

The light-content issue can be a real problem. Some sites are designed to be light on content, and sometimes this approach is perfectly valid in terms of design and usability. However, search engines have a bias for content, for text they can read. (I discuss this issue in more depth in Chapter 9.) In general, the more text — with the right keywords — the better.

### Using the right keywords in the right places

Suppose that you do have text, and plenty of it. But does the text have the right keywords? The ones uncovered at Yahoo! Search Marketing earlier in this chapter? It should.

If the reference to Yahoo! Search Marketing doesn't ring a bell, check out the "Picking Good Keywords" section, earlier in this chapter.

Where keywords are placed and what they look like are also important. Search engines use position and format as clues to importance. Here are a few simple techniques you can use — but don't overdo it!

- Use particularly important keywords — those that people are using to search for your products and services — near the top of the page.
- Place keywords into <H> (heading) tags.
- Use bold and italic keywords; search engines take note of this.
- Put keywords into bulleted lists; search engines also take note of this.
- Use keywords multiple times on a page, but don't use a keyword or keyword phrase too often. If a word makes up more than, say, 8 to 10 percent of all the words on the page, it may be too much.

Make sure that the links between pages within your site contain keywords. Think about all the sites you've visited recently. How many use links with *no* keywords in them? They use buttons, graphic navigation bars, short little links that you have to guess at, *click here* links, and so on. Big mistakes.

I don't object to using the words *click here* in links. Some writers have suggested that you should never use *click here* because it sounds silly and because people know they're supposed to click. I disagree, and research shows that using the words can sometimes increase the number of clicks on a link. The bottom line is that you should rarely, if ever, use a link with only the words *click here* in the link text; you should include keywords in the link.

When you create links, include keywords in the links wherever possible. If on your rodent-racing site you're pointing to the scores page, don't create a link that says *To find the most recent rodent racing scores, <u>click here</u>* or, perhaps, *To find the most recent racing scores, go to the <u>scores page</u>*. Instead, get a few more keywords into the links, like this: *To find the most recent racing scores, go to the <u>rodent racing scores page</u>*.

# Getting Your Site Indexed

So your pages are ready, but you still have the indexing problem. Your pages are, to put in bluntly, just *not in the search engine!* How do you fix that problem?

For Yahoo! Directory and the Open Directory Project, you have to go to those sites and register directly, but before doing that, you should read Chapter 12. With Google, Yahoo! Web Search, MSN, and Ask.com, the process is a little more time consuming and complicated.

The best way to get into the search engines is to have them *find* the pages by following links pointing to the site. In some cases, you can ask or pay the search engines to come to your site and pick up your pages, but you face two main problems with this:

- ✔ If you ask search engines to index your site, they probably won't do it. And if they do come and index your site, it may take weeks or months. Asking them to come to your site is unreliable.

- ✔ If you pay search engines to index your site, you have to pay for every URL you submit. The problem with paying, of course, is that you have to pay.

If you want to submit your site to the search engines for indexing, read Chapter 11, where I provide all the details.

So how do you get indexed? The good news is that you can often get indexed by some of the search engines *very* quickly. I'm not talking about a full-blown link campaign here, with all the advantages I describe in Chapters 14 and 15. You simply want to get search engines — particularly Google, Yahoo!, MSN, and Ask.com — to pick up the site and index it.

Find another Web site to link to your site, right away. Call several friends, colleagues, and relatives who own or control a Web site, and ask them to link to your site. Of course, you want sites that are already indexed by the search engines. The searchbots have to follow the links to your site.

When you ask friends, colleagues, and relatives to link to you, specify what you want the links to say. No *click here* or company name links for you. You want to place keywords into the link text. Something like *Visit this site for all your <u>rodent racing needs - mice, rats, stoats, gerbils, and all other kinds of rodent racing</u>*. Keywords in links are a powerful way to tell a search engine what your site is about.

After the sites have links pointing to yours, it can take from a few days to a few weeks to get into the search engines. With Google, if you place the links right before Googlebot indexes one of the sites, you may be in the index in a few days. I once placed some pages on a client's Web site on a Tuesday and found them in Google on Friday. But Google can also take several weeks to index a site. The best way to increase your chances of getting into the search engines quickly is to get as many links as you can on as many sites as possible.

# Chapter 3

# Planning Your Search-Engine Strategy

There's lot to discover about generating traffic from the search engines, and sometimes it's hard to see the forest for the trees. As you discover in this book, there's page optimization and link strategies and index submissions and directory submissions and electronic press releases and blogs and this and that . . . it goes on and on. Before you jump right in, I need to discuss the big picture, to give you an idea of how all this fits together and help you decide what you should do when . . . to help you plan your strategy. In this chapter I show you how a search-engine campaign works overall.

## Don't Trust Your Web Designer

Let me start with a warning: Don't rely on your Web designer to manage your SEO project. In fact, I know that many of you are reading this book because you did just that, and have realized the error of your ways.

Last week I consulted with the owner of a small e-commerce store. He'd just paid a Web-design firm $5,000 to build his site, and before beginning he had asked them to make sure the site was "search-engine friendly." Unfortunately, that means different things to different people, and to the design firm it didn't mean much. The site they built definitely was *not* optimized for the search engines. The owner asked the firm what it was planning to do about the search engines. They told him it would cost him $5,000.

This unusual case is more egregious than most, but the first part — that your Web-design firm says it will handle the search engines, then doesn't — is *very* common. When I hire a Web designer to build a site for me, I explain exactly what I want. And you should do the same. (Thus, this book can help you even if you never write a line of HTML code.)

The problem is twofold:

✔ Web designers pretty much *have* to say they understand the search engines, because all of their competitors are saying it.

✔ Many Web designers think they *do* understand, but typically it's at a "add some meta tags and submit to the search engines" level. It won't work.

Sorry, Web designers. I don't want to be rude, but this is a simple fact, attested to by many, many site owners out there. I've seen it over and over again. Not trusting your Web designer or team is probably the first step in your search-engine strategy!

# Understanding the Limitations

You've probably received spam e-mails guaranteeing top-ten positions for your Web site in the search engines. You've probably also seen claims that you'll be ranked in hundreds or thousands of search engines. Most of this is nonsense — background noise that creates an entirely false picture. As one of my clients put it, "There's a lot of snake oil out there!" Here are the facts.

Typically, getting a high position isn't that easy. You try a couple of techniques, but they don't seem to work. So you try something else, and maybe you achieve a little success. Then you try another thing. Search engine optimization can often be *very* labor intensive, and you may not see results for weeks, and more likely, months.

## Big doesn't always equal better

By the way, don't imagine that if you're working with a large Web-design team with extensive programming experience they understand the search engines either. In fact, it's sometimes the more sophisticated design teams that get into the most trouble, building complex sites that simply won't work well with the search engines.

I consult with companies big and small, so I've advised large design teams made up of very good programmers. I can assure you that large, sophisticated teams often know as little as the independent Web designer who's been in business a few months.

## Top two in four

Sometimes it's easy to get a very high position in the search systems. But usually it isn't. A client wanted to be positioned in Google for six important key phrases. I built some pages, ensured that Google knew where those pages were (find out how to do this in Chapter 12), and waited. In just four days, the client didn't just have a top-ten position or even just a number-one position, but the top *two* positions for five of the six key phrases. But this situation is very unusual.

The degree of work required depends on the competitiveness of the keywords you are going after. Some keywords are incredibly competitive: *mortgage, insurance, attorney, real estate*, and so on, are highly competitive, with millions of people wanting some of the action. Other phrases are very easy — phrases such as *rodent racing*, for instance. If you're in the rodent-racing business, you're in luck, because you can probably rank right at the top very easily!

Although the way that search engines function is based on science, search engine optimization is more art than science. Why? Because the search engines don't want outside parties to know exactly how they rank sites. You have to just experiment. Ranking a site can be very difficult, and tremendously laborious. After all, why should it be easy? There is huge competition, so it *can't* always be easy. If it were easy for your site, then it would be easy for your competitors' sites, wouldn't it? And, after all, there can only ever be one number one.

## *Eyeing the Competition*

Some search terms are incredibly competitive. That is, many, many sites are competing for the top positions. Other search terms are far less competitive. How can you tell just how competitive your search terms are? Let me show you a few ways to figure it out:

- ✔ **Search for your terms.** This is not a terribly good method, but so commonly recommended I want to explain it. Go to Google and search for a few of your terms. (I discuss keywords in more detail in Chapter 5.) For instance, search for *personal injury lawyer*. You see a blue bar containing something like this:

```
Results 1 - 10 of about 16,300,000 for personal injury
        lawyer
```

This tells you that over 16M pages match the search terms in the Google index. Actually, most of these pages don't match well. Most of the pages don't actually have the term *personal injury lawyer.* Rather, as explained earlier, they have the words *personal, injury,* and *lawyer* scattered around the page.

✔ **Search for your terms using quotation marks.** Type search terms in quotation marks, like this: *"personal injury lawyer."* This time Google searches for the exact phrase, and comes back with a different number. When I searched, it came back with 3,200,000, because Google ignores all the pages with the words scattered around the page, and returns only pages with the exact phrase.

Here's the problem with these two techniques: While they show you how commonly used the words are, they don't show you how well the pages are optimized. Remember, you're not competing against every page with these terms; you're really competing with pages that were "optimized" for the search engines. There may be millions of pages with the term, but if none of them have been optimized, you can take your new-found SEO knowledge, create your own optimized pages, and have a good chance of ranking well.

So here's another quick technique I like to use — a simple way to get a feel for competitiveness in a few seconds. Search for a term, then scan down the page looking for the number of

✔ **PPC ads on the page.** For instance, in Figure 3-1 you see search results for the phrase *personal injury lawyer.* As you look down the page, you see three PPC ads at the top of the page, then more ads all the way down the right side of the page. Lots of PPC ads indicate lots of interest in the phrase. If people are spending money on PPC ads, many are also probably spending money on SEO.

✔ **Bold words on the page.** You'll also notice that Google bolds the words that you searched for; all the major search sites do this. Lots of bold words often mean well-optimized pages.

✔ **Bold words in the links (page titles).** Bold words in each page result's link indicate that someone has been optimizing the pages; the links are the page titles. The more bold text you see as you scan down, the more competitive the search terms are likely to be.

✔ **Complete phrases on the page.** The more frequently you see the full phrase you searched for, the more competitive the terms are likely to be; if the search engine returns mostly pages with the words scattered around, it's not very competitive.

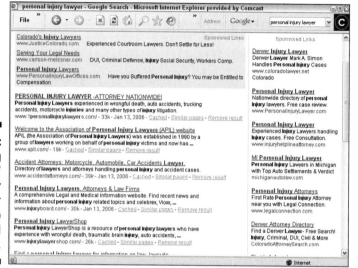

**Figure 3-1:**
Searching for *personal injury lawyer* brings up lots of bold text.

Here's another example. Search Google for *rodent racing*. What do you see? Something like that in Figure 3-2. First, notice almost no PPC ads (and the ad that does appear is not well matched to the search term). Next, notice very little bold text on the page, and *none* in the page titles (the links at the top of each search result). The matches in this case are all full phrases; but still, the other three factors suggest that this is not a very competitive term. You can see the difference between these two pages. The first search term, *personal injury lawyer,* is far more competitive than the second, *rodent racing.*

**Figure 3-2:**
Searching for *rodent racing* brings up far less bold text.

## Get your rodent running

Here's an example of how uncompetitive the phrase *rodent racing* actually is. These results are skewed somewhat, because I used the term *rodent racing* in the first edition of this book. Results 1, 2, 5, and 8 point to sample chapters from the book posted online, and to the Amazon.com book page. (Ever wondered by Amazon has recently started dropping large numbers of keywords onto their product pages?) My book has four entries out of the first ten, without even trying!

How important is competitiveness? When targeting search terms that are not very competitive, you may be able to create a few optimized pages and rank well. In very competitive areas, though, creating a few nicely optimized pages isn't enough. You *must* have links pointing to the site (perhaps to many of them), and you may also need large numbers of pages. In some really competitive areas, it may take hundreds, if not thousands, of links.

By the way, I often have clients ask me why a competitor ranks so well. "Their pages aren't better optimized than mine," I often hear. "We have more pages, and more pages with the right keywords...why is his site ranked so well?"

Without understanding all the variables — which we discuss later in this chapter, under "Controlling the Search-Engine Variables" — you can't tell for sure why a site ranks well. Is it because the site has been around much longer than yours? Is it because it has more content? Because the content is better "optimized"? Because the site has more incoming links? In fact the last of these factors is often essential; when I do a link analysis (see Chapter 15) I often discover that a poorly optimized site has a huge number of incoming links, with just the right keywords.

# Going Beyond Getting to #1

Everyone wants to rank #1 for the top keywords. Lawyers want to rank #1 for *attorney* or *lawyer.* Real estate agents want to rank #1 for *real estate.* Shoe stores want to rank #1 for *shoes,* and so on.

But what does being #1 achieve? You're trying to get people to your Web site, not to get any particular position, right? Getting ranked in the search engines is merely a way to generate that traffic to your site. People often assume that to generate traffic, they have to get #1 positions for top keywords. That's not the case. You can generate plenty of traffic to your site without ever getting to #1 for the most popular phrases. And in many cases, the traffic arriving at your site will be better — the visitors will be more appropriate for your site. There are two things to understand: *highly targeted keyword phrases*, and the *search tail*.

## Highly targeted keyword phrases

If your keywords are very competitive, look for keywords that aren't so sought after:

- ✔ **Go local.** One common strategy is, of course, to focus on local keywords. If you're a real estate agent, don't target *real estate*. Instead, target real estate in your area: *denver realtor, chicago real estate, dallas homes for sale,* and so on.

- ✔ **Focus on more specialized search terms.** A realtor might target traffic on keywords related to commercial real estate, or condos, for instance.

- ✔ **Incorporate spelling mistakes.** Some realtors target the very common misspelling *realator.*

These specialized search terms are hidden away in the search "tail," so now let's look at that concept.

## Understanding the search tail

The *search tail* is an important concept to understand. While the first few top keywords may get far more searches than any other search, when you look at the total number of searches, the top terms actually account for only a small percentage of the searches.

Look at Table 3-1 for search terms taken from Wordtracker, a great little tool that shows what search terms people are typing into the search engines. I searched for *video games* and Wordtracker returned 300 results containing that term. I don't have room for 300, so I've shown the first few.

## Table 3-1: Search Terms for *Video Games*

| | | Searches/ Day | Cumulative Searches |
|---|---|---|---|
| 1 | video games | 9,132 | 9,132 |
| 2 | music video games | 859 | 9,991 |
| 3 | adult video games | 621 | 10,612 |
| 4 | used video games | 269 | 10,881 |
| 5 | video games xbox | 240 | 11,121 |
| 6 | video games playstation 2 | 237 | 11,358 |
| 7 | violent video games | 230 | 11,588 |
| 8 | online video games | 229 | 11,817 |
| 9 | sex video games | 209 | 12,026 |
| 10 | free video games | 194 | 12,220 |
| 11 | history of video games | 186 | 12,406 |
| 12 | xxx video games | 151 | 12,557 |
| 13 | video games game cube | 145 | 12,702 |
| 14 | trade video games | 134 | 12,836 |
| 15 | violence in video games | 128 | 12,964 |
| 16 | cheap video games | 128 | 13,092 |
| 17 | nude video games | 103 | 13195 |
| 18 | video poker games | 101 | 13,296 |

Look at the Searches/Day column. It starts at 9,132 searches a day for *video games,* but immediately drops to 859 for *music video games.* By the time you get to the eighteenth search term, it's down to just 101 searches a day. Position 300 only gets 7 searches a day. This fact leads people to focus on the top phrases, where, it appears, most of the searching is going on.

But now look at the Cumulative Searches column. As you go down the list, you see the total of all searches from position one down to the current position. The first 18 keyword phrases account for 13,296 searches a day, of which 9,132 — 69 percent — are the top phrase *video games.* As you continue down, the cumulative number continues growing, of course. By the time you reach 300, the cumulative number has risen to 18,557, of which only 49 percent is the top phrase.

As you can see from the numbers in Table 3-1 and Figure 3-3, there's this big "tail"; the searches tail off. Wordtracker only gave me the first 300 search phrases; certainly thousands more contain the phrase *video games*.

For each phrase, Wordtracker gave an estimate of how often the phrase is searched upon every day. And even in this first 300 searches, most are *not* for the term *video games,* but are for phrases *containing* the term *video games*.

**Figure 3-3:**
Searches
tail off.

There's more, of course. What if you look, for instance, for the term *computer games?* How about *online games?* How about searching for the term *online video games?* You get a completely different set of 300 keyword phrases from Wordtracker.

Thus, if you only get matched with the exact phrase *video games,* you're missing 49 percent of the first 300 phrases, many of which — perhaps most — would be useful to you. Add the thousands of other, related phrases, and the primary term becomes less and less important.

It's essential that you understand that most of the action is not at the top; it's in the search tail! This means two things:

- ✔ Even if you can't rank well for a primary term, there's still plenty of room to play.

- ✔ If you focus *only* on a primary term, you're missing most of the action.

# Controlling Search-Engine Variables

You have control over five basic variables, and a sixth that waits for no man. Everything in this book fits somewhere into one of these six categories:

✔ Keywords

✔ Content

✔ Page optimization

✔ Submissions

✔ Links

✔ Time

Everything you do will be with the intention of affecting in some way one of the first five variables, and as you work the sixth, Time will keep on ticking. Here's a quick summary of each.

## Keywords

As you read in Chapter 5, and as I discuss earlier in this chapter, keywords are incredibly important. They're the very foundation of your search-engine strategy. Keywords target searchers. You place keywords in your pages and in links pointing to your pages as bait to attract people to your site. Pick the wrong keywords, and you're targeting the wrong people.

## Content

Content, from a search-engine perspective, really means text, and as you read in Chapter 9, you need content, and a lot of it. Search engines index words, and you want them to index the keywords you are interested in. The more words you have on your site — the more pages of text content — the more times your keywords can appear.

Think of a page of content as a ticket in the lottery; the more pages you have, the more lottery tickets you have. One common SEO strategy is to build huge sites, hundreds of thousands of pages, with vast amounts of text with keywords scattered through. Because of the nature of the search tail explained earlier in this chapter, each page has a chance to match a search now and then. The site has hundreds of thousands of lottery tickets.

You can play the content game a couple of ways:

✔ Create thousands of pages and hope that some of the text matches searches now and then.

✔ Create pages optimized for specific phrases that you know are used frequently.

## Page optimization

Content is just a start. Content has to be placed onto the pages in the correct way; the pages must be *optimized* to get the most out of the keywords. As you read in Chapters 2 and 6, you must place the words onto the pages in the correct places and formats.

If a search engine finds the relevant keywords on your page, that's good. If it finds the keywords in the right places on the page, that's a really powerful thing that differentiates your page from your competitors'.

## Submissions

In some ways *submissions* — submitting information to the search engines telling them where your pages can be found and asking them, in effect, to come to your site and index it — is not as important as many people imagine. Many businesses have, for a long time, promoted the idea that you have to submit your pages to the search engines, when in fact up until mid-2005 it really didn't matter much. You could submit, but the search engines would quite likely ignore the submission; links are what really counted.

However, in 2005 Google, introduced a new concept, the *sitemap*, and was quickly followed by Yahoo!. This file is placed into your Web site's root directory containing a list of links to all your pages, so the search engines could more easily find them.

These days I recommend you assume that submitting to the search engines will not get you indexed — that the way to get indexed is by making sure the search engines find links to your site — but that you also Provide Google and Yahoo! sitemaps, so those search engines can use them if they decide to (they may not). You read more about this in Chapter 11.

## Links

Links pointing to your Web site are incredibly important in a competitive keyword market. If you're targeting *rodent racing*, you probably don't need to worry too much about links (though every site needs at least some incoming links — links pointing to your site from other sites). But if you have lots of competition vying for your keywords, you won't win without links.

Links are so important, in fact, that a page can rank in the first position in any of the three major search engines, even if the page does not have the keywords that have been searched for . . . as long as links pointing to the page have the keywords. I explain this in Chapter 14. The more competitive your area, the more important links become.

## Time and the Google sandbox

Finally, the one factor you have little control over. You only really have control over time in the sense that the sooner you get started, the older your search-engine project becomes. Age is critical because the older the site, the more credibility the search engines give it.

There's something known as the *Google Sandbox* or *aging delay.* (Some people will tell you that these are actually two different types of time-related effects.) The idea is that when Google first finds your site, it puts it into a sandbox; it may index it, but it won't necessarily rank it well to begin with. It may take months before the site comes out of the sandbox. (People talk about the *Google sandbox,* but it seems likely that other search engines have something similar.)

There's a lot of debate about the effect of age; some say it's critical, and that for about eight months your site hasn't a chance of ranking well (I'm not in that camp), and others say that while the search engines may take into account age to some degree, it's by no means an overwhelming factor.

It comes down to this: The longer your domain has been registered, the better, and the longer your site has been up, the better. So you have control over this essential factor in just one way; the sooner you get started, the better. Register your domain name as soon as possible. Get a site, even a few pages, posted as soon as possible, and get links pointing from other sites to your site as soon as you can. Get new content posted as soon as possible. The sooner you start, the sooner you'll start ranking well.

### Reading history

We don't know exactly how Google handles all this, of course, but you can be fairly sure that Google uses some kind of historical data to help rank pages. In fact there's even a patent submitted in the names of various Google employees (though strangely, without Google's name itself on the patent), that discusses the idea of using historical data. (A long complicated URL takes you to the patent, so I've provided the link at www.searchenginebulletin.com.) This document is wonderful bedtime reading, if you're looking for a way to get to sleep without drugs. You won't find an explanation of how Google ranks Web pages, but you will find a lot of interesting possibilities.

# Determining Your Plan of Attack

Now you know what you're facing. As you read in Chapter 1, you can more or less forget those thousands of search sites and focus on no more than five search systems. And as I explain in this chapter, you have six essential factors to play with: keywords, content, page optimization, links, submissions, and time.

Forget about time . . . all I'll say is, get started right away! As for the other factors, how do you proceed? It depends to some degree on your budget and the competitiveness of the area you're working in.

✔ **Do a keyword analysis.** Regardless of competition or budget, you have to do one. Would you study for an exam without knowing what the exam is about? Would you plan a big meal, and then send an assistant to the grocery store without explaining which supplies you need? If you don't do a keyword analysis, you're just guessing. In my experience, you'll almost certainly fail to pick all the right keywords. See Chapter 5 for the lowdown on how to do this analysis.

✔ **Create readable pages.** If you want your site to appear, you have to create pages that the search-engine spiders or bots can read. (This isn't an issue for the search *directories,* but if you expect a bot to read your site, the pages have to be readable.) You might be surprised to hear that millions of pages on the Web cannot be read by search engines. For the lowdown on determining whether your pages are being read, see Chapter 2; to find out how to fix the problem if they're not, see Chapters 6 and 7.

✔ **Create keyworded pages.** Having readable pages is just a start. Next you have to put the keywords into the pages — in the right places and in the right format. See Chapter 6 for details.

✔ **Register with the search systems.** When your pages are ready to be indexed, you need to do two things:

• Let the search systems know where those pages are.

• Get the search systems to include the pages in their indexes and directories.

Sometimes these tasks are harder than you might expect. You can get into the search systems various ways, as described in detail in Chapters 11 and 12.

✔ **Get other sites to link to your site.** Check out Chapters 14 and 15 to find out how the number and type of links pointing to your site affect your rank.

The preceding strategies are the basics, but you may want to — or even need to — go further. I cover these additional techniques in detail later:

- ✔ **Register with other places.** You may also want to register at specialized sites that are important for your particular business. See Chapter 13.

- ✔ **Register with the shopping indexes.** If you're selling a product, it's a good idea to register with the shopping indexes. Although these indexes don't match the big search systems in volume of searches, they're still important. This is covered in Chapter 16.

- ✔ **Use Pay Per Click.** You can get noticed in the search engines two ways. You can use *natural search* — that is, get ranked in the search engines without paying — or you can use *Pay Per Click*. Many companies go straight to Pay Per Click, a system by which you get ranked well but pay each time someone clicks a link to your site. This is usually not a good idea (though sometimes it's a great way to push a product temporarily, such as a special offer), but at some point, you may want to use Pay Per Click in addition to natural search; see Chapter 17.

But there's more. If you're in a very competitive market, you may want to really push two techniques:

- ✔ **Create large amounts of content.** Make hundreds, perhaps thousands, of pages of content.

- ✔ **Go after links in a big way.** You may need hundreds, perhaps thousands, of links to rank well if your competitors have done the same.

This chapter provides an overview of the search-engine battle you're about to join. Now it's time to jump in and make it all happen, so Chapter 4 explains what search engines really like to see: Web sites that people on the Internet believe are really useful.

# Chapter 4

# Making Your Site Useful and Visible

*O*bviously, it's important to create Web pages that search engines will read and index, pages that you hope will rank well for important keywords. But if you're going to build a Web site, you need to step back and figure out what purpose the site should serve and how it can accomplish that purpose.

Creating a *useful* site is the key. Even if your sole aim is to sell a product online, the more useful the site is to visitors, the more successful it's likely to be. Take Amazon.com, for instance. It certainly wasn't the first online retailer of books and music, or any of the other products it offers. But one of Amazon's real strengths is that it doesn't just sell products; it's a really *useful* site, in many ways:

✔ It provides tons of information about the products it sells. The information is useful even if you don't buy from Amazon.

✔ You can save information for later. If you find a book you're interested in but don't want to buy right now, save a link to it and come back next month, year, or five years from now.

✔ Other site owners can become partners and make money by promoting Amazon.

✔ Other businesses can easily sell their products through Amazon.

✔ You can read sample chapters, look at tables of contents, listen to snippets of music, and so on.

✔ You can read product reviews from both professional reviewers and consumers.

Would Amazon be so successful if it just provided lists of the products it sells, rather than offering visitors a veritable cornucopia of useful stuff? Absolutely not.

Consider this: The more useful your site is, the greater the chance of success. The more people talk about your site, the more likely journalists are to write about it, the more likely it is to be mentioned on radio or TV, the more people will link to it from their Web sites. Search-engine marketing and non-search-engine marketing are both important because either form of Web site promotion can lead to more links pointing to your site. And, as you find out in Chapters 14 and 15, links to your site are critical to search-engine success.

With that in mind, this chapter focuses on the basics about what you need to do to create a successful Web site.

# Revealing the Secret but Essential Rule of Web Success

Here's a simple rule to success on the Web:

*Make your site useful and then tell people about it.*

That's not so complicated, really. Figure out how your site can be useful and then find as many ways as possible to let people know about it. You'll use the search engines, of course, but you should be using other methods, too. Remember, the search engines are not the only way to get people to your site. In fact, many Web sites have succeeded without using the search engines as their primary method of attracting visitors.

## Amazon — Success sans search

It's unlikely that search engines were a large factor in Amazon's success — Amazon grew rapidly mainly because of the enormous press attention it received, beginning in 1994. Today, I'd bet that relatively few people arrive at Amazon.com through the search engines. Rather, they already know the Amazon brand and go straight to the site, or they go through the hundreds of thousands of Amazon affiliate sites. And up until recent years, Amazon made relatively little effort to actively generate search-engine traffic. I suspect they pay more attention to it now; certainly their new Statistically Improbable Phrases (SIPs) and Capitalized Phrases (CPs) lists on their book pages help them in the search engines.

Many successful companies have done little or nothing to promote themselves through the search engines, yet they still turn up at the top when you search for their products or services. Why? Because their other promotions have helped push them higher in the search engines, by creating thousands, even tens or hundreds of thousands, of links to them around the Internet.

## The evolving, incorrect "secret"

Over the last decade, a number of popular ideas about what makes a successful Web site have been bandied around, and all were wrong to some degree. Here are some of those dated secrets to successful Web sites:

- ✔ **Links:** When the Web began booming in 1994, it was all about *links*. You would hear in the press that the secret to a successful Web site was linking to other sites.

- ✔ **Cool:** Then people started saying that the secret of success was to make your site *cool*. Cool sites were more entertaining and more likely to attract repeat visitors.

- ✔ **Community:** Then people started talking about *community;* yeah, that's the ticket! The secret to a successful Web site was creating a community where people could meet and chat with each other.

- ✔ **Content:** Then, around 2000, people discovered that the secret was *content.* By putting more stuff, particularly textual information, on your site, you could be more successful.

Specific one-size-fits-all secrets to success never make sense.

The most harmful of the preceding ideas was that your site had to be cool. This silly idea led to the expenditure of billions of dollars on useless but pretty Web sites, most of which (thankfully!) have since disappeared. Unfortunately, some of the *it's-all-about-cool* crowd is still in the Web business and still convincing businesses to spend money on ridiculous, wasteful things such as Flash intros for their Web sites.

## Uncovering the real secret

Ready to hear the real secret of site-creation success? Your Web site has to be *useful.* The problem with the secrets I just mentioned is that they're too specific, leading people to build sites that were in many cases inappropriate. Sure, links are important to Yahoo!, but they're much less so to the vast majority of Web sites. If you own an entertainment site, you may want to make it cool and entertaining. Certainly community can be an effective tool, but not every site has to have it. Content is very important, too — especially from a search-engine perspective — but many successful Web sites don't have much content. (I talk in more detail about content in the next section because it's a special case.)

I've been writing this since 1997: *Forget cool; think useful.*

When you're planning your Web site, think about what kinds of folks you want to attract to the site. Then try to come up with ideas about what features and information might be *useful* to them. Your site may end up with a lot of link pages, providing a directory of sorts for people in your industry. Or maybe you really need a cool and entertaining site. Or perhaps you decide to use discussion groups and chat rooms as a way to build community and pull the crowds into your site; that's fine. Or maybe you decide to create a huge repository of information to attract a particular type of customer. That's okay, too. Maybe you do *all* these things. But the important first step is to think about what you can do to make your site more useful.

## Showing a bias for content

Content is a special case. Search engines are biased toward ranking content-heavy Web sites well for a couple of reasons:

- Search engines were originally academic research tools designed to find *text information.* Search engines mostly index text — content.

- Search engines need something to base their judgments on. When you type a term into a search engine, it looks for the *words* you provided. So a Web site built with few words is at a disadvantage right from the start.

As you discover elsewhere in this book — such as in the discussion of PageRank in Chapter 14 — search engines do have other criteria for deciding if a Web site matches a particular search (most notably the number and type of links pointing to the site). But search engines do have a huge bias toward textual content.

Unfortunately, this bias is often a real problem. The real world simply doesn't work the way search engines see it. Here's an example: Suppose your business rents very expensive, specialized photographic equipment. Your business has the best prices and the best service of any company renting this equipment. Your local customers love you, and few other companies match your prices, service, or product range. So you decide to build a Web site to reach customers elsewhere, and ship rentals by UPS and FedEx.

The search engines base your rank, to a great degree, on the number and type of keywords in your pages.

To rank well, a competitor has added a bunch of pages about photography and photographic equipment to its site. To compete, you have to do the same. Do your customers care? No, they just want to find a particular piece of equipment that fills their need, rent it, and move on quickly. All the additional information, the content that you've added, is irrelevant to them. It's simply clutter.

This is a common scenario. I recently discussed the content issue with a client who was setting up a Web site at which people could quickly get a moving-service quote. The client wanted to build a clean, sparse site that allowed customers to get the quote within a couple of minutes. "But we don't want all that stuff, that extra text, and nor do our clients!" he told me, and he had a good point.

You can't ignore the fact that search engines like content. However, you can compete other ways. One of the most important ways is getting links from other sites, as you discover in Chapter 14. Search engines like to see links on other sites pointing to your site. Sites that have hundreds or thousands of other sites linking to them often rank well. But they still need at least *some* content for the search engines to index. And the best situation is lots of useful content with lots of incoming links.

# Making Your Site Work Well

I've been writing about site design for almost seven years, and I'm happy to say that many of the rules of good site design just happen to match what search engines like. And many of the cool tricks that designers love cause problems with the search engines. So I want to quickly review a few tips for good site design that will help both your site visitors and the search engines work with your site.

## Limiting multimedia

Most multimedia used on the Web is pointless because it rarely serves a useful purpose to the visitor. It's there because Web designers enjoy working with it and because many people are still stuck in the old "you've got to be cool" mindset.

Look at the world's most successful Web sites, and you'll find that they rarely use multimedia — Flash animations and video, for example — for purely decorative purposes. Look at Amazon: Its design is simple, clean, black text on white background, with lots of text and very little in the way of animations, video, or sound (except, for instance, where it provides music samples in the site's CD area). Look at Yahoo!, Google, CNN, or eBay — they're not cool; they just get the job done.

You can employ multimedia on a Web site in some useful ways. I think it makes a lot of sense to use Flash, for instance, to create demos and presentations. However, Flash intros are almost *always* pointless, and search engines don't like them because Flash intros don't provide indexable content. Anytime you get the feeling it would be nice to have an animation, or when your Web designer says you should have some animation, slap yourself twice on the face and then ask yourself this: Who is going to benefit: the designer or the site visitor? If that doesn't dissuade you, have someone else slap you.

## Using text, not graphics

A surprising number of Web sites use graphics to place text onto pages. Take a look at the Web site shown in Figure 4-1. Although this page appears to have a lot of text, every word is in an image file. Web designers often employ this technique so all browsers can view their carefully chosen fonts. But search engines don't read the text in the images they run across, so this page provides *no* text that can be indexed by the search engines. Although this page may contain lots of useful keywords (you find out all about keywords in Chapter 5), the search engines read *nothing*. From a usability perspective, the design is bad, too, because all those images take much longer to download than the equivalent text would take.

## Avoiding the urge to be too clever

I advise people to stay one step behind in Web technology and try not to be too clever. From a usability standpoint, the problem is that not all browser types work the same; they have different bugs and handle technical tricks differently.

If you're always working with the very latest Web-development technology, more of your visitors are likely to run into problems. Cool technology often confuses the search engines, too. As an SEO friend likes to say, "Google likes black text on a white background." In other words search engines like *simple*. The more complicated your Web pages are, the harder it is for search engines to read and categorize them.

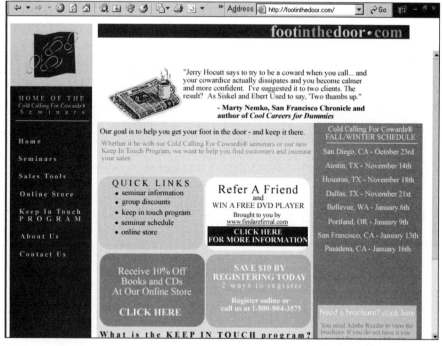

**Figure 4-1:**
This looks like text, but it's actually images that slow the page load and provide search engines nothing to read.

You must strike a compromise between employing all the latest Web-design technology and tools and ensuring the search engines can read your pages. From a search-engine perspective, in fact, one step behind probably isn't enough!

## Don't be cute

Some sites do everything they can to be cute. The Coca Cola site was a classic example of this a few years ago, though it finally got the message and changed. The site had icons labeled *Tour de Jour, Mind Candy, Curvy Canvas, Netalogue,* and so on. What do these things mean? Who knows? Certainly not the site visitor.

This sort of deranged Web design is far less common now than it used to be, but you still see it occasionally — particularly in sites designed by hip Web-design firms. One incredibly irritating technique is the hidden navigation structure. The main page contains a large image with hotspots on it. But it's unclear where the hotspots are, or what they link to, until you point at the image and move the mouse around. This strikes me as the Web-design equivalent of removing the numbers from the front of the homes in a neighborhood. You can still figure out where people live; you just have to knock on doors and ask.

Sweet and sickly cuteness doesn't help your site visitors find their way around and almost certainly hurts you with the search engines.

## Avoiding frames

Framed Web sites were very popular a few years ago; fortunately, they've fallen out of favor to a great degree. From a usability standpoint, there's nothing wrong with frames if they're used properly.

Here are a few reasons they're less prevalent today:

- Many designers misused frames, making sites hard to navigate. Too many frames in a browser window ignore the average Joe working with a small screen and low resolution.
- Some browsers simply don't handle frames well.
- Search engines don't handle frames well, for a whole list of reasons explained in Chapter 7.

I can think of few situations in which you can't use some other mechanism rather than frames, so I advise you to stay away from them.

## Making it easy to move around

Web design is constantly getting better, but it still surprises me that designers sometimes make it difficult for visitors to move around a Web site.

Think carefully about how your site is structured:

- Does it make sense from a visitor's standpoint?
- Can visitors find what they need quickly?
- Do you have *dangling* pages — pages where a visitor can't find a link to get back into your main site?

  Search engines don't like dangling pages, and consider what happens if someone on another site links directly to the page: Visitors can get to the page but not to the rest of your site.

## Providing different routes

People think differently from each other, so you need to provide them with numerous avenues for finding their way around your site. And by doing so, you're also giving more information to search engines and ensuring that search engines can navigate your site easily.

Here are some different navigational systems you can add to your site:

- ✔ **Sitemap.** This page links to the different areas of your site, or even, in the case of small sites, to every page in the site. An example is `www. peterkentconsulting.com/sitemap.htm`.

- ✔ **Table of Contents or Index page.** You can sort the page thematically or alphabetically.

- ✔ **Navigation bars.** Most sites have navigation bars these days.

- ✔ **Navigation text links.** Little links at the bottom of your pages, or along the sides, can help people find their way around . . . and the search engines, too.

I like to add simple text links near the *top,* rather than the bottom, of the page. Users with slow connections see these links quickly, and search engines are sure to find them. (Sometimes, on large and complex Web pages, search engines may miss links at the bottom of the page.)

## Using long link text

It's a proven fact that Web users like *long link text* — links that are more than just a single word and actually describe where the link takes you. Usability testing shows that long link text makes it much easier for visitors to find their way around a site. It's not surprising if you think about it; a long link provides more information to visitors about where a link will take them.

Unfortunately, many designers feel constrained by design considerations, forcing all navigation links, for instance, to conform to a particular size. You often see buttons that have only enough room for ten or so characters, forcing the designer to think about how to say complicated things in one or two words.

Long links that explain what the referenced page is about are a great thing not only for visitors but also for search engines. By using keywords in the links, you're telling the search engines what the referenced pages are about.

You also have a problem if all the links on your site are on image buttons — search engines can't read images, so image buttons provide no information about the referenced page. You can't beat a well-keyworded text link for passing information about the target page to the search engines.

## Don't keep restructuring

Try to make sure your site design is good before you get too far into the process. Sites that are constantly being restructured have numerous problems, including the following:

- Links from other Web sites into yours get broken, which is bad for potential visitors as well as for search engines (or, more precisely, bad for your position in the search engines because they won't be able to reach your site through the broken links).
- Anyone who has bookmarked your page now has a broken bookmark.

It's a good idea to create a custom 404 error page, which is displayed in your browser if the server is unable to find a page you've requested. (Ask your Web server administrator how to do this; the process varies among servers.) Create an error page with links to other areas of the site, perhaps even a sitemap, so that if visitors and searchbots can't find the right page, at least they'll be able to reach some page on your site.

## Editing and checking spelling

Check your pages for spilling and editng errors. Not only do error-free pages make your site appear more professional, they ensure that your valuable keywords are not wasted. If potential visitors are searching for *rodent racing,* for example, you don't want the term *rodint racing* in your Web pages. (Except, that is, if you are trying to catch traffic from oft-misspelled keywords, something I discuss in Chapter 5.)

# Part II
# Building Search-Engine-Friendly Sites

The 5th Wave By Rich Tennant

"Maybe your keyword search, 'legal secretary, love, fame, fortune', needs to be refined."

# In this part . . .

Time for the details. In this part, you discover things that help your site rank well in the search engines . . . and things that almost guarantee that your site won't do well in the search engines. Understand the information in this part, and you're way ahead of most Web site owners, designers, and developers.

You find out what search engines like to find in your Web pages, which are the things that are likely to help your site rank well: simplicity, text content with the right keywords, keywords in heading tags and bold text, and so on. You also discover what things have the opposite effect (making search engines stumble when they reach your site or even leave the site without reading any pages). From frames to dynamically generated pages to session IDs, these things can be the kiss of death if you're not careful.

I also let you in on a few secrets that the search engines hate, techniques that people often use to "trick" the search engines but that can also be dangerous. Many folks in the search-engine-optimization business shy away from these techniques, for fear of having their pages penalized or entire sites banned from the search engines.

Finally, this part shows you ways to quickly build the content on your site. Content is king as far as the search engines are concerned, but the problem is where to find enough text to satisfy them.

# Chapter 5

# Picking Powerful Keywords

· · · · · · · · · · · · · · · · · · · · · · · · · · · · · · · · · · · · · · · · · · · · · · ·

· · · · · · · · · · · · · · · · · · · · · · · · · · · · · · · · · · · · · · · · · · · · · · ·

*I* was talking with a client some time ago who wanted to have his site rank well in the search engines. (I've changed the details of this story a tad to protect the client's privacy.) Let's say the client is a company with annual revenues in the millions of dollars (as indeed this client is), in the business of, oh, I dunno . . . staging rodent-racing events.

I did a little research and found that most people searching for rodent-racing events use the keywords *rodent racing.* (Big surprise, huh?) I took a look at the client's Web site and discovered that the words *rodent racing* didn't appear anywhere on the site's Web pages.

"You have a little problem," I said. "Your site doesn't use the words *rodent racing,* so it's unlikely that any search engine will find your site when people search for that."

"Oh, well," was the client's reply, "Our marketing department objects to the term. We have a company policy to use the term *furry friend events.* The term rodent is too demeaning, and if we say we're racing them, the animal-rights people will get upset."

This is a true story, well, except for the bit about rodent racing and the furry friends thing. But in principle it happened. This company had a policy not to use the words that most of its potential clients were using to search for it.

You may be asking yourself how it's possible that a company can build a Web site only to discover later that the keywords its potential clients and visitors are using are not in the site. Well, I can think of a couple of reasons:

- ✔ Most sites are built without any regard for the search engines. The site designers simply don't think about the search engines or have little background knowledge about how search engines work.

- ✔ The site designers do think about the search engines, but they guess, often incorrectly, what keywords they should be using.

I can't tell you how the client and I resolved this problem because, well, we haven't yet resolved it. (Sometimes company politics trump common sense.) But I am going to tell you how to pick keywords that make sense for your site, as well as how to discover what keywords your potential site visitors are using to search for your products and services.

# Understanding the Importance of Keywords

When you go to a search engine to find something, you type in a word or words, and click the Search button. The search engine then looks in its index for those words.

Suppose that you typed the words *rodent racing.* Generally speaking, the search engine looks for various things:

- ✔ Pages that contain the exact phrase *rodent racing*

- ✔ Pages that don't have the phrase *rodent racing,* but do have the words *rodent* and *racing* in close proximity

- ✔ Pages that have the words *rodent* and *racing* somewhere, though not necessarily close together

- ✔ Pages with word stems; for instance, pages with the word *rodent* and the word *race* somewhere in the page

- ✔ Pages that have links pointing to them, in which the link text contains the phrase *rodent racing*

- ✔ Pages with links pointing to them with the link text containing the words *rodent* and *racing,* although not together

The process is actually a lot more complicated than this. The search engine doesn't necessarily show pages in the order I just listed — all the pages with the exact phrase, then all the pages with the words in close proximity, and so on. When considering ranking order, the search engine considers (in addition to hundreds of secret criteria) whether the keyword or phrase is in:

- ✔ Bold text
- ✔ Italicized text
- ✔ Bulleted lists
- ✔ Text larger than most of the other text on the page
- ✔ Heading text (<H> tags)

Despite all the various complications, however, one fact is of paramount importance: If a search engine can't relate your Web site to the words that someone searches for, it has no reason to return your Web site as part of the search results.

Picking the right keywords is critical. As Woody Allen once said, "Eighty percent of success is showing up." If you don't play the game, you can't win. And if you don't choose the right keywords, you're not even showing up to play the game.

 Understanding how to search helps you understand the role of keywords. Check out the bonus chapter I've posted at www.SearchEngineBulletin. com to find out the different ways you can search using the search engines in general and Google in particular.

# Thinking like Your Prey

It's an old concept: You should think like your prey. Companies often make mistakes with their keywords because they choose based on how they — rather than their customers — think about their products or services. You have to stop thinking that you know what customers call your products. Do some research to find out what consumers really do call your products.

Do a little keyword analysis. Check to see what people are actually searching for on the Web. You'll discover that words that you were positive people would use are rarely searched, and you'll find that you've missed a lot of common terms. Sure, you may get some of the keywords right, but if you're spending time and energy targeting particular keywords, you might as well get 'em all right!

 The term *keyword analysis* can have several meanings:

- ✔ When I use it, I'm referring to what I'm discussing in this chapter: analyzing the use of keywords by people searching for products, services, and information.

✔ Some people use the term to mean *keyword-density* analysis, which means finding out how often a keyword appears in a page. Some of the keyword-analysis tools that you run across are actually keyword-density-analysis tools.

✔ The term also may be used to refer to the process of analyzing keywords in your Web site's access logs.

# Starting Your Keyword Analysis

Do a keyword analysis — a check of what keywords people use to search on the Web — or you're wasting your time. Imagine spending hundreds of hours optimizing your site for a keyword you think is good, only to discover that another keyword or phrase gets two or three times the traffic. How would you feel? Sick? Stupid? Mad? Don't risk your mental health — do it right the first time.

## Identifying the obvious keywords

Begin by typing the obvious keywords into a text editor or word processor. Type the words you've already thought of, or, if you haven't started yet, the ones that immediately come to mind. Then study the list for a few minutes. What else can you add? What similar terms come to mind? Add them, too.

When you do your analysis, you'll find that some of the initial terms you think of aren't searched very often, but that's okay. This list is just the start.

## Looking at your Web site's access logs

Take a quick look at your Web site's access logs (often called *hit logs*). You may not realize it, but most logs show you the keywords that people used when they clicked a link to your site at a search engine. (If your logs don't contain this information, you probably need another program!) Write down the terms that are bringing people to your site.

## Examining competitors' keyword tags

You probably know who your competitors are — you should, anyway. Go to their sites and open the source code of a few pages.

1. **Choose View⇨Source from the browser's menu bar.**

2. **Look for the `<META NAME="keywords">` tag for any useful keywords.**

Often the keywords are garbage, or simply not there, but if you look at enough sites, you're likely to come up with some useful terms you hadn't thought of.

# Brainstorming with colleagues

Talk to friends and colleagues to see if they can come up with some possible keywords. Ask them something like this: "If you were looking for a site at which you could find the latest scores for rodent races around the world, what terms would you search for?" Give everyone a copy of your current keyword list and ask if they can think of anything to add to it. Usually, reading the terms will spark an idea or two, and you'll end up with a few more terms.

# Looking closely at your list

After you've put together your initial list, go through it looking for more obvious additions. Don't spend too much time on this; all you're doing here is creating a preliminary list to run through a keyword tool, which will also figure out some of these things for you.

### Obvious spelling mistakes

Scan through your list and see if you can think of any obvious spelling mistakes. Some spelling mistakes are incredibly important, with 10, 15, or 20 percent of all searches (sometimes even more) containing the word being misspelled! For example, about one-fifth of all Britney Spears–related searches are misspelled, spread out over a dozen misspellings — which might allow me to take a cheap shot, but I have no intention of doing so.

The word *calendar* is also frequently misspelled. Look at the following estimate of how often the single word *calendar* is searched for each day, in its various permutations:

> *calendar:* 10,605 times
> *calender:* 2,721
> *calander:* 1,549
> *calandar:* 256

Thirty percent of all searches on the word *calendar* are misspelled! (Where do I get these estimates, you're wondering? You find out later in this chapter, starting at "Using a keyword tool.")

If the traffic from a misspelling is significant, you may want to create a page on your site that uses that misspelling. Some sites contain what I call "Did You Mean" pages, such as the one shown in Figure 5-1. Some sites contain pages using misspellings in the <TITLE> tags, which can work very well. These don't have to be pages that many people see. After all, the only people who will see the misspelled titles in a search results page are those who misspelled the words in the first place!

One nice thing about misspellings is that often competitors have missed them, so you can grab the traffic without much trouble.

### Synonyms

Sometimes similar words are easily missed. If your business is home related, for instance, have you thought about the term *house?* Americans may easily overlook this word, using *home* instead, but other English-speaking countries use the word often. Still, add it to the list because you may find quite a few searches related to it.

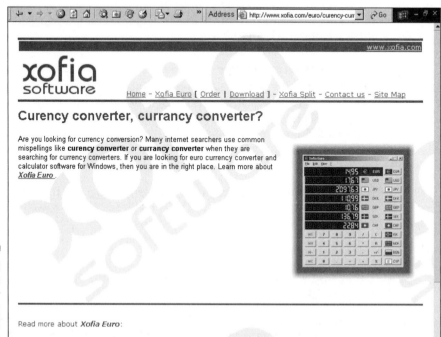

**Figure 5-1:**
A page designed for the spelling challenged!

You might even use a thesaurus to find more synonyms. However, I show you some keyword tools that will run these kinds of searches for you; see "Using a keyword tool."

### Split or merged words

You may find that although your product name is one word — *RodentRacing,* for instance — most people are searching for you using two words, *rodent* and *racing.* Remember to consider your customer's point of view.

Also, some words are employed in two ways. Some people, for instance, use the term *knowledgebase,* while others use *knowledge base.* Which is more important? Both should be on your list, but *knowledge base* is used around four to five times more often than *knowledgebase.* If you optimize your pages for *knowledgebase* (I discuss page optimization in Chapter 6), you're missing out on around 80 percent of the traffic!

### Singulars and plurals

Go through your list and add singulars and plurals. Search engines treat singulars and plurals differently. For example, searching on *rodent* and *rodents* provides different results, so it's important to know which term is searched for most often. A great example is to do a search on book (1,635 searches per day, according to Wordtracker, which is discussed later in this chapter) and books (16,475 searches per day) in Google. A search on *book* returns Barnes and Noble as the number-one result, while *books* returns Amazon.com (and has for several years now).

You don't need to worry about upper- versus lowercase letters. You can use *rodent* or *Rodent* or *RODENT,* for example. Most search engines aren't case sensitive. If you search for *rodent* (and probably almost 90 percent of all searches are in lowercase), virtually all search engines will find *Rodent* or *RODENT* — or *rODENT* or *ROdent,* for that matter.

### Hyphens

Do you see any hyphenated words on your list that could be used without the hyphen, or vice versa? Some terms are commonly used both ways, so find out what your customers are using. Here are two examples:

  ✔ The terms *ecommerce* and *e-commerce* are fairly evenly split, with a little over 50 percent of searches using the latter term.

  ✔ The dash in *e-mail* is far less frequently used, with *email* being the most common term.

Find hyphenated words, add both forms to your list, and determine which is more common because search engines treat them as different searches.

Search engines generally treat a hyphen as a space. So searching for *rodent-racing* is the same as searching for *rodent racing*. However, there is a real difference between *e-commerce* and *ecommerce*, or *rodentracing* and *rodent-racing*.

### Geo-specific terms

Is geography important to your business? Are you selling shoes in Seattle or rodents in Rochester? Don't forget to include terms that include your city, state, other nearby cities, and so on.

### Your company name

If you have a well-known company name, add that to the list, in whatever permutations you can think of (Microsoft, MS, MSFT, and so on).

### Other companies' names and product names

If people are likely to search for companies and products similar to yours, add those companies and products to your list. That's not to say you should use these keywords in your pages (you can in some conditions, as I discuss in Chapter 6), but it's nice to know what people are looking for and how often they're looking.

## Using a keyword tool

After you've put together a decent-size keyword list, the next step is to use a keyword tool. This tool enables you to discover additional terms you haven't thought of and helps you determine which terms are most important — which terms are used most often by people looking for your products and services.

Both free and paid versions of keyword tools are available. I discuss the freebies first, but I might as well cut to the chase and tell you that I recommend that you fork over the dough and use Wordtracker, the world's top search-engine keyword tool. So you can skip to that section if you want, or read on.

### The Yahoo! Search Marketing Keyword Selector tool

Yahoo! Search Marketing is a Pay Per Click service (see Chapter 17). As a service to its customers (and prospective customers), Yahoo! provides a free tool that allows you to see how often a particular search term is used each month at Yahoo!

Here's how to find and use this tool:

1. **Point your browser to** http://searchmarketing.yahoo.com/rc/srch/.

   You see the Yahoo! Search Marketing Resource Center.

2. **Click the Advertiser <u>Keyword Selector Tool</u> link on the right side of the page.**

   A small window opens with a search box.

3. **In the search box, type a keyword you think people may be using.**

4. **Press Enter.**

   The tool returns a list of keywords, showing you how often that term and related terms are used by people searching on Yahoo! and partner sites; see Figure 5-2.

I'm tired of looking for the Yahoo! keyword tool, and having to explain to people how to find it; it keeps moving! So I've placed a link on my site; go to http://searchenginebulletin.com/yahoo-keywords.html.

The number isn't terribly important; it's the relative levels that count. If one word was searched on 150,000 times last month, and another one 10,000 times, you can be pretty sure that the first term is the most important one.

Yahoo! provides other search terms, too. It looks for similar and related terms, and lists them and the number of times those terms were searched for. Clicking one of the additional terms sends Yahoo! searching on that term, bringing up similar and related terms.

For each term in your list, use the Keyword Selector Tool to find out how many times the term is used each month and to find related terms. Add to your list any related terms that look like they may be appropriate for you (and note the number of times they're searched for).

This process takes what is referred to in the search-engine optimization business as *a bloody long time.* (Well, the business in England, anyway.) This is why I suggest that you use Wordtracker, which I discuss shortly.

### Other keyword tools

Other keyword-analysis tools are available from other PPC services, but unlike Yahoo!, you generally can't get to the tool until you have already set up an account or gone through some preliminary sign-up process. Google has a pretty good tool, for instance, but you have to jump through some hoops to get to it if you haven't set up a PPC account with Google AdWords (adwords.google.com).

To find some of the other software tools and Web-based services, do a search on *keyword* or *keyword analysis.* The top tool is Wordtracker, which is discussed in the next section.

**Figure 5-2:**
The Yahoo!
Keyword
Selector
Tool.

# Using Wordtracker

Wordtracker (www.wordtracker.com) is the tool that virtually all SEO professionals use. (SEO professionals also like to throw the term *SEO* around, rather than use the more unwieldy but clearer *search engine optimization.*)

Wordtracker, owned by a company in London, England, has access to data from several very large metacrawlers. A *metacrawler* is a system that searches multiple search engines for you. For example, type a word into Dogpile's search box (www.dogpile.com), and the system searches at Google, Yahoo!, MSN, and Ask.com.

Wordtracker gets the information about what people are searching for from Metacrawler.com, Dogpile.com, and others, for a total of over 120 million searches each month. It stores 100 days of searches in its databases — somewhere around 400 million searches. Wordtracker combines the data for the last 100 days and then allows its customers to search this database. Ask Wordtracker how often someone searched for the term *rodent,* and it tells you that it was searched for (at the time of writing) 129 times over the last 100 days but that the term *rodents* is far more popular, with 544 searches over the last 100 days.

## Endorsement disclaimer

I generally don't like endorsing a product in this manner; elsewhere in this book, I mention products and even state that they're good. But Wordtracker is a special case. I know of no other tool that matches it or that is anywhere near as popular. And it's cheap to use, so I recommend that you do so. Disclaimer: I've done a little work for this firm. In fact, you may find some of my writing on the Wordtracker site. However, I mentioned Wordtracker in glowing terms in the first edition of this book, *before* I ever did business with the company.

Certain searches are seasonal: *pools* in the summer, *heaters* in the winter, and so on. Because Wordtracker has only the last 60 days of information, it may not be representative for a full year for some terms. And some searches may be influenced by the media. While searches for *paris hilton* were very high in November and December 2003, when I wrote the first edition of this book . . . oh, bad example, they're still absurdly high, unfortunately. Okay, here's another example. While searches are currently very high for *King Kong*, they'll drop once the media interest wanes.

Here's what information Wordtracker can provide:

- ✔ The number of times in the last 100 days that the exact phrase you enter was searched for out of 400 million or so searches
- ✔ An estimate of how many times each day the phrase is used throughout all the Web's search engines
- ✔ Similar terms and synonyms, and the usage statistics about these terms
- ✔ Terms used in hundreds of competing sites' KEYWORDS meta tags, ranked according to frequency
- ✔ Common misspellings
- ✔ A comparison of how often a term is searched for with how many pages appear for that term — a nice way to find terms with relatively little competition

Do metacrawlers provide better results? Here's what Wordtracker claims:

- ✔ **Search results at the big search engines are skewed.** Many Web site owners use them to check their sites' rankings, sometimes several times a week. Thus, many searches are not true searches. Metacrawlers can't easily be used for this purpose, so they provide cleaner results.

> ✔ **Wordtracker analyzes searches to find what appear to be fake, auto-mated searches.** Some companies carry out hundreds of searches an hour on particular keywords — company or product names, for instance — in an attempt to trick search engines into thinking these keywords generate a lot of interest.

Wordtracker is well worth the price. You can pay for access by the

> ✔ Day for £4.20, around $7.32 currently
> ✔ Week for £14/$24.39
> ✔ Month for £28/$48.78
> ✔ Year for £140/$243.86

Many professionals in the SEO business have a regular account with Wordtracker, but for individual sites, it may be worth just getting a day or two of access. One strategy is to build your list first, as described in this chapter, and then sign up for a day and run Wordtracker for that day. You may get enough done in a couple of hours; if not, you can always sign up for another day. (Of course these prices may change, so check the Wordtracker site.)

Anyone heavily involved in the Web and search engines can easily get addicted to this tool. Sometimes you've just got to know exactly how often people are searching for *paris hilton* (21,5315 times a day), *jack abramoff* (466), or *skyscout* (1987).

## *Creating a Wordtracker project*

Wordtracker lets you create projects so you can store different groups of terms — perhaps one for each Web site or, if you're a consultant, one for each client. The first thing you should do — after plunking down your money and setting up the standard username and password stuff — is create a project. Here's how:

1. **Log in and click the Projects button on the main navigation page.**

   The Projects page appears, as shown in Figure 5-3.

2. **Give your project a name and then click the Change Project Name button to save the new name.**

   Wordtracker allows you to have seven projects, storing different key-word lists. You can empty old projects and rename them as you move on to new Web projects. This may be an important feature if you're an SEO professional or a Web designer working on multiple Web sites.

Type your new project name here.          Click here to set the new name.

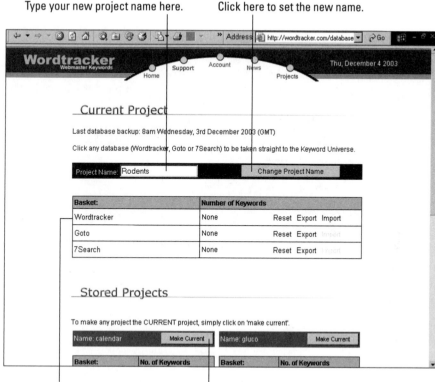

Click here to view the words          Click here to load the selected project.
stored in the project.

**3. Click the Import button, then copy and paste the words from the list into the large text box.**

You get one entry per line, as shown in Figure 5-4.

**4. Click the Submit button.**

I recommend that you leave the Compressed Import option button selected. Doing so changes all the entries to lowercase, regardless of how you typed them.

Most search systems are not case sensitive, so *Rodent* is the same as *rodent*.

After the list is imported, another page opens, showing your list with a number in parentheses next to each keyword or keyword phrase; this is the *count,* or the number of times the word or phrase appears in the database.

Paste your keyword list here.

**Figure 5-4:**
The Import
page.

# Adding keywords to your initial project list

To use Wordtracker to find more words that might be appropriate, follow these steps:

1. **Click the Home button in the navigation bar at the top of any Wordtracker page.**

   You are taken to the Wordtracker home page.

2. **Click the Keyword Universe link.**

   You see the page shown in Figure 5-5.

3. **Type the first keyword in your list into the box on the left.**

4. **Click the Proceed button.**

   Both the Lateral and Thesaurus check boxes are selected by default. Here's the lowdown on these options:

- Lateral: Wordtracker looks for 200 Web sites it thinks are related to the word you typed, and grabs keywords from their KEYWORDS meta tags. (You find out more about the KEYWORDS meta tags in Chapter 6.)

- Thesaurus: Wordtracker looks up the word in a thesaurus.

After clicking the Proceed button, wait a few minutes while Wordtracker builds a list. Then scroll down the left frame to see the list.

5. **Click a word in the left frame to load the corresponding table in the right frame.**

The table shows you actual searches from the Wordtracker database containing the word you clicked, and other keyword phrases containing that word. So, for instance, if you click *rodent,* you see search terms such as *rodents, rodent control, rodents revenge, rodent, rodent repellent, rodent pictures,* and so on.

Type a word here and click Proceed.

Click here to add all the words to your project.

**Figure 5-5:**
The
Keyword
Universe
page.

Click a word to add to your list.

Click a word to load the list in the right frame.

Next to each term in the table, you see two numbers:

- **Count:** The number of times Wordtracker found the search term in its database. The database contains searches for 100 days — more than 400 million searches. So the count is the number of times the term was used in the last two months in the search engines from which Wordtracker builds its database.

- **Predict:** An estimate of how many times this term is likely to be used each day, in all the Internet search engines combined.

Wordtracker assumes that the search engines it's working with account for a certain percentage of all searches, so it simply takes the count number and multiplies accordingly.

I believe these numbers are too low. From what I've seen and heard, these terms may actually be searched for 50 to 100 percent more often than the predict number. However, what counts is the relative, rather than absolute, number. If one phrase has a predict value of 12,000 times a day, and another one 6,000 times a day, the actual numbers may be 24,000 and 12,000, but what really matters is that one is much more than the other.

Here's what you can do with the list of search terms in the right frame:

- Click the Click Here to Add All Keywords to Your Basket link to add all the keyword phrases to your project. (The number next to the basket in the bottom frame increases as you add phrases to the project.)

- Click a term to add just that term to the project.

- Click the shovel icon in the Dig column to see similar terms. Click the shovel in the _rodents revenge_ row, for example, to see a smaller list containing _download rodents revenge, rodents revenge download, download rodents revenge game,_ and so on.

Should you add all the words in the list at once, or one by one? That depends. If the list contains mostly words that seem relevant, click the All link. You can remove the few that are no good later. If most of the list seems to be garbage, scroll down the list and add only the useful words.

After you've finished tweaking the list, here are a couple of other things you can do:

- Click another phrase in the left frame to load a new list in the right frame with search terms related to that phrase.

✔ Type another word from your original list into the box at the top of the left frame. Wordtracker retrieves more terms related to it from the thesaurus and KEYWORDS meta tags.

✔ Type a term into the text box at the top of the right frame and click the Go button to create a list based on that term.

The left frame is handy because it runs your words through a thesaurus and grabs words from KEYWORDS meta tags. But I also like to use the text box at the top of the right frame: I grab a few keyword phrases from my list and copy them into the box. (Each one needs to be on a separate line.) This is a quick way to find matching phrases for the terms already in your list. Typing a word into the text box at the top of the right frame is the same thing as clicking a word in the left frame — Wordtracker looks for real search phrases that include the word. Type (or paste) multiple words into that text box, and Wordtracker looks for matches for each of those words.

## Cleaning up the list

After you've worked through your list, checking for relevant terms, click the Click Here for Step 3 link at the bottom of the page. On the Step 3 page, you see the first 100 words in your project, with the most common appearing first; see Figure 5-6.

Scroll through this list carefully. Look for any keywords that really aren't appropriate. It's possible you'll find some, especially if you clicked the All link on the previous page. To delete a term, select the check box to the right of the unwanted term and click the Delete button at the top. Then scroll to the bottom of the list and work your way up; if you delete 15 terms from the page, 15 more are pulled from the next page, so you need to check them as well. Use the right-pointing triangle at the top of the list to move to the next page.

Remove only those terms that are totally inappropriate. Don't worry too much right now about terms that are not used much or terms that may be too general. I get to that topic in a moment.

## Exporting the list

When you're satisfied with your list, you can export it from Wordtracker. At the top of the Step 3 page, click the Export Keywords button to open a window that contains your compiled list. The window contains a list of keyword phrases — a simple list with no numbers. To display the list with the count and predict numbers, click the <u>Click Here to Get a Tab Delimited List of Keywords</u> link.

| Number of keywords in Rodents (28) | | Wordtracker ▾ | Go |
|---|---|---|---|

| Export Keywords | Email Keywords | Competition Search |
|---|---|---|

| ◀ Keywords 1 - 28 ▾ of 28 ▶ | Count | Delete |
|---|---|---|
| ▶ gerbils | 640 | ☐ |
| ▶ gerbil | 295 | ☐ |
| ▶ rat race | 90 | ☐ |
| ▶ gerbil cages | 70 | ☐ |
| ▶ gerbil care | 66 | ☐ |
| ▶ mouse trap race car | 34 | ☐ |
| ▶ rodentia | 27 | ☐ |
| ▶ gerbil breeding | 18 | ☐ |
| ▶ mongolian gerbils | 17 | ☐ |
| ▶ information on gerbils | 17 | ☐ |
| ▶ mouse trap race cars | 16 | ☐ |
| ▶ gerbils for sale | 16 | ☐ |
| ▶ gerbil newscast | 16 | ☐ |

**Figure 5-6:**
Clean your
keyword-
phrase list
here.

You can highlight the Wordtracker list and copy and paste it into a word processor or text editor. You can also click the Email Keywords button at the top of the Step 3 page to e-mail the list to yourself or a colleague.

## Performing competitive analysis

By doing a competitive analysis, you can identify terms that are searched for frequently but yield few results. If you then use these keywords on your pages, your pages are more likely to rank high in the search engines because you face little competition from other sites.

To do a competitive analysis, follow these steps:

1. **Click `Click here for step 3` at the bottom of the Keyword Universe page.**

   The Step 3 page appears.

2. **Click the Competition Search button at the top of the Step 3 page.**

   Another page appears, as shown in Figure 5-7.

3. **Check various search engines and directories, two at a time.**

Wordtracker tells you how often the term is searched for and how often the keyword phrase appears in Web pages in the indexes you selected.

**Figure 5-7:**
The
Competition
Search
page.

Keep these options turned on.

Select two search systems in which Wordtracker checks for competing pages.

At the bottom of the Competition Search page, you find the KEI Analysis and Quotes drop-down list boxes. You generally want to keep these options turned on:

✔ **Quotes:** Wordtracker encloses your search term in quotation marks when entering it into the selected search engines. For instance, if your phrase is *rodent racing,* Wordtracker searches for *"rodent racing".* The quotation marks tell the search engine that you want to find only those pages that contain the exact term *rodent racing,* providing a better idea of your true competition. If you search for the term without using quotation marks, you get all the pages with the word *rodent* or *racing* somewhere in the page, which returns far more results because the terms don't necessarily appear together or in order. You want to leave the Quotes option turned on because you're competing with sites that have the exact term in their pages.

✔ **KEI Analysis:** Wordtracker calculates the *KEI (Keyword Effectiveness Index)*, which is a comparison of the number of people searching for a term and the number of Web pages returned by a search engine for that term. See Figure 5-8. The higher the KEI, the more powerful the term.

KEI is not always useful. A term that has few competing pages and is searched upon infrequently can generate a high KEI. This term would have little benefit to you because although the competition is low, the number of searches is also low. Also, it doesn't factor in how many people are actually optimizing their pages for the keyword; that's the real competition. See Chapter 3 for a discussion of this issue.

The Competition Search also provides information on *pay-per-click (PPC)* services, which allow you to buy a position in the search results, as discussed in Chapter 17. Wordtracker shows you the prices that you'd pay for these terms in a variety of PPC systems. Some people like to run a PPC check even if they're not doing a PPC campaign because it may give them an idea of what terms other people think are effective for sales. However, just because others are spending a lot of money on a particular term doesn't mean they're actually making money from it!

The KEI indicates a phrase with a very high Count : Competition ratio.

**BEST SEARCH TERMS FOR GOOGLE**

Google gets 35.1100% of all search engine traffic (approx. 112 million a day).

What do these headings mean? Click here

The KEI was invented by search engine positioning specialist Sumantra Roy of 1stSearchRanking.com.

| 0 | 10 | 100 | 400+ |
|---|---|---|---|
| → Poor Keyword | → Good Keyword | → | Excellent Keyword |

| No. | Keyword (Why quotes? Click here) | KEI Analysis | Count | 24Hrs | Competing ❓ |
|---|---|---|---|---|---|
| 1 | "gerbil newscast" | 256.000 | 16 | 6 | 1 |
| 2 | "how to build a mouse trap race car" | 64.000 | 8 | 3 | 0 |
| 3 | "designs for a mouse trap race cars" | 36.000 | 6 | 2 | 0 |
| 4 | "human rat race greetings" | 36.000 | 6 | 2 | 0 |
| 5 | "designs for a mouse trap race car" | 36.000 | 6 | 2 | 0 |
| 6 | "mouse trap race car designs" | 25.000 | 5 | 2 | 0 |
| 7 | "mouse trap races" | 24.000 | 12 | 4 | 6 |
| 8 | "mouse trap race cars" | 18.286 | 16 | 6 | 14 |
| 9 | "how to make a mouse trap race car" | 16.000 | 4 | 1 | 0 |
| 10 | "gerbil cages" | 10.938 | 70 | 25 | 448 |
| 11 | "gerbil in a blender" | 7.682 | 13 | 5 | 22 |
| 12 | "mouse trap race car" | 6.494 | 34 | 12 | 178 |

**Figure 5-8:** The Competition Report.

## Finding keywords more ways

Wordtracker has a number of other search tools available, although I use mainly those discussed earlier in the chapter:

- ✔ **Full Search:** Wordtracker returns similar terms in the same conceptual ballpark (a very large ballpark, though).

- ✔ **Simple Search:** You can dump a bunch of keyword phrases into a text box to find actual search terms that include those keywords. For example, *rat* turns up *rat terrier, pet rats, naked mole rat,* and so on.

- ✔ **Exact/Precise Search:** This is a mixture of several tools, including the Exact Search, the Compressed Exact Search, and the Precise Search.

- ✔ **Compressed Search:** This is useful for finding plurals and singulars of words from a single list.

- ✔ **Comprehensive Search:** You can dig out a few useful related terms mixed in with a large number of unrelated terms.

- ✔ **Misspelling Search:** This is a good way to find common misspellings of your keywords.

# Choosing Your Keywords

When you've finished working with a keyword tool, look at the final list to determine how popular a keyword phrase actually is. You may find that many of your original terms are not worth bothering with. My clients often have terms on their preliminary lists — the lists they put together without the use of a keyword tool — that are virtually never used. You'll also find other terms near the top of the final list that you hadn't thought about. The next several sections help you clean up this list.

## Removing ambiguous terms

Scan through your list for keyword phrases that probably won't do you any good for various reasons.

### You missed the target

Take a look at your list to determine whether you have any words that may have different meanings to different people. Sometimes you can immediately spot such terms.

---

# Cam again?

One of my clients thought he should use the term *cam* on his site. To him, the term referred to *Complementary and Alternative Medicine.* But to the vast majority of searchers, *cam* means something different. Search Wordtracker on the term *cam*, and you come up with phrases such as *web cams, web cam, free web cams, live* *web cams, cam, cams, live cams, live web cams,* and so on. To most searchers, the term *cam* refers to *Web cams,* cameras used to place pictures and videos online. The phrases from this example generate a tremendous amount of competition, but few of them would be useful to my client.

---

### Ambiguous terms

A client of mine wanted to promote a product designed for controlling fires. One common term he came up with was *fire control system.* However, he discovered that when he searched on that term, most sites that turned up don't promote products relating to stopping fires. Rather, they're sites related to *fire control* in the military sense: weapons-fire control.

This kind of ambiguity is something you really can't determine from a system such as Wordtracker, which tells you how often people search on a term. In fact, it's often hard to spot such terms even by searching to see what turns up when you use the phrase. If a particular type of Web site turns up when you search for the phrase, does that mean people using the phrase are looking for that type of site? You can't say for sure. A detailed analysis of your Web site's access logs may give you an idea; see Chapter 20 for the details.

### Very broad terms

Look at your list for terms that are incredibly broad. You may be tempted to go after high-ranking words, but make sure that people are really searching for your products when they type in the word.

Suppose that your site is promoting *degrees in information technology.* You discover that around 40 people search for this term each day, but approximately 1,500 people a day search on the term *information technology.* Do you think many people searching on the term *information technology* are really looking for a degree? Probably not. Although the term generates 40,000 to 50,000 searches a month, few of these will be your targets.

Here are a few reasons to forgo a term that's too broad:

 ✔ **Tough to rank.** It's probably a very competitive term, which means ranking well on it would be difficult.

> ✔ **Relevance is elsewhere.** You may be better off spending the time and effort focusing on another, more relevant term.
>
> ✔ **Maintaining focus.** It's difficult to optimize Web pages for a whole bunch of search terms (see Chapter 6), so if you optimize for one term, you won't be optimizing for another, perhaps more appropriate, term.

## Picking combinations

Sometimes it's a good idea to target terms lower down on your list, rather than the ones up top, because the lower terms *include* the higher terms.

Suppose that you're selling an e-commerce system and find the following list. The numbers are the *predict* numbers — the number of times Wordtracker believes the term is used each day:

```
1828        e-commerce
1098        ecommerce
 881        shopping cart
 574        shopping cart software
 428        shopping carts
 260        ecommerce software
 130        ecommerce solutions
 109        e-commerce software
  92        e-commerce solutions
  58        shopping carts and accessories
  26        ecommerce software solution
```

Notice the term *e-commerce*. This is probably not a great term to target because it's very general and has a lot of competition. But lower down on the list is the term *e-commerce solutions*. This term is a combination of two keyword phrases: *e-commerce* and *e-commerce solutions*. Thus, you can combine the predict numbers: 1,828 searches a day plus 130 a day. If you target *e-commerce solutions* and optimize your Web pages for that term, you're also optimizing for *e-commerce*.

Notice also the term *ecommerce* (which search engines regard as different from *e-commerce*) and the term a little lower on the list, *ecommerce software*. A term even lower down encompasses both of these terms: *ecommerce software solution*. Optimize your pages for *ecommerce software solution,* and you've just optimized for three terms at once.

Use the keyword-analysis procedure I describe in this chapter, and you'll have a much better picture of your keyword landscape. Unlike the majority of Web site owners, you'll have a good view of how people are searching for your products and services.

# Chapter 6

# Creating Pages That Search Engines Love

*I*n this chapter, you find out how to create Web pages that search engines *really* like — pages that can be read and indexed and that put your best foot forward. Before you begin creating pages, I recommend that you read not only this chapter but also Chapter 7 to find out how to avoid things that search engines hate. There are a lot of ways to make a Web site work, and ways to break it, too. Before you get started creating your pages, you should be aware of the problems you may face and what you can do to avoid them.

I'm assuming that you or your Web designer understands HTML and can create Web pages. I focus on the most important search-engine-related things you need to know while creating your pages. It's beyond the scope of this book to cover basic HTML and Cascading Style Sheets.

## Preparing Your Site

When creating a Web site, the first thing to consider is *where* to put your site. By that, I mean the Web server and the domain name.

## Finding a hosting company

Although many large companies place their Web sites on their own Web servers, most companies don't. They shouldn't do this, in fact, because there's simply no way you can do it anywhere near as cheaply and reliably as a good hosting company can do it. Rather, a hosting company places sites on servers owned by a hosting company. Although you have to take into consideration many factors when selecting a hosting company, I focus on the factors that are related to search engine optimization.

When looking for a hosting company, make sure that it offers the following features:

✔ **Allows you to upload Web pages that you've created all by your lonesome.** Some services provide simple tools you can use to create Web pages; it's fine if they provide these tools as long as you also have the ability to create pages yourself. You must have control over the HTML in your pages.

✔ **Provides an access-log-analysis tool or, if you plan to use your own analysis tool, a way to get to the raw access logs.** A log-analysis tool shows you how many people visit your site and how they get there. See Chapter 20 for more information.

✔ **Allows you to use your own domain name.** Don't get an account in which you have a subdirectory of the hosting company's domain name.

You need to consider many issues when selecting a hosting company, most of which are not directly related to the search engine issue. If you want to find out more about what to look for in a hosting company, I've posted an article about selecting a host on my Web site, at www.SearchEngineBulletin.com.

## Picking a domain name

Search engines actually read *uniform resource locators (URLs),* looking for keywords in them. For instance, if you have a Web site with the domain name *rodent-racing.com* and someone searches at Google for *rodent racing*, Google sees *rodent-racing.com* as a match. Because a dash appears between the two words, Google recognizes the words in the domain name. (Google also interprets periods and slashes as word separators.) If, however, you use an underscore or some other character, or if you run the words together (*rodent_racing_events.com* or *rodentracingevents.com*), Google doesn't regard the individual words as individual words; it sees them as part of the same word. That's not to say that Google can't find text *within* words — it can, and you'll sometimes see words on the search-results pages partially bolded, when Google does just that — but when ranking the page, it's not going to regard the word it found inside another word as the same as finding the word itself.

To see this concept in action, use the *allinurl:* search syntax at Google. Type *allinurl:rodent,* for example, and Google finds URLs that contain the word *rodent* (including the directory names and filenames).

So putting keywords into the domain name and separating keywords with dashes do provide a small benefit. Another advantage to adding dashes between words is that it's relatively easy to come up with a domain name that's not already taken. Although it may seem like most of the good names were taken long ago, you can pretty easily come up with some kind of keyword phrase, separated with dashes, that is still available. Furthermore, the search engines don't care what first-level domain you use; you can have a *.com*, *.net*, *.biz*, *.tv*, or whatever; it doesn't matter.

Now, having said all that, let me tell you my philosophy regarding domain names. In the search engine optimization field, it has become popular to use dashes and keywords in domain names, but the lift provided by keywords in domain names is very small, and you should take into consideration other, more important factors when choosing a domain name:

- **A domain name should be short, easy to spell, and easy to remember.** And it should pass the "radio test." Imagine you're being interviewed on the radio and want to tell listeners your URL. You want something that is instantly understandable, without having to be spelled. You don't want to have to say "rodent dash racing dash events dot com"; it's better to say "rodent racing events dot com."

- **In almost all cases, you should get the** *.com* **version of a domain name.** If the *.com* version is taken, do *not* try to use the *.net* or *.org* version for branding purposes! People remember *.com*, even if you say *.org* or *.net* or whatever. So if you're planning to promote your Web site in print, on the radio, on TV, on billboards, and so on, you need the *.com* version.

## Read the fine print

Several years ago, I recommended that a nonprofit client of mine register the *.com* version of their domain name. (They'd been using *.org* for years.) During the few hours that the *.com* domain was not yet pointing to their site, but was pointing to the domain registrar's site, the company received several calls from people trying to get to its Web site. These people wanted to let the company know that something was wrong with its server because its domain name was pointing to the wrong place. For years, the company printed all its materials using *.org*; they had never printed anything with *.com* because they didn't own it; however, people were still trying to get to *.com*.

A classic example is Rent.com and Rent.net. These were two different Web sites, owned by two different companies. Rent.net spent millions of dollars on advertising; every time I saw a Rent.net ad on a bus, I had to wonder how much of the traffic generated by these ads actually went to Rent.com! (Rent.net is now out of business — it was bought by Homestore.com — while Rent.com isn't. I don't know if that's a coincidence!)

Are keyworded domain names worth the trouble? Because the lift provided by keywords in the domain name is rather small — and, in fact, putting too many keywords into a name can actually hurt your placement. It's probably better to focus on a single, brandable domain name (a *.com* version).

Don't use a domain-forwarding service for Web sites you want to turn up in the search engines. Many registrars now allow you to simply forward browsers to a particular site: A user types *www.domain1.com*, and the registrar forwards the browser to *www.domain2.com*, for instance. Such forwarding systems often use frames (discussed in Chapter 7), which means the search engines won't index the site properly. Your site should be properly configured by using the nameserver settings, not a simple forward.

# Seeing Through a Search Engine's Eyes

What a search engine sees when it loads one of your pages is not the same as what your browser sees. To understand why, you need to understand how a Web page is created. See Figure 6-1 and read this quick explanation:

1. A user types a URL into his browser, or clicks a link, causing the browser to send a message to the Web server asking for a particular page.

2. The Web server grabs the page and quickly reads it to see if it needs to do anything to the page before sending it.

3. The Web server compiles the page, if necessary.

   In some cases, the Web server may have to run ASP or PHP scripts, for instance, or it may have to find an *SSI (server-side include)*, an instruction telling it to grab something from another page and insert it into the one it's about to send.

4. After the server has completed any instructions, it sends the page to the browser.

5. When the browser receives the page, it reads through the page looking for instructions and, if necessary, further compiles the page.

6. When it's finished, the browser displays the page for the user to read.

# Scripting

*ASP* and *PHP* scripts are little programs that are written into Web pages. The scripts are read by a program working in association with the Web server when a page is requested. The searchbots see the results of the scripts because the scripts have been run by the time the Web server sends the page. *Server-side includes* *(SSIs)* are simple statements placed into the HTML pages that name another file and, in effect, say to the Web server, "Grab the information in this file and drop it into the Web page here." Again, the searchbots see the information in the SSI because the Web server inserts the information before sending the Web page.

Here are a few examples of instructions the browser may receive:

- It may find a <SCRIPT> tag telling it to load a JavaScript from another file. It must then request this file from the server.

- It may find JavaScripts embedded into the file, in which case it runs those scripts.

- It may find references to images or other forms of media, and have to pull those into the page and read *Cascading Style Sheets (CSS)* instructions to see how the text should be formatted.

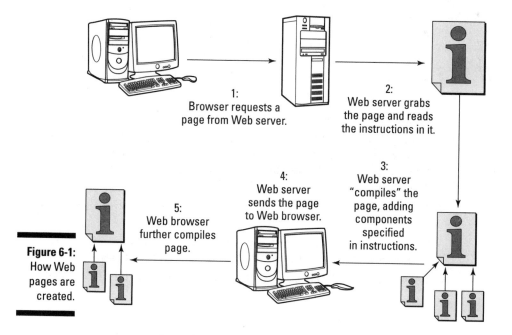

**Figure 6-1:** How Web pages are created.

1: Browser requests a page from Web server.

2: Web server grabs the page and reads the instructions in it.

3: Web server "compiles" the page, adding components specified in instructions.

4: Web server sends the page to Web browser.

5: Web browser further compiles page.

So, that's what happens normally when Web pages are created. But the *searchbots,* used by the search engines to index pages, work differently. When they request a page, the server does what it normally does, constructing the page according to instructions, and sends it to the searchbot. But the search-bot doesn't follow all the instructions in the page — it just reads the page. So, for example, it doesn't run scripts in the page.

You can add instructions that build the page in two ways:

- **Browser-side (or *client-side*) instructions:** Browser-side instructions are generally ignored by searchbots. For instance, if you create a page with a navigation system that is built with JavaScript, the search engines won't see it. Some people can even use browser-side instructions to *intentionally* hide things from the search engines.

- **Server-side instructions:** If you use an SSI to place navigation into the site, the searchbots *will* see it because the Web server uses the SSI before sending the information to the searchbots.

Of course, it's possible for an SSI to place browser-side instructions into a page. In this case, the searchbot sees the instructions — because the server has placed them there — but will ignore them.

This is a very important concept:

Server side = visible to searchbots

Browser side = not visible to searchbots

# Understanding Keyword Concepts

Here's the basic concept: You're putting keywords into your Web pages in such a manner that the search engines can get to them, read them, and regard them as significant.

Your keyword list is probably very long, perhaps hundreds of keywords, so you need to pick a few to work with. (If you haven't yet developed a keyword list, page back to Chapter 5 for details.) The keywords you pick should be either

- Words near the top of the list that have many searches.

- Words lower on the list that may be worth targeting because you have relatively few competitors. That is, when someone searches for the key-word phrase using an exact search (*"rodent racing"* rather than *rodent racing*), the search engine finds relatively few pages.

It's often easy to create pages that rank well for the keywords at the bottom of your list because they're unusual terms that don't appear in many Web pages. However, they're at the bottom of your list because *people don't search for them very often!* So you have to decide whether the effort is worth it to rank well on a search term that is only searched for once or twice a month.

## Picking one or two phrases per page

You're going to optimize each page for one or two keyword phrases. By *optimize,* I mean create the page in such a manner that it has a good chance of ranking well for the chosen keyword phrase or phrases, when someone actually uses them in a search engine.

You can't optimize a page well for more than one keyword phrase at a time. The TITLE tag is one of the most important components on a Web page, and the best position for a keyword is right at the beginning of that tag. And only one phrase can be placed at the beginning of the tag, right? (However, sometimes, as you find out in Chapter 5, you can combine keyword phrases — optimizing for *rodent racing scores* also, in effect, optimizes for *rodent racing.*)

Have a primary and a secondary keyword phrase in mind for each page you're creating, but also consider all the keywords you're interested in working into the pages. For instance, you might create a page that you plan to optimize for the phrase *rodent racing.* But you also have several other keywords you want to have scattered around your site: *rodent racing scores, handicap, gerbil, rodentia, furry friend events,* and so on. Typically, you pick one main phrase for each page, but incorporate the other keyword phrases throughout the page, where appropriate.

Place your keyword list into a word processor, enlarge the font, and then print the list and tape it to the wall. Occasionally, while creating your pages, glance at the list to remind yourself of what words you need to weave into your pages.

## Checking prominence

The term *prominence* refers to where the keyword appears — how prominent it is within a page component (the body text, the TITLE tag, and so on). A word near the top of the page is more prominent than one near the bottom; a word at the beginning of a TITLE tag is more prominent than one at the end; a word at the beginning of the DESCRIPTION meta tag is more prominent than one at the end; and so on.

Prominence is good. If you're creating a page with a particular keyword or keyword phrase in mind, make that term prominent — in the body text, in the TITLE tag, in the DESCRIPTION meta tag, and elsewhere — to convey to the search engines that the keyword phrase is important in this particular page. Consider this title tag:

```
<TITLE>Everything about Rodents - Looking after Them,
       Feeding Them, Rodent Racing, and more.</TITLE>
```

When you read this, you can see that *Rodent Racing* is just one of several terms the page is related to. The search engine comes to the same conclusion because the term is at the end of the title, meaning it's probably not the predominant term. But what about the following tag?

```
<TITLE>Rodent Racing - Looking after Your Rodents, Feeding
       them, Everything You Need to Know</TITLE>
```

Placing *Rodent Racing* at the beginning of the tag places the stress on that concept; the search engines are likely to conclude that the page is mainly about Rodent Racing.

## Watching density

Another important concept is *keyword density*. When a user searches for a keyword phrase, the search engine looks at all the pages that contain the phrase and checks the *density* — the ratio of the search phrase to the total number of words in the page.

For instance, suppose that you search for *rodent racing* and the search engine finds a page that contains 400 words, with the phrase *rodent racing* appearing 10 times — that's a total of 20 words. Because 20 is 5 percent of 400, the keyword density is 5 percent.

Keyword density is important, but you can overdo it. If the search engine finds that the search phrase makes up 50 percent of the words in the page, it may decide that the page was created purely to grab the search engine's attention for that phrase and then ignore it. On the other hand, if the density is too low, you risk having the search engines regard other pages as more relevant for the search.

You can get hung up on keyword density, and some people use special tools to check the density on every page. This can be very time consuming, especially for large sites. You're probably better off eyeballing the density in most cases. If the phrase for which you're optimizing appears an awful lot, you've overdone it. If the text sounds clumsy because of the repetition, you've overdone it.

## Placing keywords throughout your site

Suppose that someone searches for *rodent racing* and the search engine finds two sites that use the term. One site has a single page in which the term occurs, and the other site has dozens of pages containing the term. Which site will the search engine think is most relevant? The one that has many pages related to the subject, of course.

Some search engines — such as Google — often provide two results from a site, one indented below the other. So if your site has only one page related to the subject, this can't happen.

To see how this works in the real world of search engines, refer to Figure 6-2, which appears a little later in the chapter. You'll notice that Google provides two pages from the Britney Spears Guide to Semiconductor Physics. (The site's owner has done a great job of getting his site ranked high in the search engines. After all, Britney Spears's lectures — on semiconductor physics, radiative and non-radiative transitions, edge emitting lasers, and VCSELs — are not what she is best known for and probably of little interest to most of her fans. Yet this site appears in positions 2 and 3 when people search for *britney spears.*)

In most cases, you're not likely to grab a top position simply by creating a single page optimized for the keyword phrase. You may need dozens, perhaps hundreds, of pages to grab the search engines' attention.

# Creating Your Web Pages

When you're creating your Web pages, you need to focus on two essential elements:

- ✔ The underlying structure of the pages
- ✔ The text you plunk down on the pages

The next sections fill you in on what you need to look out for.

## Naming files

Search engines do get clues about the nature of a site from its domain name as well as from the site's directory structure. The added lift is probably not large, but every little bit counts, right? You might as well name directories, Web pages, and images by using keywords.

So, for example, rather than creating a file named *gb123.jpg*, you can use a more descriptive name, such as *rodent-racing-scores.jpg*. Don't have too many dashes in the filenames, though. Using more than a couple means the search engine is likely to ignore the name, if not *penalize* the page by omitting it from the index.

You can separate keywords in a name with dashes or periods, but not underscores. Search engines also see the / symbol in a URL as a separator.

## Creating directory structure

It may be a good idea to keep a *flat* directory structure in your Web site. Keep your pages as close to the root domain as possible, rather than have a complicated multilevel directory tree. Create a directory for each navigation tab and keep all the files in that directory.

Many observers believe that search engines downgrade pages that are lower in the directory structure. This effect is probably relatively small, but in general, you're better off using a structure with two or three sublevels, rather than five or ten. For instance, the first page that follows would be weighted more highly than the second page:

```
http://www.domainname.com/dir1/page.html
```

```
http://www.domainname.com/dir1/dir2/dir3/dir4/page.html
```

## Viewing TITLE tags

Most search engines use the site's TITLE tag as the link and main title of the site's listing on the search results page, as shown in Figure 6-2.

TITLE tags not only tell a browser what text to display in the browser's title bar, but they're also very important for search engines. Searchbots read the page titles and use the information to determine what the pages are about. If you have a keyword between your TITLE tags that competing pages don't have, you have a good chance of getting at or near the top of the search results.

The TITLE is one of the most important components as far as search engines are concerned. However, these tags are usually wasted because few sites bother placing useful keywords in them. Titles are often pretty generic: *Welcome to Acme, Inc.*, or *Acme Inc. - Home Page.* Such titles are not beneficial for search engine optimization.

**Figure 6-2:**
Search
results from
Google,
showing
where
components
come from.

I searched at Google for *intitle:welcome* to find out how many pages have the word *welcome* in their TITLE tags. The result? Around 102 million! Around 77 million have *welcome to* in the title (*allintitle:"welcome to"*). Having *Welcome to* as the first words in your title is a waste of space — only slightly more wasteful than your company name! Give the search engines a really strong clue about your site's content by using a keyword phrase in the TITLE tags. Here's how:

1. **Place your TITLE tags immediately below the <HEAD> tag.**

2. **Place 40 to 60 characters between the <TITLE> and </TITLE> tags, including spaces.**

3. **Put the keyword phrase you want to focus on for this page at the very beginning of the TITLE.**

   If you want, you can repeat the primary keywords once. Limit the number of two-letter words and very common words (known as *stop words*), such as *as, the,* and *a,* because the search engines ignore them.

Here is an example TITLE:

```
<TITLE>Rodent Racing Info. Rats, Mice, Gerbils, Stoats,
         all kinds of Rodent Racing</TITLE>
```

The TITLE and often the DESCRIPTION (explained in the next section) appear on the search results page, so they should encourage people to visit your site.

# Using the DESCRIPTION meta tag

*Meta tags* are special HTML tags that can be used to carry information, which can then be read by browsers or other programs. When search engines began, Webmasters included meta tags in their pages to make it easy for search engines to determine what the pages were about. Search engines also used these meta tags when deciding how to rank the page for different keywords.

The DESCRIPTION meta tag describes the Web page to the search engines. The search engines use this meta tag two ways:

- They read and index the text in the tag.
- In many cases, they use the text verbatim in the search results page. That is, if your Web page is returned in the search results page, the search engine grabs the text from the DESCRIPTION tag and places it under the text from the TITLE tag so the searcher can read your description.

In most cases, Google *doesn't* use the text from the DESCRIPTION meta tag in its search results page. Rather, Google grabs a block of text near where it found the search keywords on the page, and then uses that text in the results page. And as explained in Chapter 12, sometimes search engines use the site description from a Web directory in the index search results.

Still, using the DESCRIPTION meta tag is important for the following reasons:

- Sometimes search engines *do* use the DESCRIPTION you provide. If it can't find the keywords in the page (perhaps it found the page based on its TITLE tag or links pointing at the page rather than page content, for instance), a search engine may use the DESCRIPTION.
- Search engines index the DESCRIPTION.
- Some smaller search engines use the DESCRIPTION tag in the results.

The DESCRIPTION meta tag is pretty important, so you should use it. Place the DESCRIPTION tag immediately below the TITLE tags and then create a nice keyworded description of up to 250 characters (again, including spaces).

Here's an example:

```
<META NAME="description" CONTENT="Rodent Racing - Scores,
        Schedules, everything Rodent Racing. Whether
        you're into mouse racing, stoat racing, rats,
        or gerbils, our site provides everything you'll
        ever need to know about Rodent Racing and
        caring for your racers.">
```

It's okay to duplicate your most important keywords once, but don't overdo it, or you'll upset the search engines. Don't, for instance, do this:

```
<META NAME="description" CONTENT="Rodent Racing, Rodent
        Racing, Rodent Racing, Rodent Racing, Rodent
        Racing, Rodent Racing, Rodent Racing, Rodent
        Racing, Rodent Racing, Rodent Racing">
```

Overloading your DESCRIPTION (or any other page component) with the same keyword or keyword phrase is known as *spamming* (a term I hate, but hey, I don't make the rules), and trying such tricks may get your page penalized; rather than *help* your page's search engine position, it may actually cause search engines to omit it from their indexes.

Sometimes Web developers switch the attributes in the tag: <META CONTENT="your description goes here" NAME="description"> for instance, rather than <META NAME="description" CONTENT="your description goes here">. Make sure that your tags don't do the former because some search engines choke on such tags.

## Tapping into the KEYWORDS meta tag

The KEYWORDS meta tag was originally created as an indexing tool: a way for the page author to tell search engines what the page is about by listing (yep) keywords. Although quite important many years past, this meta tag isn't so important these days. Some search engines may use it, but many don't. Still, you might as well include the KEYWORDS meta tag. You do have a list of keywords, after all.

Don't worry too much about the tag — it's not worth spending a lot of time over. Here are a few points to consider:

- ✔ **Limit the tag to 10 to 12 words.** Originally, the KEYWORDS tag could be very large, up to 1,000 characters. These days many search engine observers are wary of appearing to be spamming the search engines by stuffing keywords into any page component, and so recommend that you use short KEYWORDS tags.

- ✔ **You can separate each keyword with a comma and a space.** However, you don't have to use both — you can have a comma and no space, or a space and no comma.

- ✔ **Make sure that most of the keywords in the tag are also in the body text.** If they aren't, I don't believe you'll be penalized, but it probably won't do you any good either. Many people also use the KEYWORDS tag as a good place to stuff spelling mistakes that are commonly searched.

✔ **Don't use a lot of repetition.** You shouldn't do this, for instance: *Rodent Racing, Rodent Racing, Rodent Racing, Rodent Racing, Rodent Racing, Rodent Racing,* or even *Rodent Racing, Rodent Racing Scores, Rodent Racing, Gerbils, Rodent Racing Scores, Rodent Racing . . . .*

✔ **Don't use the same** KEYWORD **tag in all your pages.** You could create a primary tag to use in your first page and then copy it to other pages and move terms around in the tag.

Here's an example of a well-constructed KEYWORD tag:

```
<META NAME="keywords" CONTENT="rodent racing, racing
        rodents, gerbils, mice, mose, raceing, mouse,
        rodent races, rat races, mouse races, stoat,
        stoat racing">
```

## Using other meta tags

What about other meta tags? Sometimes if you look at the source of a page, you see all sorts of meta tags, as shown in Figure 6-3. Meta tags are useful for various reasons, but from a search engine perspective, you can forget almost all of them. (And most meta tags really aren't of much use for any purpose.)

**Figure 6-3:**
An example
of all sorts
of meta
tags you
generally
don't need.
I've bolded
the names
to make
them easier
to see.

```
<meta name="resource-type" content="document">
<meta http-equiv="pragma" content="no-cache">
<meta name="revisit-after" content="1">
<meta name="classification" content="Arts and Crafts">
<meta name="description"
content="New York Alive! Photographs is an online gallery containing dozens of signed, original, custom-
printed black and white photographs of New York City, its landmarks, buildings, neighborhoods, people,
and places. Buy original images for home or office direct from the photographers.">
<meta name="keywords"
content=" New York City, New York, New York NY, NYC, skyline, landmarks, buildings, Manhattan,
Brooklyn, neighborhood, neighbourhood, neighborhoods, neighbourhoods, photography, fine, fine art, art,
artist, artists, artistic, arts, photo, photographic, photographs, photograph, photographer, photographers,
pictures, black, black and white, white, images, imagery, image, gallery, galleries, virtual, online, on-line,
exhibits, exibits, exhibition, exhibitions, exhibit, contemporary, Central Park, Greenwich Village, Soho,
Wall Street, Statue of Liberty, Harlem, Washington Heights, Lower East Side, Ethnic, Empire State
Building, Flatiron, Flat Iron, Building, Chrysler, Brooklyn Bridge, Wall Street, New York Stock Exchange,
Chinatown, Little Italy, Yankees, people">
<meta name="robots" content="ALL">
<meta name="distribution" content="Global">
<meta name="rating" content="General">
<meta name="copyright" content="(c) Naomi Diamant, 2000. All rights reserved.">
<meta name="author" content="Abacus Consultants">
<meta http-equiv="reply-to" content="abacusconsultants@yahoo.com">
<meta name="language" content="English">
<meta name="doc-type" content="Public" ">
<meta name="doc-class" content="Completed">
<meta name="doc-rights" content="Copywritten Work">
```

You've heard about DESCRIPTION and KEYWORDS meta tags, but also of relevance to search engine optimization are the REVISIT-AFTER and ROBOTS meta tags:

✔ REVISIT-AFTER tells search engines how often to reindex the page. Save the electrons; don't expect search engines to follow your instructions. Search engines reindex pages on their own schedules.

✔ ROBOTS blocks search engines from indexing pages. (I discuss this topic in detail later in this chapter.) But many Web authors use it to *tell* search engines to index a page. Here's an example:

```
<META NAME="robots" CONTENT="ALL">
```

This tag is a waste of time. If a search engine finds your page and wants to index it, and hasn't been blocked from doing so, it will. And if it doesn't want to index the page, it won't. Telling the search engine to do so doesn't make a difference.

Here's a special Google meta tag that you can use a couple of ways:

```
<META NAME="googlebot" CONTENT="nosnippet">
```

This meta tag tells Google not to use the description *snippet,* the piece of information it grabs from within a Web page to use as the description; instead it will use the DESCRIPTION meta tag. However, it will also remove the page from Google's cache. Here's another example:

```
<META NAME="googlebot" CONTENT="noarchive">
```

This meta tag tells Google not to place a copy of the page into the cache. If you have an average corporate attorney on staff who doesn't like the idea of Google storing a copy of your company's information on its servers, you can tell Google not to. (By the way, it seems likely that Google's automatic caching feature breaks copyright law, though this is an issue that hasn't been tested yet.)

These Google meta tags may work, but a number of users report that sometimes they don't.

## *Including image ALT text*

You use the <IMG> tag to insert images into Web pages. This tag can include the ALT= attribute, which means *alternative* text. (For a page to comply with HTML 4.01 standards, you must include this attribute.) ALT text was originally text displayed if the browser viewing the page could not display images. These days, the `ALT` text is also used by programs that speak the page (for blind people). In many browsers, the `ALT` text also appears in a little pop-up box when you hold your mouse over an image for a few moments.

`ALT` tags are also read by search engines. Why? Because these tags offer another clue about the content of the Web page. How much do `ALT` tags help? Almost not at all these days, because some Web designers have abused the technique by stuffing `ALT` attributes with tons of keywords. But using `ALT` tags can't hurt (assuming you *don't* stuff them with tons of keywords, but simply drop a few in here and there) and may even help push your page up a little in the search engine rankings.

You can place keywords in your `ALT` attributes like this:

```
<IMG SRC="rodent-racing-1.jpg" ALT="Rodent Racing - Ratty
          winners of our latest Rodent Racing event">
```

## Flush the Flash animation

Using Flash animations sometimes makes sense, but usually it doesn't. Many Web designers place fancy Flash animations on their home pages just to make them look cool. But rarely do these animations serve any purpose beyond making site visitors wait a little longer to get into the site. Some search engines can now read and index Flash stuff (albeit not well), but generally Flash animations don't contain any useful text for indexing. So if you include Flash on your home page, the most important page on your site, the page is worthless from a search engine perspective.

Even if a page with Flash animation *does* appear in the search results — perhaps because you used the perfect `TITLE` tag — the search engine won't have much to work with. For example, in Figure 6-4, the search engine may grab the following text:

*Skip Intro. The Celtic Bard is optimized for a 56k modem and above. If you are running a 28.8 modem please be advised you will have to wait for the Flash elements to download.*

This text is probably not what you want the search engine to index.

Most home-page Flash animations automatically forward the browser to the next page — the *real* home page — after they've finished running. If you do decide to include Flash, make sure that you include a clearly visible Skip Intro link somewhere on the page.

**Figure 6-4:**
A classic example of a Flash animation. At least this site designer is honest in explaining that some site visitors will have to wait.

Search engines can index Flash files, but generally not well. If you create a page based on Flash, there are a few things you can do to help with indexing:

- ✓ Make sure you use your TITLE tags and DESCRIPTION and KEYWORDS meta tag.

- ✓ Put text between <NOSCRIPT> and </NOSCRIPT> tags. You could use the text displayed in the Flash within these tags, or if using audio a transcription of the text audio.

## Avoiding embedded text in images

Many sites use images heavily. The overuse of images is often the sign of an inexperienced Web designer, in particular one who is very familiar with graphic-design tools — perhaps a graphic artist who has accidentally run into some Web business. Such designers often create their entire pages in a graphic-design program, including the text, and then save images and insert them into the Web page.

The advantage of this approach is that it gives the designer much more control over the appearance of the page — and is often much faster than using HTML to lay out a few images and real text.

But putting text into graphics has significant drawbacks. Such pages transfer across the Internet much more slowly, and because the pages contain no real text, the search engines don't have anything to index.

For example, the text in Figure 6-5 isn't real text; the text is part of one large image. This may be the perfect text to get you ranked highly for your most important keyword phrase, but because it's a picture, it won't do you any good.

## Adding body text

You need text in your page. How much? More than a little, but not too much. Maybe 100 to 250 words are good. Don't get too hung up on these numbers, though. If you put an article in a page, and the article is 1,000 words, that's fine. But in general, something in the 100–250 word range is good. That amount of content allows you to really define what the page is about and will help the search engine understand what the page is about.

**Figure 6-5:**
This entire page is invisible to the search engines. It's made up of one large image and a JavaScript navigation tool.

Keep in mind that a Web site needs content in order to be noticed by the search engines. (For more on this topic, see Chapter 9.) If the site doesn't have much content for the search engine to read, the search engine will have trouble determining what the page is about and may not properly rank it. In effect, the page loses points in the contest for search engine ranking. Certainly keywords in content are not all there is to being ranked in the search engines; as you find out in Chapters 14 and 15, for instance, linking to the pages is also very important. But keywords in content are very significant, so the search engines have a natural bias toward Web sites with a large amount of content.

This bias toward content could be considered very unfair. After all, your site may be the perfect fit for a particular keyword search, even if you don't have much content in your site. In fact, inappropriate sites often appear in searches simply because they have a lot of pages, some of which have the right keywords.

Suppose that your Rodent Racing Web site is the only site in the world at which you can buy tickets for rodent-racing events. Your site doesn't provide a lot of content because rodent-racing fans simply want to be able to buy the tickets. However, because your site has less content than other sites, it is at a disadvantage to sites that have lots of content related to rodent racing, even if these other sites are not directly related to the subject.

You really can't do much to confront this problem, except to add more content! (Try to get into a habit of adding one page of quality content per day to your site.) You can find some ideas on where to get content in Chapter 9.

## Creating headers: CSS versus <H> tags

Back when the Web began, browsers defined what pages looked like. A designer could say, "I want body text here, and a heading there, and an address over there," but the designer had no way to define what the page actually looked like. The browser decided. The browser defined what a header looked like, what body text looked like, and so on. The page might appear one way in one browser program, and another way in a different program.

These days, designers have a great new tool available to them: *Cascading Style Sheets (CSS).* With CSS, designers can define exactly what each element should look like on a page.

Now, here's the problem. HTML has several tags that define headers: <H1>, <H2>, <H3>, and so on. These headers are useful in search engine optimization, because when you put keywords into a heading, you're saying to a search engine, "These keywords are so important that they appear in my heading text." Search engines pay more attention to them, weighing them more heavily than keywords in body text.

But many designers have given up on using the <H> tags and rely solely on CSS to make headers look the way they want them to. The plain <H> tags are often rather ugly when displayed in browsers, so designers don't like to use them. <H> tags also cause spacing issues; for example, an <H1> tag always includes a space above and below the text contained in the tag.

However, there's no reason you can't use both <H> tags *and* CSS. You can use style sheets two basic ways:

✔ Create a style class and then assign that class to the text you want to format.

✔ Define the style for a particular HTML tag.

Many designers do the former; they create a style class in the style sheet, like in the following example:

```
.headtext { font-family: Verdana, Arial, Helvetica, sans-
          serif; font-size: 16px; font-weight: bold;
          color: #3D3D3D }
```

Then they assign the style class to a piece of text like this:

```
<DIV CLASS="headtext">Rodent Racing for the New
          Millennium!</div>
```

In this example, the `headtext` class makes the text appear the way the designer wants the headings to appear. But as far as the search engines are concerned, this is just normal body text.

A better way is to define the <H> tags in the style sheets, as in the following example:

```
H1 {
font-family: Verdana, Arial, Helvetica, sans-serif;
font-size: 16px;
font-weight: bold;
color: #3D3D3D
}
```

Now, whenever you add an <H1> tag to your pages, the browser reads the style sheet and knows exactly what font family, size, weight, and color you want. It's the best of both worlds — you get the appearance you want, and the search engines know it's an <H1> tag.

## Formatting text

You can also tell the search engines that a particular word might be significant several other ways. If the text is in some way different from most of the other text in the page, the search engines may assume that it's been set off for some reason, that the Web designer has treated it differently because it *is* in some way different and more significant than the other words.

Here are a few things you can do to set your keywords apart from the other words on the page:

- ✔ Make the text **bold.**
- ✔ Make the text *italic.*
- ✔ Uppercase the First Letter in Each Word, and lowercase the other letters in the word.
- ✔ Put the keywords in bullet lists.

For each page, you have a particular keyword phrase in mind; this is the phrase for which you use the preceding techniques.

Another way to emphasize the text is to make a piece of text larger than the surrounding text (just make sure that you do this in a way that doesn't look tacky). For example, you can use <H> tags for headers, but also use slightly larger text at the beginning of a paragraph or for subheaders.

## Creating links

Links in your pages serve several purposes:

- ✔ They help searchbots find other pages in your site.
- ✔ Keywords in links tell search engines about the pages that the links are pointing at.
- ✔ Keywords in links also tell the search engines about the page containing the links.

You need links into — and out of — your pages. You don't want *dangling* pages — pages with links into them but no links out. All your pages should be part of the navigation structure. But it's also a good idea to have links within the body text, too.

Search engines read link text not only for clues about the page being referred to, but also for hints about the page containing the link. I've seen situations in which links convinced a search engine that the page the links pointed to were relevant for the keywords used in the links, even though the page didn't contain those words. The classic example was an intentional manipulation of Google, late in 2003, to get it to display George Bush's bio (`www.whitehouse.gov/president/gwbbio.html`) when people searched for the term *miserable failure*. This was done by a small group of people using links in blog pages. Despite the fact that this page contains neither the word *miserable,* nor the word *failure,* and certainly not the term *miserable failure,* a few dozen links with the words *miserable failure* in the link text were enough to trick Google.

So when you're creating pages, create links on the page to other pages, and make sure that other pages within your site link back to the page you're creating, using the keywords that you have placed in your TITLE.

Don't create simple <u>Click Here</u> links or <u>You'll Find More Information Here</u> links. These words don't help you. Instead, create links like these:

> For more information, see our <u>*rodent-racing scores page*</u>.
>
> Our <u>*rodent-racing background page*</u> will provide you the information you're looking for.
>
> Visit our <u>*rat events*</u> and <u>*mouse events*</u> pages for more info.

Links are critical. Web developers have played all sorts of tricks with keywords — overloading TITLE tags, DESCRIPTION tags, ALT attributes, and so on — and all these tricks are well known to the search engines and don't do much anymore. The search engines constantly look for new ways to analyze and index pages, and link text is a good way for them to do that. In the same way that it's hard for a Web designer to manipulate a TITLE tag — because search engines can easily spot overloading — it's also difficult to manipulate link text.

In Chapters 14 and 15, you find out about another aspect of links: getting links from other sites to point back to yours.

## Using other company and product names

Here's a common scenario: Many of your prospective visitors and customers are searching online for other companies' names, or the names of products produced or sold by other companies. Can you use these names in your pages? Yes, but be careful how you use them.

Many large companies are aware of this practice, and a number of lawsuits have been filed that relate to the use of keywords by companies other than the trademark owners. Here are a few examples:

- A law firm that deals with Internet domain disputes sued Web-design and Web-hosting firms for using its name, Oppedahl & Larson, in their KEYWORDS meta tags. These firms thought that merely having the words in the tags could bring traffic to their sites. The law firm won. Duh! (Didn't anyone ever tell you not to upset large law firms?)

- Playboy Enterprises sued Web sites that were using the terms *playboy* and *playmates* throughout their pages, site names, domain names, and meta tags to successfully boost their positions. Not surprisingly, Playboy won.

- Insituform Technologies Inc. sued National Envirotech Group after discovering that Envirotech was using its name in its meta tags. Envirotech lost. The judge felt that using the name in the meta tag without having any relevant information in the body of the pages was clearly a strategy for misdirecting people to the Envirotech site.

So, yes, you can get sued. But then again, you can get sued for anything. In some instances, the plaintiff loses. Playboy won against a number of sites, but lost against former playmate Terri Welles. Playboy didn't want her to use the terms *playboy* and *playmate* on her Web site, but she believed she had the right to, as a former Playboy Playmate. A judge agreed with her. The real point of this Terri Welles case is that nobody owns a word, a product name, or a company name. They merely own the right to use it in certain contexts. Thus, Playboy doesn't own the word *playboy* — you can say *playboy,* and you can use it in print. But Playboy does own the right to use it in certain contexts and to stop other people from using it in those same contexts.

If you use product and company names to mislead or misrepresent, you could be in trouble. But you can use the terms in a valid, nonfraudulent manner. For instance, you can have a product page in which you compare your products to another, named competitor. That's perfectly legal. No, I'm not a lawyer, but I'm perfectly willing to play one on TV given the opportunity. And I would bet that you won't be seeing the courts banning product comparisons on Web sites.

If you have information about competing products and companies on your pages, used in a valid manner, you can also include the keywords in the TITLE, DESCRIPTION, and KEYWORDS, as Terri Welles has done:

```
<META NAME="keywords" CONTENT=" terri, welles, playmate,
        playboy, model, models, semi-nudity, naked,
        censored by editors, censored by editors,
        censored by editors, censored by editors,
        censored by editors, censored by editors,
        censored by editors, censored by editors">
```

And there's nuthin' Playboy can do about it.

To some degree, all this is a moot point, anyway. Just stuffing a competitor's name into the KEYWORDS tag won't do much for your search engine ranking, although some companies drop competitor's names into the body text in a totally irrelevant way. The bigger debate is the question of whether companies should be allowed to buy keywords related to competing products and companies. (See Chapter 17 for information on buying keywords.)

## Creating navigation structures that search engines can read

Your navigation structure needs to be visible to the search engines. As I explain earlier in this chapter, some page components are simply invisible to search engines. For instance, a navigation structure created with JavaScript won't work for the search engines. If the only way to navigate your Web site is with the JavaScript navigation, you have a problem. The only pages the search engines will find are the ones with links pointing to them from other Web sites; the search engines won't be able to find their way around your site.

Here are a few tips for search-engine-friendly navigation:

- ✔ If you use JavaScript navigation, or some other technique that is invisible (which is covered in more detail in Chapter 7), make sure that you have a plain HTML navigation system, too, such as basic text links at the bottom of your pages.

- ✔ Even if your navigation structure is visible to search engines, you may want to have these bottom-of-page links as well. They're convenient for site visitors and provide another chance for the search engines to find your other pages.

  Yet another reason for bottom-of-page, basic text navigation: If you have some kind of image-button navigation, you don't have any keywords in the navigation for the search engines to read.

- ✔ Add a site map page and link to it from your main navigation. It provides another way for search engines to find all your pages.

- ✔ Whenever possible, provide keywords in text links as part of the navigation structure.

## Blocking searchbots

You may want to block particular pages, or even entire areas of your Web site, from being indexed. Here are a few examples of pages or areas you may want to block:

 ✔ Pages that are under construction.

 ✔ Pages with information that is for internal use. (You should probably password-protect that area of the site, too.)

 ✔ Directories in which you store scripts and CSS style sheets.

Using the ROBOTS meta tag or the *robots.txt* file, you can tell the search engines to stay away. The meta tag looks like this:

```
<META NAME="robots" CONTENT="noindex, nofollow">
```

This tag does two things: `noindex` means don't index this page, and `nofollow` means don't follow the links from this page.

To block entire directories on your Web site, create a text file called *robots.txt* and place it in your site's root directory — which is the same directory as your home page. When a search engine comes to a site, it generally requests the *robots.txt* file first; it requests `http://www.domainame.com/robots.txt`.

The *robots.txt* file allows you to block specific search engines and allow others, although this is rarely done. In the file, you specify which search engine (user agent) you want to block and from which directories or files. Here's how:

```
User-agent: *
Disallow: /includes/
Disallow: /scripts/
Disallow: /info/scripts/
Disallow: /staff.html
```

Because `User-agent` is set to *, all searchbots are blocked from *www.domainname.com/includes/*, *www.domainname.com/scripts/*, *www.domain name.com/info/scripts/directories*, and the *www.domainname.com/staff.html* file. (If you know the name of a particular searchbot you want to block, replace the asterisk with that name.)

Be careful with your *robots.txt* file. If you make incomplete changes and end up with the following code, you've just blocked all the search engines from your entire site:

```
User-agent: *
Disallow: /
```

In fact, this technique is sometimes used nefariously; I know of one case in which someone hacked into a site and placed the `Disallow: /` command into the *robots.txt* file . . . and Google dropped the site from its index!

# Chapter 7

# Avoiding Things That Search Engines Hate

*I*t is possible to look at your Web site in terms of its *search engine friendliness.* (Chapter 6 of this book does just that.) It is equally possible, however, to look at the flip side of the coin — things people often do that hurt their Web site's chances with search engines, and in some cases even making their Web sites invisible to the search engines.

This tendency on the part of Web site owners to shoot themselves in the foot is very common. In fact, as you read through this chapter, you are quite likely to find things that you're doing that are hurting you. Paradoxically, serious problems are especially likely for sites created by mid- to large-size companies using sophisticated Web technologies.

Steering you clear of the major design potholes is what this chapter is all about. Guided by the principle, First Do No Harm, the following sections show you the major things to avoid when setting up your Web site.

## Dealing with Frames

Frames were very popular a few years ago, but they are much less so these days, I'm glad to say. A *framed* site is one in which the browser window is broken into two or more parts, each of which holds a Web page (as shown in Figure 7-1).

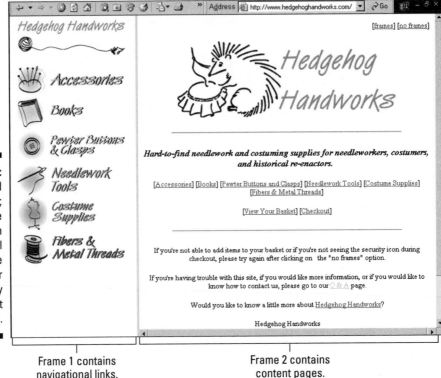

**Figure 7-1:**
A framed
Web site;
each frame
has an
individual
page. The
scroll bar
moves only
the right
frame.

Frame 1 contains
navigational links.

Frame 2 contains
content pages.

Frames cause a number of problems. Some browsers don't handle them well — in fact, the first frame-enabled browsers weren't that enabled and often crashed when loading frames. In addition, many designers created framed sites without properly testing them. They built the sites on large, high-resolution screens, so they didn't realize that they were creating sites that would be almost unusable on small, low-resolution screens.

From a search engine perspective, frames create the following problems:

✔ Some search engines have trouble getting through the frame-definition or frameset page to the actual Web pages.

✔ If the search engine gets through, it indexes individual pages, not framesets. Each page is indexed separately, so pages that make sense only as part of the frameset end up in the search engines as independent pages. (Jump ahead to Figure 7-2 to see an example of a page, indexed by Google, that belongs inside a frameset.)

✔ You can't point to a particular page in your site. This may be a problem in the following situations:

## Refraining

Here's what the top search engine had to say when the technical editor on the first edition of this book, Micah Baldwin of Current Wisdom, asked about frames:

"Google does support frames to the extent that it can. Frames can cause problems for search engines because frames don't correspond to the conceptual model of the Web. In this model, one page displays only one URL. Pages that use frames display several URLs (one for each frame) within a single page. If Google determines that a user's query matches the page as a whole, it will return the entire frameset. However, if the user's query matches an individual frame within the larger frameset, Google returns only the relevant frame. In this case, the entire frameset of the page will not appear."

Google often does just that, returning a page pulled out of its frame; the page is, in effect, "orphaned."

- Linking campaigns (see Chapters 14 and 15). Other sites can link to only the front of your site; they can't link to specific pages during link campaigns.

- Pay-per-click campaigns (see Chapter 17). If you're running a *pay-per-click (PPC)* campaign, you can't link directly to a page related to a particular product.

- Placing your products in shopping directories, which is described in Chapter 16. In this case, you need to link to a particular product page.

Search engines index URLs — single pages, in other words. By definition, a framed site is a collection of URLs, and as such, search engines don't know how to properly index the pages.

# The HTML Nitty-Gritty of Frames

Here's an example of a *frame-definition*, or *frameset*, document:

```
<HTML>
<HEAD>
</HEAD>
<FRAMESET ROWS="110,*">
<FRAME SRC="navbar.htm">
<FRAME SRC="main.htm">
</FRAMESET>
</HTML>
```

This document describes how the frames should be created. It tells the browser to create two rows, one 110 pixels high and the other * high — that is, whatever room is left over. It also tells the browser to grab the *navbar.htm* document and place it in the first frame — the top row — and place *main.htm* into the bottom frame.

Most of the bigger search engines can find their way through the frameset to the *navbar.htm* and *main.htm* documents, so Google, for instance, indexes those documents. Some older systems may not, however, effectively making the site invisible to them.

But suppose the pages *are* indexed. Pages that were intended for use inside a frameset are individually indexed in the search engine. In Figure 7-2, you can see a page that I reached from Google — first (on the left) in the condition that I found it and then (on the right) in the frameset it was designed for.

I found this page indexed in Google . . .                    . . . it really belongs in this frame.

**Figure 7-2:** The document on the left, which I found through Google, actually belongs in the frameset shown on the right.

This is not a pretty sight — or site, as it were. But you can work around this mess by doing the following:

✔ Provide information in the frame-definition document to help search engines index it.

✔ Ensure that all search engines can find their way through this page into the main site.

✔ Make sure that pages are open in the correct frameset (perhaps).

The next sections give you the details for following these strategies.

## Providing search engines with the necessary information

The first thing you can do is provide information in the frame-definition document for the search engines to index. First, add a TITLE and your meta tags, like this:

```
<HTML>
<HEAD>
<TITLE>Rodent Racing - Scores, Mouse Events, Rat Events,
        Gerbil Events - Everything about Rodent
        Racing</TITLE>
<meta name="description" content="Rodent Racing - Scores,
        Schedules, everything Rodent Racing. Whether
        you're into mouse racing, stoat racing, rats,
        or gerbils, our site provides everything you'll
        ever need to know about Rodent Racing and
        caring for your racers.">
<META NAME="keywords" CONTENT="Rodent Racing, Racing
        Rodents, Gerbils, Mice, Mouse, Rodent Races,
        Rat Races, Mouse Races, Stoat, Stoat Racing,
        Rats, Gerbils">
</HEAD>
<FRAMESET ROWS="110,*">
<FRAME SRC="navbar.htm">
<FRAME SRC="main.htm">
</FRAMESET>
</HTML>
```

Then at the bottom of the FRAMESET, add <NOFRAMES> tags — <NOFRAMES> tags were originally designed to enclose text that would be displayed by a browser that couldn't handle frames — with <BODY> tags and information inside, like this:

```
<FRAMESET ROWS="110,*">
<FRAME SRC="navbar.htm">
<FRAME SRC="main.htm">
<NOFRAMES>
<BODY>
<H1>Rodent Racing - Everything You Ever Wanted to Know
        about Rodent Racing Events and the Rodent
        Racing Lifestyle</H1>
<P>[This site uses frames, so if you are reading this,
        your browser doesn't handle frames]</P>
<P>This is the world's top rodent-racing Web site. You
        won't find more information about the world's
        top rodent-racing events anywhere else ...[more
        info]
</BODY>
</NOFRAMES>
</FRAMESET>
</HTML>
```

The <NOFRAMES></NOFRAMES> tags were originally intended to display text
for browsers that don't handle frames. Although few people still use such
browsers, you can use the NOFRAMES tags to provide information to the
search engines that they can index. For example, you can take the information from *main.htm* and place it into the NOFRAMES area. Provide 200 to 400
words of keyword-rich text to give the search engines something to work
with. Make sure that the content between the <NOFRAMES> tags is about your
site, and is descriptive and useful to visitors.

Google suggests that the <NOFRAMES> area should be for alternate content
(though as every good editor knows, it probably means *alternative*), and
says that

> If you use wording such as 'This site requires the use of frames,' or 'Upgrade
> your browser,' instead of providing alternate content on your site, then you
> will exclude both search engines and people who have disabled frames on
> their browsers. For example, audio Web browsers, such as those used in
> automobiles and by the visually impaired, typically do not deal with such
> frames. You read more about the <NOFRAMES> tag in the HTML standard
> here at the following URL: www.w3.org/TR/REC-html40/present/frames.
> html#h-16.4. . . .

Unfortunately, many Web designers use the NOFRAMES tags as a convenient
place to add keywords, even if the page is not a frame-definition document.
For this reason, search engines may treat the text within the tags in one of
three ways: Ignore it if it's not within FRAMESET tags; downgrade it, awarding
fewer points to text in a FRAMESET; or ignore it altogether.

## Providing a navigation path

You can easily provide a navigation path in the NOFRAMES area. Simply add links in your text to other pages in the site. Include a simple text-link navigation system on the page and remember to link to your sitemap.

Remember also to do the following:

✔ Give *all* your pages unique <TITLE> and meta tags, as shown in Figure 7-3. Many designers don't bother to do this for pages in frames because browsers read only the TITLE in the frame-definition document. But search engines index these pages individually, not as part of a frameset, so they should all have this information.

✔ Give *all* your pages simple text navigation systems so that a search engine can find its way through your site.

**Figure 7-3:** All pages that are loaded into frames should contain TITLE tags, meta tags, and navigation links.

Pages loaded into frames should contain TITLEs, meta tags, and simple text navigation links to help the search engines index the pages and travel through the site.

You'll run into one problem using these links inside the pages. The links work fine for people who arrive at the page directly through the search engines, and any link that simply points at another page works fine in that situation or for someone who arrives at your home page and sees the pages in the frames. But any link that points at a frame-definition document rather than another page won't work properly (unless you use the fix I'm about to describe) if someone is viewing the page in a frame.

Suppose that you have a link back to the frame-definition document for your home page. If someone is viewing one of your pages inside a frame, as you intended it to be viewed, and clicks the link, the frame definition loads the new frameset into the existing frameset. Now, rather than seeing, say, two frames, the visitor sees three frames — the two new frames are loaded into the current frame. To get around this problem, use the _top target, like this:

```
<a href="index.html" TARGET = "_top">Home</a>
```

This "breaks" the frames, opening the *index.html* document alone in the browser window.

## Opening pages in a frameset

Given the way search engines work, pages in a Web site will be indexed individually. (Refer to Figure 7-3.) If you've created a site by using frames (hey, it takes all kinds!), presumably you want the site displayed in frames. You don't want individual pages pulled out of the frames and displayed, well, individually.

You can use JavaScript to force the browser to load the frameset. Of course, this won't work for the small percentage of users working with browsers that don't handle JavaScript . . . but those browsers probably don't handle frames, either. It also won't work for the small percentage of people who turn off JavaScript; but hey, you can't have everything.

You have to place a small piece of JavaScript into each page so that when the browser loads the page, it reads the JavaScript and loads the frame-definition document. It's a simple little JavaScript that goes something like this:

```
<script language="javascript">
<!--
if (top == self) self.location.href = "index.html";
// -->
</script>
```

Admittedly, this JavaScript causes two problems:

- ✔ The browser loads the frameset defined in *index.html*, which may not include the page that was indexed in the search engine. Visitors may have to use the navigation to find the page that, presumably, had the content they were looking for.

- ✔ The Back button doesn't work correctly, because each time the browser sees the JavaScript, it loads the *index.html* file again.

Another option is to have a programmer create a customized script that loads the frame-definition document and drops the specific page into the correct frame. If you work for a company with a Web-development department, this is a real possibility.

The only really good fix is to not use frames in the first place! I've spent a lot of time on frames, for one purpose really: so that you can quickly fix a site that is using frames. But you shouldn't build Web sites with frames. You may need to fix what someone else did or what you did in earlier, less knowledgeable, days. In general, though, frames are used far less today than they were five years ago for good reason: They are an unnecessary nuisance. Sure, frames may be appropriate in a few instances, but the general rule is this: If you think it is a good idea to build a Web site using frames, you're almost certainly wrong!

# Handling iframes

The iframe is an Internet Explorer feature and not something that is as common as normal frames. An *iframe* is an inline floating frame. It allows you to grab content from one page and drop it into another, in the same way you can grab an image and drop it into the page. The tag looks like this:

```
<iframe src ="page.html">
</iframe>
```

It has similar problems to regular frames. In particular, some search engines don't see the content in the iframe, and the ones that do index it separately.

You can add a link within the <IFRAME> tag so that older searchbots will find the document, like this:

```
<iframe src="page.html"><a href="page.html"
        target="_blank">Click here for more Rodent
        Racing information if your browser doesn't
        display content in this internal
        frame.</a></iframe>
```

You can also use the JavaScript discussed in the preceding section to load your home page and to provide a link at the bottom of the iframe content that people can use to load your home page.

# Fixing Invisible Navigation Systems

Navigation systems that never show up on search engines' radar screens are a common problem, probably even more common than the frames problem I cover in the previous section. Fortunately, you can deal with a navigation system problem very easily.

Many Web sites use navigation systems that are invisible to search engines. In Chapter 6 I explain the difference between *browser-side* and *server-side* processes, and this issue is related. A Web page is compiled in two places — on the server and in the browser. If the navigation system is created in the browser, it's probably not visible to a search engine.

Examples of such systems include those created using

- ✔ Java applets
- ✔ JavaScripts
- ✔ Macromedia Flash

How can you tell if your navigation is invisible to search engines? If you created the pages yourself, you probably know how you built the navigation (although you may be using an authoring tool that did it all for you). So if that's the case, or if you're examining a site that was built by someone else, here are a few ways to figure out how the navigation is built:

- ✔ If navigation is created with a Java applet, when the page loads you probably see a gray box where the navigation sits for a moment or two, with a message such as Loading Java Applet.
- ✔ Look in the page's source code and see how its navigation is created.
- ✔ Turn off the display of JavaScript and other active scripting and then reload the page to see if the navigation is still there. I explain how to do this under "Turning off scripting and Java," a little later in this chapter.

## Looking at the source code

Take a look at the source code of the document to see how it's created. Open the raw HTML file or choose View➪Source from the browser's main menu, and then dig through the file looking for the navigation.

If the page is large and complex, or if your HTML skills are correspondingly small and simple, you may want to try the technique under "Turning off scripting and Java."

Here's an example. Suppose that you find the following code where the navigation should be:

```
<applet code="MenuApplet" width="160" height="400"
        archive="http://www.yourdomain.com/menu.jar">
```

This is a navigation system created with a Java applet. Search engines don't read applet files, so they won't see the navigation. Here's another example:

```
<script type="javascript" src="/menu/menu.js"></script>
```

This one is a navigation tool created with JavaScript. Search engines have difficulty reading JavaScript, so they won't see this navigation system either.

Here's an example of a Flash-based navigation system. Links in Flash navigation systems can't be read by many search engines.

```
<embed src="flash/rcbank_nav02.swf" quality=high
        pluginspage="http://www.macromedia.com/shockwav
        e/download/index.cgi?P1_Prod_Version=ShockwaveF
        lash" type="application/x-shockwave-flash"
        width="750" height="84"></embed>
```

The preceding examples are pretty easy to identify. The script calls a Java applet or JavaScript, and you know that the searchbots don't read these, so they won't see the navigation. Here's another form that can create a problem:

```
<a href="javascript:void(0)"
        onclick="Javascript:window.open('http://yourdom
        ain.com/rat-race/','Rat
        Race','width=550,height=600,left=20,
        top=20,screenX=0,screenY=100,resizable=yes,
        scrollbars=yes')"
        onMouseOut="MM_swapImgRestore()"onMouseOver="MM
        _swapImage('rat_race','','images/rat_race2.gif'
        ,1)"> <img src="images/rat_race1.gif"
        alt="Living and Shopping" name="rat_race"></a>
```

This link uses JavaScript *event handlers* to do several things when triggered by particular events:

- ✔ onclick runs when someone (guess!) clicks the link. This opens a new window and places the referenced document in that window.

- ✔ onMouseOver runs when someone points at the link. In this case, it runs the MM_swapImage function, which changes the image file used for this navigation button.

✔ onMouseOut runs when the mouse is moved away from the link. In this case, it runs the MM_swapImgRestore function, presumably to display the original image.

This is a real link, but it won't work if JavaScript is turned off because the URL normally goes in the href= attribute of the anchor tag (the <A> tag); href= is disabled in this link because it uses JavaScript to do all the work. Search engines won't follow a link like this.

## Turning off scripting and Java

You can also turn off scripting and Java in the browser, and then look at the pages. If the navigation has simply disappeared, or if it's there but doesn't work anymore, you've got a problem.

Here's how to disable the settings in Internet Explorer. Other browsers are similar.

1. **Choose Tools⇨Internet Options from the main menu.**

   The Internet Options dialog box appears.

2. **Click the Security tab.**

   The Security options appear, as shown in Figure 7-4.

3. **Click the Custom Level button.**

   The Security Settings dialog box opens.

4. **Select the Microsoft VM⇨Java Permissions⇨Disable Java option button.**

   This stops Java applets from running.

5. **Select the Active Scripting⇨Disable option button, as shown in Figure 7-5.**

   This disables JavaScripts and other similar scripts.

6. **Click the OK button and answer Yes in the message box.**

7. **Click the OK button again in the Internet Options dialog box.**

Now reload the page that you want to check — use the Reload or Refresh button — and see if the navigation is still there. If it is, try to use it. Does it still work? If the navigation has gone or if it's broken, this is something that the search engines will have a problem with. (Figures 7-6 and 7-7 show you how effective this little trick can be. Navigation bar? Now you see it, now you don't.)

When you reload the page, you may notice that other page components disappear, if they're created with scripts. You may find that other things important for the search engines have gone, too.

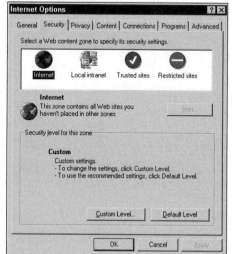

**Figure 7-4:**
The Internet
Options
dialog box.

Disabling scripting and Java doesn't stop Flash from working, and unfortunately there is no simple, quick, and temporary way to stop Flash from working in Internet Explorer. Some other browsers do have such a tool, though. Your best option for Internet Explorer is to install some other kind of blocking software, such as PopUpCop (www.popupcop.com) or jTFlashManager (www.jtedley.com/jtflashmanager).

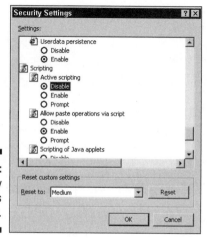

**Figure 7-5:**
The Security
Settings
dialog box.

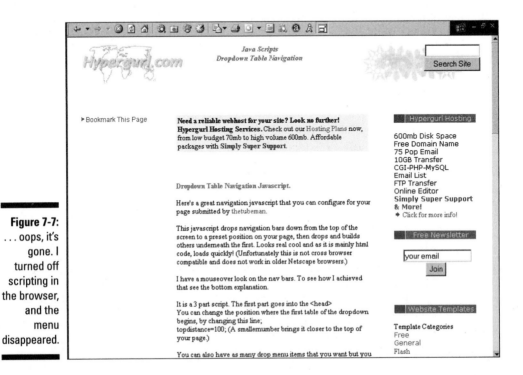

## *Fixing the problem*

If you want, you can continue to use these invisible menus and navigation tools. They can be attractive and effective. The search engines won't see them, but that's okay because you can add a secondary form of navigation that duplicates the top navigation.

You can duplicate the navigation structure by using simple text links at the bottom of the page, for instance. If you have long pages or extremely cluttered HTML, you may want to place small text links near the top of the page to make sure search engines get to them, perhaps in the leftmost table column. (Table columns on the right are lower down on the page as far as the HTML is concerned, and search engines read the text in the HTML instead of viewing the page as people do.)

# *Reducing the Clutter in Your Web Pages*

Simple is good; cluttered is bad. The more cluttered your pages, the more work it is for search engines to dig through them. What do I mean by *clutter?* I'm referring to everything in a Web page that is used to create the page but that is not actual page content.

For instance, one of my clients had a very cluttered site. The HTML source document for the home page had 21,414 characters, of which 19,418 were characters other than spaces. However, the home page did not contain a lot of text: 1,196 characters, not including the spaces between the words.

So if 1,196 characters were used to create the words on the page, what were the other 18,222 characters used for?! Things like this:

- ✔ JavaScripts: 4,251 characters
- ✔ JavaScript event handlers on links: 1,822 characters
- ✔ The top navigation bar: 6,018 characters
- ✔ Text used to embed a Flash animation near the top of the page: 808 characters

The rest is the normal clutter that you always have in HTML: tags used to format text, create tables, and so on. The problem with this page was that a search engine had to read 18,701 characters (including spaces) *before it ever reached the page content.* Of course, the page did not have much content, and what was there was hidden away below all that HTML.

This clutter above the page content means that some search engines may not reach it. Fortunately, you can use some simple methods to unclutter this and other pages. (There were some very obvious ways to remove around 11,000 text characters without much effort.)

## Use external JavaScripts

You don't need to put JavaScripts inside a page. JavaScripts generally should be placed in an *external file* — a tag in the Web page "calls" a script that is pulled from another file on the Web server — for various reasons:

- ✔ **They're actually safer outside the HTML file.** By that, I mean they're less likely to be damaged while making changes to the HTML.

- ✔ **They're easier to manage externally.** Why not have a nice library of all the scripts in your site in one directory?

- ✔ **The download time is slightly shorter.** If you use the same script in multiple pages, the browser downloads the script once and caches it.

- ✔ **They're easier to reuse.** You don't need to copy scripts from one page to another and fix all the pages when you have to make a change to the script. Just store the script externally and change the external file to automatically change the script in any number of pages.

- ✔ **Doing so removes clutter from your pages!**

Creating external JavaScript files is easy. Simply take the text between the <SCRIPT></SCRIPT> tags, save it in a text editor, and save that file on your Web server (as a *.js* file — *mouseover_script.js*, for instance).

Then add an src= attribute to your <SCRIPT> tag to refer to the external file, like this:

```
<script language="JavaScript" type="text/javascript"
        src="/scripts/mouseover_script.js"></script>
```

In this example, placing scripts in external files would have removed over 20 percent of the text characters from the file.

## Use document.write to remove problem code

If you have a complicated top navigation bar — one with text colors in the main bar that change when you point at a menu or drop-down lists, also with changing colors — you can easily get code character counts up to 6,000 characters or so. That's a lot of characters! Add some Flash animation, and you're probably up to 7,000 characters, which can easily end up being a significant portion of the overall code for the page. You can easily remove all this clutter by using JavaScript to write the text into the page. Here's how:

1. **In an external text file, type this text:**

```
<!--
document.write("")
//-->
```

2. **Grab the entire code you want to remove from the HTML page and then paste it between the following quotation marks:**

```
document.write("place code here")
```

3. **Save this file and place it on your Web server.**

4. **Call the file from the HTML page by adding an `src=` attribute to your `<SCRIPT>` tag to refer to the external file, like this:**

```
<script language="JavaScript" src="/scripts/navbar.js"
        type="text/javascript"></script>
```

Of course, if you remove the navigation — remember, the searchbots won't read these JavaScripts, so they won't see the navigation — from the page, you won't have navigation that the search engines can follow. So remember to add simple text navigation somewhere else on the page (maybe at the bottom, now that the page is much smaller). Simple text navigation takes up much less room than a complex navigation bar.

## Use external CSS files

If you can stick JavaScript stuff into an external file, it shouldn't surprise you that you can do the same thing — drop stuff into a file that is then referred to in the HTML file proper — with *Cascading Style Sheet (CSS)* information. For reasons that are unclear to me, many designers place CSS information directly into the page, despite the fact that the ideal use of a style sheet is *external*. Just think about it — one of the basic ideas behind style sheets is to allow you to make formatting changes to an entire site very quickly. If you want to change the size of the body text or the color of the heading text, you make one small change in the CSS file, and it affects the whole site immediately. If you have your CSS information in each page, though, you have to change each and every page. Rather defeats the object of CSS, doesn't it?

Here's how to remove CSS information from the main block of HTML code. Simply place the targeted text in an external file — everything between and including the `<STYLE></STYLE>` tags — and then call the file in your HTML pages by using the `<LINK>` tag, like this:

```
<link rel="stylesheet" href="site.css" type="text/css">
```

## Move image maps to the bottom of the page

*Image maps* (described in detail later in the chapter) are images that contain multiple links. One way to clean up clutter in a page is to move the code that defines the links to the bottom of the Web page, right before the `</BODY>` tag. Doing so doesn't remove the clutter from the page, but moves the clutter to the end of the page where it won't get between the top of the page and the page content. That makes it more likely that the search engines will reach the content.

## Don't copy and paste from MS Word

That's right. Don't copy text directly from Microsoft Word and drop it into a Web page. You'll end up with *all sorts* of formatting clutter in your page!

Here's one way to get around this problem:

1. **Save the file as an HTML file.**

   Word provides various options to do this, but you want to use the simplest: Web Page (Filtered).

2. **In your HTML-authoring program, look for a Word-cleaning tool.**

   Word has such a bad reputation that HTML programs are now starting to add tools to help you clean the text before you use it. Dreamweaver has such a thing, and even Microsoft's own HTML-authoring tool, FrontPage, has one. It's in the Optimize HTML dialog box, on the Options menu.

# Managing Dynamic Web Pages

Chapter 6 explains how your standard, meat-and-potatoes Web page gets assembled in your browser so that you, the surfer, can actually see it. But you can assemble a Web page more than one way. For example, the process can go like this:

1. The Web browser requests a Web page.

2. The Web server sends a message to a database program requesting the page.

3. The database program reads the URL to see exactly what is requested, compiles the page, and sends it to the server.

4. The server reads any instructions inside the page.

5. The server compiles the page, adding information specified in *server side includes (SSIs)* or scripts.

6. The server sends the file to the browser.

Pages pulled from databases are known as *dynamic pages,* as opposed to the normal *static pages* that don't come from the database. They're dynamic because they're created *on the fly,* when requested. The page doesn't exist until a browser requests it, at which point the data is grabbed from a database and put together with a CGI, an ASP, or a PHP program, for instance, or one of the many content-management systems (such as BroadVision, Ektron CMS, or ATG Dynamo).

Unfortunately, dynamic pages can create problems. Even the best search engines sometimes don't read them. Of course, a Web page is a Web page, whether created on the fly or days beforehand. After the searchbot receives the page, the page is already complete. So why don't search engines always read dynamic pages? Because search engines don't want to read them (or their programmers don't want them to, that is). Of course, they *can* read dynamic pages. Again, a page is a page.

The search engine programmers have discovered that dynamic pages are often problem pages. Here are a few of the problems searchbots can run into reading dynamic pages:

✔ Dynamic pages often have only minor changes in them. A searchbot reading these pages may end up with hundreds of pages that are almost exactly the same, with nothing more than minor differences to distinguish one from the other.

✔ The search engines are concerned that databased pages might change frequently, making search results inaccurate.

✔ Searchbots sometimes get stuck in the dynamic system, going from page to page to page among tens of thousands of pages. On occasion, this happens when a Web programmer hasn't properly written the link code, and the database continually feeds data to the search engine, even crashing your server.

✔ Hitting a database for thousands of pages can slow down the server, so searchbots often avoid getting into situations in which that is likely to happen.

✔ Sometimes URLs can change (I talk about *session IDs* in a moment), so even if the search engine does index the page, the next time someone tries to get there, it'll be gone; and search engines don't want to index dead links.

# Are your dynamic pages scaring off search engines?

You can often tell if search engines are likely to omit your pages just by looking at the URL. Go deep into the site; if it's a product catalog, for instance, go to the furthest subcategory you can find. Then look at the URL. Suppose that you have a URL like this:

```
http://www.yourdomain.edu/rodent-racing-scores/march/
          index.php
```

This is a normal URL that should have few problems. It's a static page — or at least looks like a static page, which is what counts. Compare this URL with the next one:

```
http://www.yourdomain.edu/rodent-racing/scores.php?prg=1
```

This filename ends with *?prg=1*. This is almost certainly a databased dynamic page; ?prg=1 is a *parameter* that is being sent to the server to let it know what information is needed for the Web page. This URL is probably okay, especially for the major search engines, although a few smaller search engines may not like it. Now look at the following URL:

```
http://yourdomain.com/products/index.html?&DID=18&CATID=13
          &ObjectGroup_ID=79
```

This URL is worse. It contains three parameters: DID=18, CATID=13, and ObjectGroup_ID=79. Three parameters may be too much. These days Google may index this page; at one point it probably wouldn't have. Some major search engines, though — Yahoo!, for instance — are far less likely to do so.

If you have a *clean* URL with no parameters, the search engines should be able to get to it. If you have a single parameter, it's probably okay for the major search engines, though not necessarily for older systems. If you have two parameters, it may be a problem, or it may not, although two parameters are more likely to be a problem than a single parameter. Three parameters are almost certainly a problem for some systems, and reduce the likelihood that the page will be indexed.

You can also find out if a page in your site is indexed by using the following techniques:

✔ If you have the Google Toolbar, open the page you want to check, click the i button, and select Cached Snapshot of Page. Or go to Google and type **cache:** *YourURL*, where *YourURL* is the site you're interested in. If Google displays a cached page, it's there, of course. If Google doesn't display it, move to the next technique. (For more on the Google Toolbar — including where to download it — see Chapter 1.)

✔ Go to Google and type the URL of the page into the text box and click Search. If the page is in the index, Google displays some information about it.

✔ Use similar techniques with other search engines if you want to check them for your page. Take a look at their help pages for more information.

## Fixing your dynamic Web page problem

So, how do you get search engines to take a look at your state-of-the-art dynamic Web site? Here are a few ideas:

✔ **Find out if the database program has a built-in way to create static HTML.** Some e-commerce systems, for instance, will spit out a static copy of their catalog pages, which is intended for search engines. When visitors click a Buy button, they're taken back into the dynamic system.

✔ **Modify URLs so they don't look like they're pointing to dynamic pages.** You can often help fix the problem by removing characters such as ?, #, !, *, %, and & and reducing the number of parameters to one. Talk with the programmer who is responsible for the database system for the specifics.

✔ **Use a URL rewrite trick — a technique for changing the way URLs look.** Different servers have different tools available; mod_rewrite, for instance, is a tool used by the Apache Web server (a very popular system). *Rewriting* is a system whereby the server can convert fake URLs into real URLs. The server might see, for instance, a request for a page at

```
http://yourdomain.com/showprod/20121.html
```

The server knows that this page doesn't exist and that it really refers to the following URL:

```
http://yourdomain.com/
       showprod.cfm?&DID=7&User_ID=2382175&st=6642&st
       2=45931500&st3=-
       43564544&topcat_id=20018&catid=20071&objectgro
       up_id=20121.
```

In other words, this technique allows you to use what appear to be static URLs, yet still grab pages from a database. This is complicated stuff, so if your server administrator doesn't understand it, it may take him or her a few days to figure it all out.

✔ **Find out if the programmer can create static pages from the database.** Rather than creating a single Web page each time it's requested, the database could "spit out" the entire site periodically — each night for instance, or when the database is updated — creating static pages with normal URLs.

✔ **You can get your information into Yahoo! using an XML feed (often known as a *trusted feed*).** However, note that if you use a trusted feed, you'll be charged for every click to your site — and even then, it wouldn't get you anywhere with Google, the world's most popular search engine, because Google does not have this service, nor with MSN or Ask.com. See Chapter 11 for more information.

Want to find out more about URL rewriting? Here are a couple of places to look:

✔ `www.asp101.com/articles/wayne/extendingnames`

✔ `httpd.apache.org/docs/mod/mod_rewrite.html`

# Using Session IDs in URLs

Just as dynamic Web pages can throw a monkey wrench into the search engine machinery, session IDs can make search engine life equally interesting. A *session ID* identifies a particular person visiting the site at a particular time, which enables the server to track what pages the visitor looks at and what actions the visitor takes during the session.

If you request a page from a Web site — by clicking a link on a Web page, for instance — the Web server that has the page sends it to your browser. Then if you request another page, the server sends that page, too, but the server doesn't know that you are the same person. If the server needs to know who you are, it needs a way to identify you each time you request a page. It does that by using session IDs.

Session IDs are used for a variety of reasons, but the main purpose is to allow Web developers to create various types of interactive sites. For instance, if the developers have created a secure environment, they may want to force visitors to go through the home page first. Or the developers may want a way to pick up a session where it left off. By setting cookies on the visitor's computer containing the session ID, the developers can see where the visitor was in the site at the end of the visitor's last session. (A *cookie* is a text file containing information that can be read only by the server that set the cookie.)

Session IDs are common when running a software application that has any kind of security (such as requiring a login), or needs to store variables, or wants to defeat the browser cache — that is, ensure that the browser always displays information from the server, never from its own cache. Shopping cart systems typically use session IDs — that's how the system can allow you to place an item in the shopping cart and then go away and continue shopping. It *recognizes* you based on your session ID.

Session IDs can be created in two ways:

✔ They can be stored in cookies.

✔ They can be displayed in the URL itself.

Some systems are set up to store the session ID in a cookie but then use a URL session ID if the user's browser is set to not accept cookies. (Relatively few browsers, perhaps a percent or two, don't accept cookies.) Here's an example of a URL containing a session ID:

```
http://yourdomain.com/index.jsp;jsessionid=07D3CCD4D9A6A9F
        3CF9CAD4F9A728F44
```

The `07D3CCD4D9A6A9F3CF9CAD4F9A728F44` piece of the URL is the unique identifier assigned to the session.

If a search engine recognizes a URL as including a session ID, it probably won't read the referenced page because the server can handle a session ID two different ways when the searchbot returns. Each time the searchbot returns to your site, the session ID will have expired, so the server could do either of the following:

✔ **Display an error page, rather than the indexed page, or perhaps the site's default page (generally the home page).** In other words, the search engine has indexed a page that won't be there if someone clicks the link in the search results page. This is admittedly less common than the next server behavior.

✔ **Assign a new session ID.** The URL that the searchbot originally used has expired, so the server replaces the ID with another one, changing the URL. So the spider could be fed multiple URLs for the same page.

Even if the searchbot does read the referenced page (and sometimes they do), it probably won't index it or won't index much of your site. Webmasters sometimes complain that a search engine entered their site, requested the same page over and over, and left without indexing most of the site. The searchbot simply got confused and left. Or sometimes the search engine doesn't recognize a session ID in a URL. One of my clients has hundreds of URLs indexed by Google, but because they are all long-expired session IDs, they all point to the site's main page.

Dealing with session IDs is like a magic trick. Sites that were invisible to search engines suddenly become visible! One site owner in a search engine discussion group described how his site had never had more than six pages indexed by Google, yet within a week of removing session IDs, Google had indexed over 600 pages.

When sites are run through URLs with session IDs, you can do various things:

- ✔ **Instead of using session IDs in the URL, store session information in a cookie on the user's computer.** Each time a page is requested, the server can check the cookie to see if session information is stored there. (Few people change their browser settings to block cookies.) However, the server shouldn't *require* cookies, or you could run into further problems (as you find out in a moment).

- ✔ **Get your programmer to omit session IDs if the device requesting a Web page from the server is a searchbot.** The server will deliver the same page to the searchbot but won't assign a session ID, so the searchbot can travel throughout the site without using session IDs. (Every device requesting a page from a Web server identifies itself, so it's possible for a programmer to send different pages according to the requestor — something I talk more about in Chapter 8.) This is known as *User-Agent delivery*. User-Agent refers to the device — browser, searchbot, or some other kind program — that is requesting a page.

The User-Agent method does have one potential problem. It's a technique sometimes known as *cloaking* — where a server sends one page to the search engines and another to real site visitors. Search engines generally don't like cloaking because Web designers often try to trick the search engines by providing different content from what the site visitor sees. Of course, in the context of using the technique to avoid the session-ID problem, that is not the intent; it's a way to show the *same* content that the site visitor sees, so it isn't true cloaking. However, the (slight) danger is that the search engines may view it as cloaking if they discover what is happening. For more on cloaking, see Chapter 8.

# Examining Cookie-Based Navigation

*Cookies* — the small text files that a Web server can store on a site visitor's hard drive — can often prove as indigestible to search engines as dynamic Web pages and session IDs. Imagine this scenario: You visit a site that is using cookies, and at some point, the server decides to store a cookie. It sends the information to your browser, and the browser duly creates a text file, which it then stores on your computer's hard drive. This text file might contain a session ID (as discussed in the preceding section) or something else. Cookies enable systems to remember who you are so you don't have to log in each time you visit.

Cookies are sometimes used for navigation purposes. For instance, you may have seen *crumb trails,* a series of links showing where you have been as you travel through the site. Crumb trails look something like this:

```
Home->Rodents->Rats->Racing
```

This is generally information being stored in a cookie and is read each time you load a new page. Or the server may read the cookie to determine how many times you've visited the site or what you did the last time you were on the site, and direct you to a particular page based on that information.

If you're using Internet Explorer on Microsoft Windows, follow these steps to see what these cookie files look like:

1. **Choose Tools⇨Internet Options from the main menu.**

   The Internet Options dialog box appears.

2. **In the Internet Options dialog box, make sure that the General tab is selected.**

3. **Click the Settings button in the Temporary Internet Files area.**

   The Settings dialog box appears.

4. **In the Settings dialog box, click the View Files button.**

   A Windows Explorer window opens, displaying the directory containing your temporary files, including cookies. The files are named *Cookies:username@domainname.com.* For instance, when I visited the www.nokiausa.com Web site, the server created a cookie called *Cookie:peter kent@nokiausa.com.*

5. **Double-click any of these cookie files.**

   View the file's contents. A warning message appears, but ignore it.

6. **Click Yes.**

   The cookie opens in Notepad.

Here are the contents of the cookie that was set by www.nokiausa.com. This cookie contains a session ID:

```
session_idA_da6Bj6pwoLg=_nokiausa.com/_1536_1240627200_303
         94925_36557520_29597255_*
```

There's nothing wrong with using cookies, *unless* they're *required* in order to navigate through your site. A server can be set up to simply refuse to send a Web page to a site visitor if the visitor's browser doesn't accept cookies. That's a problem for several reasons:

> ✔ A few browsers simply don't accept cookies.
>
> ✔ A small number of people have changed their browser settings to refuse to accept cookies.
>
> ✔ Searchbots can't accept cookies.

If your Web site *demands* the use of cookies, you won't get indexed. That's all there is to it! The searchbot will request a page, your server will try to set a cookie, and the searchbot won't be able to accept it. The server won't send the page, so the searchbot won't index it.

How can you check to see if your site has this problem? Change your browser's cookies setting and see if you can travel through the Web site. Here's how (for Internet Explorer):

1. **Choose Tools⇨Internet Options from the main menu.**

   The Internet Options dialog box appears.

2. **In the Internet Options dialog box, click the Privacy tab.**

3. **On the Privacy tab, click the Advanced button.**

   The Advanced Privacy Settings dialog box appears, as shown in Figure 7-8.

4. **Select the Override Automatic Cookie Handling checkbox if it's not already selected.**

5. **Select both of the Prompt option buttons.**

   You want to get prompts from both first-party cookies and third-party cookies. I recommend that you select Prompt rather than Block to make it easier to test your site. Now each time a server tries to set a cookie, you see a warning box, and you can accept or block the cookie at will.

6. **Click OK to close the Advanced Privacy Settings dialog box.**

7. **In the Internet Options dialog box, click the General tab.**

8. **On the General tab, click the Delete Cookies button.**

   Note that some sites won't recognize you when you revisit them, until you log in again and they reset their cookies.

9. **Click the OK button in the confirmation message box.**

10. **Click the OK button to close the dialog box.**

Now go to your Web site and see what happens. Each time the site tries to set a cookie, you see a message box, as shown in Figure 7-9. Block the cookie and then see if you can still travel around the site. If you can't, the searchbots can't navigate it either.

**Figure 7-8:**
The
Advanced
Privacy
Settings
dialog box.

Select these two option buttons.

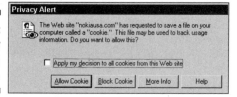

**Figure 7-9:**
The Privacy
Alert dialog
box.

How do you fix this problem?

- ✔ **Don't require cookies.** Ask your site programmers to find some other way to handle what you're doing with cookies, or do without the fancy navigation trick.

- ✔ **As with session IDs, you can use a User-Agent script that treats search-bots differently.** If the server sees a normal visitor, it requires cookies; if it's a searchbot, it doesn't.

# *Fixing Bits and Pieces*

Forwarded pages, image maps, and special characters can also cause problems for search engines.

## *Forwarded pages*

Search engines don't want to index pages that automatically forward to other pages. You've undoubtedly seen pages telling you that something has moved to another location and that you can click a link or wait a few seconds for the

page to automatically forward the browser to another page. This is often
done with a REFRESH meta tag, like this:

```
<meta http-equiv="refresh" content="0;
        url=http://yourdomain.com">
```

This meta tag forwards the browser immediately to *yourdomain*.com. Quite
reasonably, search engines don't like these pages. Why index a page that
doesn't contain information but forwards visitors to the page *with* the information? Why not index the target page? That's just what search engines do.

If you use the REFRESH meta tag, you can expect search engines to ignore the
page (unless it's a very slow refresh rate of over ten seconds, which is specified by the number immediately after content=).

## *Image maps*

An *image map* is an image that has multiple links. You might create the image
like this:

```
<img name="main" src="images/main.gif" usemap="#m_main">
```

The usemap= parameter refers to the map instructions. You can create the
information defining the *hotspots* on the image — the individual links — by
using a <MAP> tag, like this:

```
<map name="m_main">
<area shape="rect" coords="238,159,350,183"
        href="page1.html">
<area shape="rect" coords="204,189,387,214" href="
        page2.html">
<area shape="rect" coords="207,245,387,343" href="
        page3.html">
<area shape="rect" coords="41,331,155,345" href="
        page4.html">
<area shape="rect" coords="40,190,115,202" href="
        page5.html">
<area shape="rect" coords="42,174,148,186" href="
        page6.html">
<area shape="rect" coords="40,154,172,169" href="
        page7.html">
<area shape="rect" coords="43,137,142,148" href="
        page8.html">
<area shape="rect" coords="45,122,165,131" href="
        page9.html">
```

```
<area shape="rect" coords="4,481,389,493" href="
        page10.html">
<area shape="rect" coords="408,329,588,342" href="
        page11.html">
    <area shape="rect" coords="410,354,584,391" href="
        page12.html">
    </map>
```

Will search engines follow these links? Many search engines don't read image maps, although the problem is not as serious as it was a few years ago. The solution is simple: Use additional simple text links in the document.

## Special characters

Don't use special characters, such as accents, in your text. To use unusual characters, you have to use special codes in HTML, and the search engines generally don't like these codes. If you want to write the word *rôle,* for example, you can do it three ways:

```
R&ocirc;le
```

```
R&#244;le
```

```
rôle
```

Note that the third method displays okay in Internet Explorer but not in a number of other browsers. But you probably shouldn't use any of these forms because the search engines don't much like them, and so won't index these words. Stick to basic characters.

# Chapter 8

# Dirty Deeds, Done Dirt Cheap

*E*veryone wants to fool the search engines. And the search engines know it. That's why search engine optimization is such a strange business — a hybrid of technology and, oh, I dunno . . . industrial espionage, perhaps? The search engines don't want you to know exactly how they rank pages because if you did, you would know exactly how to trick them into giving you top positions.

Now for a bit of history. When this whole search engine business started out, the search engines just wanted people to follow some basic guidelines — make the Web site readable, provide a TITLE tag, provide a few keywords related to the page's subject matter, and so on — and then the search engines would take it from there.

What happened, though, is that Web sites started jostling for position. For example, although the KEYWORDS meta tag seemed like a great idea, so many people misused it (by repeating words and using words that *weren't* related to the subject matter) that it eventually became irrelevant to the search engines. Eventually, the major search engines stopped giving much weight to the tag or just ignored it altogether.

The search engines try to hide their methods as much as they can, but it sometimes becomes apparent what the search engines want, and at that point, people start trying to give it to them in a manner the search engines regard as manipulative. This chapter discusses what things you should avoid doing because you risk upsetting the search engines and getting penalized — potentially even getting booted from a search engine for life!

# Tricking the Search Engines

Before getting down to the nitty-gritty details about tricking the search engines, I focus on two topics: why you need to understand the dangers of using dirty tricks and what the overriding principles behind tricking the search engines are based on.

## Deciding whether to trick

Should you use the tricks in this chapter, and if not, why not? You'll hear several reasons for not using tricks. The first I'm not going to belabor, because I'm not sure the argument behind this reason is very strong: ethics. You'll hear from many people that the tricks in this chapter are unethical, that those who use them are cheating and one step on the evolutionary ladder above pond scum (or one step below pond scum, depending on the commentator).

Self-righteousness is in ample supply on the Internet. Maybe these people are right, maybe not. I do know that many people who try such tricks also have great reasons for doing so and are not the Internet's equivalent of Pol Pot or Attila the Hun. They're simply trying to put their best foot forward in a difficult technical environment.

Many people have tried search engine tricks because they've invested a lot of money in Web sites that turn out to be invisible to the search engines. These folks can't afford to abandon their sites and start again. (See Chapter 7 for a discussion of why search engines sometimes can't read Web pages.) You can, rightly so, point out that these folks can deal with the problem in other ways, but that just means the people involved are misinformed, not evil. The argument made by these tricksters might go something like this: Who gave the search engines the right to set the rules, anyway?

One could argue that doing pretty much anything beyond the basics is cheating. After all, smart Webmasters armed with a little knowledge can make the sorts of adjustments discussed elsewhere in this book, pushing their Web sites up in the ranks above sites that are more appropriate for a particular keyword phrase yet are owned by folks with less knowledge.

Ethics aside, the really good reason for avoiding egregious trickery is that it may have the opposite effect and *harm* your search engine position. And a corollary to that reason is that other, legitimate ways exist to get a good search engine ranking. (Unfortunately, these are often more complicated and time-consuming.)

# Figuring out the tricks

The idea behind most search engine tricks is simple: to confuse the search engines into thinking your site is more appropriate for certain keyword phrases than they would otherwise believe, generally by showing the search engine something that the site visitor doesn't see.

The search engines want to see what the site visitors see, yet at the same time they know they can't. It will be a long, long time before search engines will be able to see and understand the images in a Web page, for instance. Right now, they can't even read text in the images, although that's something that could be possible soon. But to view and understand the images as a real person sees them? Michael Jackson could well be President of the United States before that happens.

The search engine designers have started with this basic principle:

> What you see — with the exception of certain things you're not interested in (images, JavaScript navigation systems, and so on) and of certain technical issues that are not important to the visitor (the DESCRIPTION meta tag, what <H> tag has been applied to a heading, and so on) — should be what the user sees.

For various reasons, the searchbots are not terribly sophisticated. They generally don't read JavaScript, Cascading Style Sheets (CSS), and so on, because of the complexity of doing so. In theory, they could read these things, but it would greatly increase the time and hardware required. So by necessity, they ignore certain components.

Here's one other important principle: The text on the page should be there for the benefit of the site visitor, not the search engines.

Ideally, the search engine designers want Web designers to act as if the search engines don't exist. (Of course, this is *exactly* what many Web designers have done and the reason why so many sites rank poorly in the search engines!) The search engine designers want their programs to determine which pages are the most relevant for a particular search query. They want you — the Web designer — to focus on creating a site that serves your visitors' needs and let the search engines determine which site is most appropriate for which searcher.

What the search engines don't want is for you to show one version of a page to visitors and another version to the search engines because you feel that version is what the search engine will like most.

## Do these tricks work?

For the moment, all the tricks in this chapter do work, at least in some circumstances for some search engines. This may be a little surprising, considering that some of these tricks are very crude and have been known to the search engines for a long time. You'll still find crudely keyword-stuffed pages and pages with hidden text sometimes ranking well in the search engines. Some of this search engine spam does filter through. But most major search engines are much better at recognizing the tricks and eliminating those pages.

Could you use every trick in the book and rank first for your keyword? Sure, but your rank may not last long, and the penalty it could incur will last for a long time. (Although in most cases the pages will simply drop in rank as the search engines apply an algorithm that recognizes the trick, in some cases a search engine could decide to remove all pages from a particular site from the index, permanently.)

As Micah Baldwin, the technical editor for the first edition, likes to point out, "If your competitors are ranking higher than you, it's not because of the tricks they played. It's because of the good, solid search engine optimization work you didn't do." These tricks can be dangerous. You may get caught in one of several ways:

- ✔ A search engine algorithm may discover your trickery, and your page or your entire site could be dropped from the search engine.

- ✔ A competitor might discover what you're doing and report you to the search engines. Google has stated that it prefers to let its algorithms track down cheaters and uses reports of search engine spamming to tune these algorithms, but Google will take direct action in some cases.

- ✔ Your trick may work well for a while, until a major search engine changes its algorithm to discover the trickery . . . at which point your site's ranking will drop like a rock.

If you follow the advice from the rest of this book, you'll surpass 80 percent of your competitors.

# Concrete Shoes, Cyanide, TNT — An Arsenal for Dirty Deeds

The next few sections take a look at some of the search engine tricks that are employed on the Web.

# Keyword stacking and stuffing

You may run across pages that contain the same word or term, or maybe several words or terms, repeated over and over again, often in hidden areas of the page (such as the <KEYWORD> tag), though sometimes visible to visitors. This is one of the earliest and crudest forms of a dirty deed, one that the search engines have been aware of for years. You'd think keyword stacking wouldn't work, but the search engines aren't perfect, and sometimes keyword-stacked pages slip through.

Take a look at Figure 8-1. The Web designer has repeated the word *glucosamine* numerous times, each one in a hyperlink to give it a little extra oomph. I found this page in Google by searching for the term *glucosamine glucosamine glucosamine,* which shows that the page hasn't been kicked out of the index. It's possible it may have been penalized in some way — it doesn't turn up in the first 900 results at Google.

Look at this tactic from the search engine's perspective. Repeating the word glucosamine over and over isn't of any use to a site visitor, so it's understandable why search engine designers don't appreciate this kind of thing. My impression is that this sort of trick is working less frequently than it used to just a couple of years ago, and sites doing this are also becoming less abundant.

**Figure 8-1:**
The person creating this page stacked it with the word *gluco-samine.*

The terms *keyword stacking* and *keyword stuffing* are often used inter-changeably, though some people regard keyword stuffing as something a little different — placing inappropriate keywords inside image ALT attributes and in hidden layers.

## Hiding (and shrinking) keywords

Another old (and very crude) trick is to hide text. This trick, often combined with keyword stuffing, involves placing large amounts of text into a page and hiding it from view. For instance, take a look at Figure 8-2. I found this page in Google (also by searching for *glucosamine glucosamine glucosamine*). It has hidden text at the bottom of the page.

If you suspect that someone has hidden text on a page, you can often make it visible by clicking inside text at the top of the page and dragging the mouse to the bottom of the page to highlight everything in between. You can also look in the page's source code.

How did this designer make the text disappear? Down at the bottom of the source code (choose View➪Source), I found this:

```
<FONT SIZE=7 COLOR="#ffffff"><H6>glucosamine glucosamine
         glucosamine glucosamine glucosamine emu oil emu
         oil emu oil kyolic kyolic kyolic wakunaga
         wakunaga wakunaga</H6></FONT>
```

Notice the COLOR="#ffffff" piece; #ffffff is hexadecimal color code for the color white. The page background is white, so, abracadabra, the text disappears.

Here are some other tricks used for hiding text:

- ✔ **Placing the text inside** <NOFRAMES> **tags.** Some designers do this even if the page isn't a frame-definition document.

- ✔ **Using hidden fields.** Sometimes designers hide words in a form's hidden field (<INPUT TYPE="HIDDEN">).

- ✔ **Using hidden layers.** Style sheets can be used to position a text layer underneath the visible layer or outside the browser.

Because hidden text takes up space, designers often use a very small font size. This is another trick that search engines may look for and penalize.

Here's another variation: Some Web designers make the text color just a little different from the background color to make it hard for the browser to catch. However, the text remains invisible, especially if it's at the bottom of the page preceded by several blank lines. Search engines can look for ranges of colors to determine if this trick is being employed.

There's a big space at the bottom of this page . . .

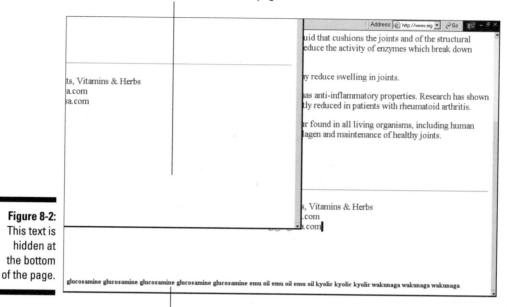

**Figure 8-2:**
This text is
hidden at
the bottom
of the page.

. . . but if you drag the cursor down from the end of the text, you'll see the hidden text.

# Using <NOSCRIPT> tags

This is another way to hide text, but I mention it separately because I suspect it still has more effect than most other hidden-text methods. The <NOSCRIPT></NOSCRIPT> tags are used to put text on a page that can be read by browsers that don't work with JavaScript. Some Web-site owners use them to simply give more text to the search engines to read, and from what I've seen the major search engines often do read this text. However, I also believe that the text inside these tags is not given as much weight as other text on a page, and it may well be that over time the text is being given less and less weight.

# Hiding links

A variation on the old hidden text trick is to hide links. As you discover in Chapters 14 and 15, links provide important clues to search engines about the site's purpose. Some Web designers create links specifically for the search engines to find, but not intended for site visitors. Links can be made to look exactly like all the other text on a page or may even be hidden on punctuation marks — visitors are unlikely to click a link on a period, so the link can be made invisible. Links may be placed in transparent images or invisible layers, in small images, or in `<NOFRAMES><NOSCRIPT>` tags, or hidden in any of the ways discussed earlier for hiding ordinary text.

## Using unrelated keywords

This is a crude and perhaps little-used technique: using keywords that you know are being searched upon frequently, yet which have little or nothing to do with the subject of your site. A few years ago, many Web designers thought it was clever to place the word *sex* in their KEYWORDS meta tag or hide it somewhere in the page. This technique is used less frequently these days because these words are so incredibly competitive. Anyway, it's better to focus on keywords that can actually attract the right kind of visitor.

## Duplicating pages and sites

If content with keywords is good, then twice as much content is better, and three times as much is better still, right? Some site developers have duplicated pages and even entire sites, making virtual photocopies and adding the pages to the site or placing duplicated sites at different domain names.

Sometimes called *mirror pages* or *mirror sites,* these duplicate pages are intended to help a site gain more than one or two entries in the top positions. If you can create three or four Web sites that rank well, you can dominate the first page of the search results, with from four to eight entries out of the first ten. (Google, for instance, will display one or two pages from a site.)

Some people who use this trick try to modify each page just a little to make it harder for the search engines to recognize duplicates. The search engines, in particular Google, have designed tools to find duplication and will often drop a page from their indexes if they find it's a duplicate of another page at the same site. Duplicate pages found across different sites are often okay, which is why content syndication (see Chapter 15) can work well, but entire duplicate sites are something the search engines frown on.

## Page swapping and page jacking

Here are a couple of variations on the duplication theme:

> ✔ **Page swapping:** This is a little-used technique of placing one page at a site and then, after the page has attained a good position, removing it and replacing it with a less-optimized page. One serious problem with this technique is that some search engines now reindex pages very quickly, and it's impossible to know *when* the search engines will return.

> ✔ **Page jacking:** Some truly unethical search engine marketers have employed the technique of using other peoples' high-ranking Web pages, in effect stealing pages that perform well for a while. This is known as *page jacking.*

# Doorway and Information Pages

A *doorway page* is created solely as an entrance from a search engine to your Web site. Doorway pages are sometimes known as *gateway pages* and *ghost pages.* The idea is to create highly optimized pages that are picked up and indexed by the search engines and, hopefully, will rank well and thus channel traffic to the site.

Search engines hate doorway pages because they break one of the cardinal rules: They're intended for search engines, not visitors. The sole purpose of a doorway page is to channel people from the search engines to the real Web site.

One man's doorway page is another man's *information page* — or what some people call *affiliate pages, advertising pages,* or *marketing pages.* The difference between a doorway page and an information page is that the information page is designed for use by the visitor in such a manner that the search engines will rank it well, whereas the doorway page is designed in such a manner that it's utterly useless to the visitor because it's intended purely for the search engine; in fact, originally doorway pages were stuffed full of keywords, duplicated hundreds of times.

Doorway pages typically don't look like the rest of the site, having been created very quickly or even by some kind of program. Doorway pages are part of other strategies. The pages used in *redirects* and *cloaking* (discussed in the next section) are, in effect, doorway pages.

Where do you draw the line between a doorway page and an information page? That's a question I'm not going to answer; it's for you to ponder and remains a matter of debate in the search engine optimization field. If a client asks me to help him in the search engine race and I create pages designed to rank well in the search engines but in such a manner that they're still useful to the visitor, have I created information pages or doorway pages? Most people would say that I've created legitimate information pages.

Suppose, however, that I create lots of pages designed for use by the site visitor, pages that, until my client started thinking about search engine optimization, would have been deemed unnecessary. Surely these pages are, by *intent,* doorway pages, aren't they, even if one could argue that they're useful in some way?

Varying degrees of utility exist, and I know people in the business of creating "information" pages that are useful to the visitor in the author's opinion only! Also, a number of search engine optimization companies create doorway pages that they simply *call* information pages.

Still, an important distinction exists between the two types of pages, and creating information pages is a widely used strategy. The search engines don't know your *intent,* so if you create pages that appear to be useful, are not duplicated dozens or hundreds of times, and don't break any other rules, chances are they'll be fine.

Here's a good reality check. Be honest: Are the pages you just created really of use to your site visitors? If you submitted these pages to Yahoo! or the Open Directory Project for review by a human, would the site be accepted? If the answer is no, the pages probably are not informational.

# Using Redirects and Cloaking

*Redirects* and *cloaking* are pretty much the same thing. The intention is to show one page to the search engines but a completely different page to the site visitor. Why do people want to do this? Here are a few reasons:

- ✔ If a site has been built in a manner that makes it invisible to search engines, cloaking allows the site owner to deliver indexable pages to the search engines while retaining the original site.

- ✔ The site may not have much textual content, making it a poor fit for the search engine algorithms. Although search engine designers might argue that this fact means the site isn't a good fit for a search, this argument clearly doesn't stand up to analysis and debate.

- ✔ Each search engine prefers something slightly different. As long as the search engines can't agree on what makes a good search match, why should they expect site owners and developers to accept good results in some search engines and bad results in others?

I've heard comments such as the following from site owners, and I can understand the frustration: "The search engines are defining how my site should work and what it should look like, and if the manner in which I want to design my site isn't what they like to see, that's not my fault! Who gave them the right to set the rules of commerce on the Internet?!"

What might frustrate and anger site owners more is if they realized that one major search engine actually *does* accept cloaking, as long as you pay them. (See the information on trusted feeds in Chapter 11; a trusted feed is, in effect, a form of cloaking.) So cloaking is a crime, but one search engine says, pay us, and we'll help you do it. (Is that a fee, a bribe, or a protection-racket payment?)

## *Understanding redirects*

A *redirect* is the automatic loading of a page without user intervention. You click a link to load a Web page into your browser, and within seconds, the page you loaded disappears, and a new one appears. Designers often create pages that are designed for the search engines — optimized, keyword-rich pages — that redirect visitors to the real Web site which is not so well optimized. The search engines read the page, but the visitors never really see it.

Redirects can be carried out in various ways:

- By using the REFRESH meta tag. But this is an old trick the search engines discovered long ago; most search engines won't index a page that has a REFRESH tag that bounces the visitor to another page in less than ten seconds or so.

- By using JavaScript to automatically grab the next page within a split second.

- By using JavaScript that is tripped by a user action that is almost certain to occur. In Figure 8-3 you can see an example of this at work. The large button on this page has a JavaScript mouseover event associated with it; when users move their mice over the image — as they're almost certain to do — the mouseover event triggers, loading the next page.

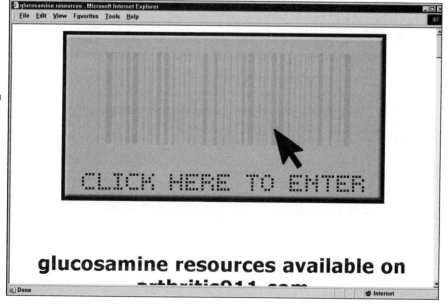

**Figure 8-3:**
The mouse pointer triggers a JavaScript mouse over event on the image, loading another page.

You're unlikely to get penalized for using a redirect. But a search engine may ignore the redirect page. That is, if the search engine discovers that a page is redirecting to another page — and, to be honest, the search engines often don't find these redirect pages unless they use a REFRESH meta tag — it simply ignores the redirect page and indexes the destination page. Search engines reasonably assume that redirect pages are merely a way station on the route to the real content.

## Examining cloaking

*Cloaking* is a more sophisticated trick than a redirect, and harder for the search engines to uncover than a basic REFRESH meta tag redirect. When browsers or searchbots request a Web page, they send information about themselves to the site hosting the page — for example, "I'm Version 6.1 of Internet Explorer," or "I'm Googlebot." The cloaking program quickly looks in its list of searchbots for the device requesting the page. If the device isn't listed, the cloaking program tells the Web server to send the regular Web page, the one intended for site visitors. But if the device name is listed in the searchbot list — as it would be for Googlebot, for instance — the cloaking program sends a *different* page, one that the designer feels is better optimized for that particular search engine. (The cloaking program may have a library of pages, each designed for a particular search engine or group of engines.)

Here's how the two page versions differ:

- ✔ **Pages provided to the search engine:** Often much simpler; created in a way to make them easy for the search engines to read; have lots of heavily keyword-laden text that would sound clumsy to a real person

- ✔ **Pages presented to visitors:** Often much more attractive, graphic-heavy pages, with less text and more complicated structures and navigation systems

The search engines don't like cloaking. Conservative search engine marketers steer well clear of this technique. Here's how Google defines cloaking:

> *The term "cloaking" is used to describe a Web site that returns altered Web pages to search engines crawling the site.*

Well, that's pretty clear; cloaking is cloaking is cloaking. But wait a minute . . .

> *In other words, the Web server is programmed to return different content to Google than it returns to regular users, usually in an attempt to distort search engine rankings.*

Hang on, these two definitions are not the same thing. The term "in an attempt to distort" is critical. If I "return altered pages" without intending to distort rankings, am I cloaking? Here's more from Google:

*This can mislead users about what they'll find when they click on a search result. To preserve the accuracy and quality of our search results, Google may permanently ban from our index any sites or site authors that engage in cloaking to distort their search rankings.*

Notice a few important qualifications: *altered pages . . . usually in an attempt to distort search engine rankings . . . cloaking to distort their search engine rankings.*

This verbiage is a little ambiguous and seems to indicate that Google doesn't totally outlaw the technical use of cloaking; it just doesn't like you to use cloaking in order to cheat. Some would say that using cloaking to present to Google dynamic pages that are otherwise invisible, for instance (see Chapter 7), would be an acceptable practice. Indeed, however, as I've pointed out, many in the business disagree and advise that you never use cloaking in any circumstance.

# Paying the Ultimate Penalty

Just how much trouble can you get into by breaking the rules? The most likely penalty isn't really a penalty. It's just that your pages won't work well with a search engine's algorithm, so they won't rank well.

It is possible to get the ultimate penalty: having your entire site booted from the index. Here's what Google has to say about it:

*We investigate each report of deceptive practices thoroughly and take appropriate action when abuse is uncovered. At minimum, we will use the data from each spam report to improve our site ranking and filtering algorithms. The result of this should be visible over time as the quality of our searches gets even better.*

Google is describing what I just explained — that it will tweak its algorithm to downgrade pages that use certain techniques. But . . .

*In especially egregious cases, we will remove spammers from our index immediately so they don't show up in search results at all. Other steps will be taken as necessary.*

One of the dangers, then, of using tricks, is that someone might report you, and if the trick is bad enough, you get the boot. Where will they report you?

- Google at `www.google.com/contact/spamreport.html`
- Yahoo! at `http://add.yahoo.com/fast/help/us/ysearch/cgi_reportsearchspam`
- MSN at `http://feedback.search.msn.com/`
- Ask.com at `http://webk.ask.com/feedback`

People reporting spam are also investigated, so don't throw stones in a glass house.

What do you do if you think you've been penalized? For example, suppose your site is dropped from Google. It may not be a penalty — perhaps your site was not available at the point at which Google tried to reach it. But if the site doesn't return to the index after a few weeks (Google will try again later and if it finds it reindex), then you may have been penalized.

Sometimes sites get penalized due to unintentional mistakes. Perhaps you hired a Web-development team that implemented various tricks without your knowing, or perhaps your company gave you a site to look after long after the tricks were used. Or maybe you purchased a domain name that was penalized due to dirty tricks in the past. (Just changing owners is not enough to automatically lift the penalty.) Stuff happens: Be truthful and explain the situation to the folks at Google.

If you think your site has been banned, follow these steps:

1. **Clean away any dirty tricks from your site.**

2. **E-mail** `help@google.com` **to explain that you fixed your site.**

   Don't expect a rapid reply.

3. **Wait a couple of weeks and then try again.**

4. **Still no reply? Try again after another couple of weeks.**

5. **If you still can't get a response, try calling 650-330-0100 and then pressing 0.**

6. **Ask the operator who you can talk to about the problem.**

   You may be given another e-mail address to try, along with a password to put in the Subject line. (The password is changed each day.) By the way, I've heard from some site owners that if you have a *pay-per-click (PPC)* account with Google, you may be able to reach someone who can help by talking with your PPC account manager.

# Chapter 9

# Bulking Up Your Site — Competing with Content

. . . . . . . . . . . . . . . . . . . . . . . . . . . . . . . . . . . . . . . . . . . .

. . . . . . . . . . . . . . . . . . . . . . . . . . . . . . . . . . . . . . . . . . . .

*C*ontent is often a very important factor in getting a high ranking in the search engines. (Not convinced? Check out Chapter 4, where I present my definitive argument for the primacy of content.) What do I mean by content? *Content,* in the broadest sense, is a geeky Web term that means "stuff on your Web site." A *content-rich* Web site is one that contains lots and lots of information for people to see, read, and use.

For search engines, content has a more narrow definition: words, and lots of 'em. So if you're interested in search engine optimization, you should concentrate on the *text* part of your Web site's content (the right text, of course, using the keywords you find out about in Chapter 5). You don't need to care about pictures, video, or sound — at least as far as the search engines are concerned — because those forms of content don't help you get higher rankings. You don't need Flash animations, either, because although some search engines are starting to index them, most do not. Moreover, Flash animations generally don't contain much indexable text, and rarely index well.

What you should be concerned about is text — words that the search engines can read. Now, it's not *always* necessary to bulk up your site by adding textual content — in some cases, it's possible to get high search engine rankings with a small number of keyword-laden pages. If that's your situation, congratulations. Sit back and enjoy the fruits of your rather minimal labors, and skip this chapter. But if you don't find yourself in this happy situation, this chapter helps you get there.

You may find that your competitors have Web sites stacked full of content. They have scores of pages, perhaps even hundreds of pages — or hundreds of thousands — full of text that is nicely laden with all the juicy keywords you're interested in. That's tough to compete with.

Content is not a subject covered in many books, newsletters, or Web sites related to search engine optimization and ranking. Most publications say, "You need content, so create some." But I believe this issue is critical and shouldn't be glossed over with such trite comments, especially when several simple ways exist to *find* content. If you know the shortcuts, creating content doesn't have to be difficult. This chapter describes a slew of shortcuts to free and low-cost content, such as government materials, marketing and technical documents from manufacturers, and even something new called *copyleft*.

## Creating Content Three Ways

You can compete in the search engines several different ways. You can create well-optimized pages, get lots of links into your site, target keywords that competitors have missed, or put content on your site. (Chapter 3 has more on such "basic" strategies.) In some cases, when going up against a well-entrenched competitor, you may have no choice but to fight on several fronts. You may find that you *must* do something to stack your site with content.

You may be wondering at what point you should stop adding content. I recommend evaluating competing sites to help you make that determination. Compare your site to competitors that rank well in search engines. All major search engines now use some kind of link popularity to rate Web pages. If you're sure that your site has more well-optimized pages than those competing sites, it may be time to stop adding content. Instead, you may want to focus on getting links into your site and thereby raising your Google PageRank. (For more on Google PageRank, check out Chapter 14.)

I've got some bad news and some good news about creating content.

> ✔ **The bad news:** The obvious way to create content — writing it yourself or getting someone else to write it for you — is a huge problem for many people. Most people find writing difficult, and even if they find it easy, the results are often less than appealing. Perhaps you know someone who can write well and you can convince this person to write a few paragraphs for you. But are your powers of persuasion sufficient to get you 10, 20, or 50 pages? You can always pay someone for content, but the problem with paying is that it costs money.

✔ **The good news:** You can use some shortcuts to create content. Tricks of the trade can help you quickly bulk up your Web site (even if your writing skills match those of a dyslexic gerbil and your funds make the Queen of England's bikini budget look large in comparison). Note, though, that these tricks involve using *someone else's content.*

Here are the three different ways to get content for your site.

✔ Write your own content.

✔ Convince (force, bribe) someone else to create your content.

✔ Find existing content from somewhere else.

# Writing Your Own Stuff

The obvious way to create content, for many small-site owners anyway, is to start writing articles. That's not a terrible idea in many cases. Thousands of sites rank well using content from the sites' owners.

If you use the write-it-yourself approach, keep the following points in mind:

✔ **Writing content is time consuming, even for good writers.** You may want to evaluate whether you can devote the time to writing and maintaining your own content and then allocate time in your schedule to do so.

✔ **Many people are *not* good writers.** Not only is the writing process time consuming, but also the results are often rather pathetic (so I won't go into detail on this one).

✔ **If you *do* write your own stuff, pleeze spill chuck it.** Then have it edited by someone who has more than a third-grade education, and then spill chuck it again.

Do *not* rely on a word processor's grammar checker. This tool is worse than useless for most writers. Grammar checkers are of benefit only to those what already has a good grasp of grammar.

## Summarizing online articles

Here's a quick way to get keywords onto your page:

1. **Use the search engines to track down articles related to your subject area.**

2. **Create a library area on your Web site in which you link to these articles.**

3. **For each link, write a short, keyword-laden summary of what the article is all about.**

The advantage to this kind of writing is that it's fairly quick and easy.

You may want to include the first few sentences of the article. This comes under the gray area of copyright *fair use* (which you find out about in the appendix for this book). What really counts is what the article's owner thinks. In most cases, if you contact the article's owner (and you really don't *have* to contact the owner), the owner is happy to have you summarize the article, excerpt a small portion of it, and link to his or her site. Most people recognize that *this is good for them!* However, occasionally you'll find someone who just doesn't get it and creates a fuss. Just remove the link and move on.

You may want to approach the owners of the sites you're linking to and ask them to add a link back to your site. See Chapter 15 for more information.

Ideally, you don't want to link out of your site too much, though don't get paranoid about how much is too much. Just be aware that linking out of your site *leaks* PageRank out of the site. (Not sure what this PageRank business is all about? Check out Chapter 14, which gives you all the messy details.)

## Reviewing Web sites

Similar to the summarizing, you can link to useful Web sites and write short (yes, keyword-laden) reviews of each one. Before you undertake such a program, read Chapter 15 to find out about gathering links from other sites.

## Reviewing products

Write short (um, keyword-laden) reviews of products related to the subject matter covered by your site. An additional benefit of such a program is that eventually people may start sending you free stuff to review.

# Convincing Someone Else to Write It

You may find that having articles written (by others) specifically for your site is rather appealing for two reasons. First, someone else does the work, not you. Second, if it doesn't turn out well, someone else (not you) gets blamed.

One approach, assuming you can't force someone to write for you, is to pay someone. Luckily (for you), writers are cheap. For some reason, people often have a bizarre idea of a glamorous writing life that's awaiting them. (It's been over a decade since I wrote my first bestseller, and I'm still waiting for the groupies to turn up.) So you may be able to find someone to write for you for $10 or $12 an hour, depending on where you live and how well you lie. Or maybe you can find a high-school kid who can string a few coherent words together and is willing to work for less.

If you work for a large corporation, you may be able to convince a variety of people to write for you — people who may assume it's actually part of their job (again, depending on how well you lie). Spread the work throughout various departments — marketing, technical support, sales, and so on — and it may turn into a decent amount of content. Still, you can use quicker and easier ways to get content, as described in the next section.

If you pay someone to write for you, get a simple contract saying that the work is a _work for hire_ and that you are buying all rights to it. Otherwise, you don't own it and can use it only for limited purposes that are either stated in the contract or are more or less obvious. If you ask someone to write an article for your Web site and don't get a contract giving you full rights, you can't later decide to syndicate the article on other sites or in newsletters. (Chapter 15 has more on this syndication stuff.) If an employee writes the material for you on company time, the work is generally considered a work for hire and company property. However, if you have a very small company with an informal employment relationship and the writing is outside the scope of the employee's normal work, you should get the employee to sign a contract.

# Using OPC — Other People's Content

Writing or hiring is the slow way to create content. Using someone else's content — now that's the quick way. See the following list of quick content sources for your site. I explain the details later in the chapter.

- **Product information:** Contact the manufacturer or distributor of the products you sell on your site for marketing and sales materials, technical documentation, and so on.

- **Web sites and e-mail newsletters:** Contact the owners of other sites and e-mail newsletters and ask them if you can use their work.

- **Government sources:** Check U.S. Government Web sites for free materials.

- **Content syndication sites:** A number of sites provide free content for the asking.

✔ **Traditional syndication services:** Numerous companies sell materials you can use on your site.

✔ **RSS syndication feeds:** This is a new, geeky technique for feeding syndicated content into Web sites.

✔ **Open content and copyleft:** This is an unusual new movement probably based on the old Internet maxim, "Information wants to be free."

✔ **Search pages:** You can search at a site to generate a search-results page with your favorite keywords.

✔ **Press releases:** You may be able to find press releases related to your area of business. These are copyright free, and you can use them as you wish.

✔ **A Q&A area on your site:** This is a way to serve your site visitors *and* get keywords onto the site.

✔ **Forums or message boards:** With forums and message boards on your site, your visitors create the keywords for you.

✔ **Blogs:** From the term *Weblogs,* these journals provide another way to let people create content for you.

This list gives you a good idea of the sources of content, and the "Hunting for Other People's Content" section, later in this chapter, explores how you find, evaluate, and procure content from these sources.

Before I show you how to help yourself to someone else's content, I need to warn you about a critical legal issue: copyright law. You must have a working knowledge of copyright restrictions so that you can properly evaluate whether (and how) it's appropriate to use the content that you find. The next section gives you an overview of what you need to know, and the appendix for this book goes into excruciating detail, if you're curious.

# Understanding Copyright — It's Not Yours!

I'm constantly amazed at how few people understand copyright — even people who should know better.

When I speak to clients about adding content to a Web site, I sometimes hear something like this: "How about that magazine article I read last week? Let's put that up there!" Or maybe, "Such and such a site has some great information, let's use some of that." That's called *copyright infringement.* It's against the law, and although serious harm is unlikely to befall you in most cases, you *can* get sued or prosecuted.

Let me quickly summarize copyright law so that you have a better idea of what you can and can't use on your site:

✔ As soon as someone creates a work — writes an article, writes a song, composes a tune, or whatever — copyright is automatic. There's no need to register copyright; the creator owns the copyright whether or not it has been registered. Most copyright works, in fact, are not registered, which is a good thing. If they were, the Library of Congress, which houses the Copyright Office and stores copyright registrations, would be the size of Alabama.

✔ If you don't see a copyright notice attached, it doesn't mean the work's copyright isn't owned by someone. Current copyright law does not require such notices.

✔ If someone owns the copyright, that person has the right to say what can be done with, um, copies. What this means is that you generally can't take an article you find in a newspaper, magazine, or Web site and use it without permission. (There are exceptions, which you find out about later in this chapter.)

✔ In the United States, certain kinds of copyright infringement are felonies. You may not only get sued but also prosecuted.

✔ If you don't know whether you have the right to use something, assume that you *don't.*

✔ You can't just take something and rewrite it. *Derivative works* are also protected. If the result is clearly derived from the original, you could be in trouble.

✔ Copyright has to be expressly assigned. If you hire me to write an article for your Web site and don't get a contract saying that you own *all rights,* or that the work was a *work for hire,* you only have the right to place it on your Web site. I still have the right to use the article elsewhere.

A number of exceptions can prove *very* important when you're gathering content, so listen closely:

✔ **If it's really old, you can use it.** Copyright eventually expires. Anything created before 1923 (at the time of writing, in 2006), for instance, is free for the taking.

✔ **If the guvmint created it, you can use it.** The U.S. Government spends millions of dollars creating *content.* This content is almost never copyright protected.

✔ **If it's donated, you can use it.** Authors often *want* you to use their materials. If they have given the public permission to use it, you can use it.

✔ **It's only fair.** Copyright law has a *fair use* exception that allows you to use small parts of a work, without permission, under particular conditions.

I strongly suggest that you read the appendix for this book to get the details on copyright, and make sure that you beg or borrow, but not steal, other people's work.

# Hunting for Other People's Content

In this chapter I list different types of other people's content and I warn you about copyright. Now it's time to get out there and grab some content. You're about to find some great places to get tons of content.

## Remembering the keywords

When you're out on your content hunt, remember that the purpose is *keywords*. You're trying to add keywords to your site. You can do that several ways:

- **Find content with the keywords already in it.** You want content that has at least *some* of your keywords, though you'll often find it's not enough.

- **Add keywords to the content you get.** In some cases, you shouldn't edit the content because you'll be expected to use the content without changes. In other cases, you may be allowed to modify the content. You can, for instance, modify *open content* (described later in the chapter), and some syndicators allow it. As syndicator Featurewell says, "Clients can make minor edits to stories and photos, provided they do not modify or change the meaning, tone or general context of the articles. . . ." Thus you could replace a few words here and there with your keywords, as long as the article still makes sense and retains the same tone and context.

- **Chunk up the article.** Break it into smaller, Web-friendly pieces and separating each piece with a heading (containing keywords, of course).

Newspapers often modify content they buy. A syndicated column you read in New York may be different from the same column run in a paper in Los Angeles, because newspapers will cut and modify for space reasons or because they don't like the way something is worded.

When adding content, you're generally interested in adding pages with a variety of keywords sprinkled throughout. Remember, if you have a rodent-racing site, you'll want lots of pages with the words *rodent, racing, race, event, mouse, rat,* and so on.

# Product information

Does your Web site sell products that you buy from a wholesaler or manufacturer? If so, contact your source and find out what materials are available: brochures, spec sheets, technical documentation, or user manuals. Take a look at anything the manufacturer has available.

In many cases, the material may available in Adobe Acrobat PDF files. You can post these files on your site within seconds, and they will be indexed by some search engines — Google, for instance. However, the ideal approach is to also convert the work to HTML files because you have more opportunities to insert keywords — in the TITLE, DESCRIPTION, and KEYWORDS tags, and so on — and to stress keywords by putting them in bold, italic, <H> tags, and so on.

# Web sites and e-mail newsletters

The Web is so full of content that it's about to sink (well, not your site obviously, or you wouldn't be reading this chapter). Why not grab a few articles you like from other sites or from the e-mail newsletters you subscribe to? In fact, you may want to go hunting to find articles for this very purpose.

If you ask nicely, many people are happy to let you use their content. In fact, as I explain in Chapter 15, many people use content syndication as a strategy for site promotion. They *want* people to use their stuff, as long as the sites using the material provide *attribution* — meaning they clearly state where the material is from and who wrote it, and provide a link back to the site of origin.

Asking for permission is quite easy. Simply contact the owner of the article you saw on a site or in a newsletter, and ask whether you can use it. I did this recently and, within *ten minutes,* got a positive response. Within 15 minutes, I had an article on my site that was loaded with keywords and that ranked very highly in the search engines in its own right. (I later realized that the author's page was ranking #3 for one of my critical keywords. Thus within minutes, I had a page that had the potential of ranking very highly for some important keywords.)

When you talk to the article's owner, make sure that you praise the article. (After all, you do like it, don't you, or you wouldn't be asking? There's too much good content out there to be using trash.) Also, clearly state that you will provide a bio at the bottom of the article and a link back to the owner's site.

Those of you who own your own sites have it easy. You can simply save the e-mail response from the article's author as evidence of permission to use the article. Those of you working for large corporations with legal departments have a bigger problem. Your lawyers, working under the principle of "common sense is dead," will expect you to get the article's author to sign a 32-page document providing permission, declaring that he or she has the right to give permission, and signing over exclusive and lifetime rights to the article and any spinoff toys or clothing derived from it. Sorry, I don't know how to help you here. I would tell you to just remember what Shakespeare said — "First thing we do, let's kill all the lawyers" — except I'm sure my publisher's legal department would complain.

Where can you find these articles? For Web site articles, search for sites that are likely to have the type of information you need. I suggest that you avoid sites that are directly competing. Also keep your eyes open for newsletters while you're doing your Web search, or look for appropriate newsletters at some of these sites:

- **Coollist:** www.coollist.com
- **EzineHub:** www.ezinehub.com
- **E-Zine-List:** www.e-zine-list.com/
- **Ezine-Universe:** www.ezine-universe.com
- **listTool:** www.listtool.com
- **NewJour:** gort.ucsd.edu/newjour
- **Newsletter Access:** www.newsletteraccess.com
- **Tile.Net:** http://tile.net
- **Topica:** www.topica.com
- **WebScout Lists:** www.webscoutlists.com

Try searching for a combination of one of your keyword phrases and the words *article* and *newsletter* — for instance, *rodent racing article* and *rodent racing newsletter*.

How do you know who owns the copyright to the article? Here's a quick rule of thumb: If the article has an attribution attached to it, contact that person. For instance, many e-mail newsletters are either written by a single person (in which case you contact him or her) or have a variety of articles, each one with a bio and e-mail address (in which case you contact the author, not the newsletter itself). In the majority of cases, the author has given the newsletter one-time rights and still owns the copyright.

Some mechanisms used for syndicating content ensure that the search engines won't read the syndicated content! So you need to make sure you use the right technique. See "Content syndication sites," later in this chapter, for more information.

## Government sources

I love this source, because it's *huge,* with a surprising range of information. In general, documents created by the U.S. Federal Government are in the public domain. Under the terms of Title 17 United States Code section 105, works created by U.S. Government departments do not have copyright protection.

However, you should be aware of some important exceptions:

- ✔ The government may still hold copyrights on works that have been given to the government — bequests or assignments of some kind.

- ✔ The law is a U.S. law, making U.S. Government works copyright free. Most other governments hold copyrights on their works.

- ✔ In some cases, works that nongovernment agencies create on behalf of the government may or may not be protected by copyright — the law is not clear.

- ✔ Works created by the National Technical Information Service (NTIS; www.ntis.gov) may have a limited, five-year copyright protection.

- ✔ The United States Postal Service is exempt from these regulations. The Postal Service can have copyright protection for its works. (It doesn't want people printing their own stamps!)

- ✔ In some cases, the government may publish works that were originally privately created works. Such documents are copyright protected.

Even with these exceptions, vast quantities of juicy government content are available. Now, don't think to yourself, "Oh, there probably aren't any government documents related to *my* area!" Maybe, maybe not. But where do you think all our tax billions go? The money can't *all* go to defense and schools. It has to be spent somehow, so some of it goes to creating vast amounts of Web content!

You can take this content and place it directly on your Web site. You'll find the content in Web pages or Adobe Acrobat PDF files. You may want to convert PDF files to Web pages for several reasons:

✔ Web pages load more quickly than PDF files.

✔ Although most major search engines now index PDF files, some systems don't.

✔ You can do more keywording in Web pages.

And just *how* do you convert PDF files? If you own Adobe Acrobat, you could try to use that program, though you may not like the results. Various other programs do it for you (such as PDF-to-HTML at `http://convert-in.com/pdf2html.htm`), and PDF Online, a free system (at `www.pdfonline.com/`).

Not only will you find the sorts of documents useful for your purposes — text-heavy documents that the search engines can read — you'll also find other materials that may be useful for your site, such as videos.

Here are a few good places to find government materials:

✔ **FedWorld:** `www.fedworld.gov`

✔ **Government Printing Office:**

  • Catalog of U.S. Government Publications: `www.gpoaccess.gov/cgp`

  • New Electronic Titles: `www.access.gpo.gov/su_docs/locators/net`

✔ **Library of Congress — Browse Government Resources:** `lcweb.loc.gov/rr/news/extgovd.html`

✔ **CIA's Electronic Reading Room:** `www.foia.cia.gov`

✔ **U.S. Department of State's Electronic Reading Room:** `foia.state.gov`

✔ **U.S. Historical Documents Archive:** `www.ushda.org`

✔ **FBI's Electronic Reading Room:** `foia.fbi.gov`

## Content syndication sites

In the "Web sites and e-mail newsletters" section, earlier in this chapter, I discuss the idea of finding Web pages or e-mail newsletter articles you like and asking the owners for permission to use them. Well, here's a shortcut: Go to the content-syndication sites.

*Content-syndication sites* are places where authors post their information so that site owners or newsletter editors can pick it up and use it for free. Why? Because, in return, you agree to place a short blurb at the bottom of the article, including a link back to the author's Web site.

Here are a few places to get you started in the wonderful world of content syndication:

- ✔ **Article Dashboard:** www.articledashboard.com
- ✔ **EZineArticles.com:** ezinearticles.com
- ✔ **FreeSticky.com:** www.freesticky.com
- ✔ **GoArticles.com:** www.goarticles.com
- ✔ **IdeaMarketers.com:** www.ideamarketers.com
- ✔ **The Open Directory Project's List of Content Providers:** dmoz.org/Computers/Software/Internet/Site_Management/Content_Management/Content_Providers
- ✔ **Purple Pages:** www.purplepages.ie
- ✔ **World Wide Information Outlet:** certificate.net

Some Web sites have their own *syndication areas* — libraries from which you can pick articles you want to use. Also, see Chapter 15, where I talk about syndicating your own content and point you to other syndication sites.

Make sure that when you grab articles from a content-syndication site, you're not using a competitor's article! All these articles have links back to the author's site, so you don't want to be sending traffic to the enemy.

### Geeky stuff you must understand

I have to get into a little techno-geeky stuff right now, I'm afraid. I hate to do it, but if you don't understand this, you're just wasting your time with content syndication.

Many syndication systems use a simple piece of JavaScript to allow you to pull articles from their sites onto yours. For instance, take a look at this code I pulled from a site that syndicates news articles:

```
<script
        src="http://farmcentre.com/synd/synd.jsp?id=cfb
        mc"> </script>
```

This piece of code tells the Web browser to grab the *synd.jsp* file from the *farmcentre.com* Web site. That file uses a JavaScript to insert the article into the Web page. Articles or other forms of content are automatically embedded other ways, too. They may be inserted using Java applets, and sometimes with an <iframe> tag.

None of these ways of embedding an article into your site does you any good with the search engines. As I explain in Chapter 7, the search engine bots *don't read JavaScript!* Nor do they read Java applets. And if they do read inside the `<iframe>` tags, it doesn't help, because they follow the link that is used to pull the page into the frame and view that content as if it were on the origin Web site.

The `<iframe>` tag is used by Internet Explorer to place an internal frame inside a Web page. That frame contains information from another Web page, in this case a page on another Web site. Depending on how the iframe is set up, it can appear as if the information inside the frame is part of the original page — readers can't tell the difference.

So, the searchbot grabs the page and reads the source code. It sees the JavaScript (such as the example code you just saw) but ignores it, moving on to the next line. The syndicated article you wanted to place into the Web page *never gets placed into the page the searchbot reads!* All your time and energy placing content is wasted.

This all strikes me as quite humorous, really. Thousands of people are syndicating content or using syndicated content, partly for search engine reasons. People syndicating the content want to place their links on as many Web pages as possible for two reasons:

✔ So readers will see the links and click them

✔ So the search engines will see the links and rank the home site higher

And people using the syndicated content are doing so because they want content, stuffed with good keywords, for the search engines to read.

In many cases, both the syndicators and the people using syndicated content are wasting their time because the search engines aren't placing the content, aren't seeing the keywords, and aren't reading the links!

How do you avoid JavaScript?

✔ **Don't use browser-side inclusion techniques.** That includes JavaScript, Java, or iframes.

✔ **Use server-side inclusion techniques**. That includes server includes, PHP, or ASP. If you're not sure whether a technique is server side or browser side, ask a knowledgeable geek — you want an inclusion technique that loads the content into the page *before* it's sent to the browser or searchbot.

✔ **Use manual inclusion techniques.** That is, copy and paste the content into your pages directly. Plenty of content relies on manual inclusion, and you may even get content owners who are using automatic-inclusion techniques to agree to let you manually copy their content.

As long as you're aware of syndicated content's pitfalls and how to avoid them, it's quite possible to find syndicated content and make it work so that you reap the search engine benefits of having that content on your site.

*Hosted-content services* are companies that host the content on their sites along with a copy of your Web site template so that it looks like the content is on your site (unless you look in the browser's Location or Address bar, where you see the company's URL). The problem with such services is that the search engines are unlikely to pick up the content because they see the same articles duplicated over and over again on the same domain. Google, for instance, will probably keep one set and ignore the duplicates.

### The problem with automatic updates

Another problem with content syndication sites involves *automatic updates.* Automatic updates allow the content owner to change the content immediately. For example, sites that provide weekly or monthly newsletters use automatic updates. This technique allows the content provider to update the content on dozens or hundreds of sites simply by changing the source file. The next time a page is loaded on one of the sites using the syndicated content, the new information appears.

But if you're adding content for keyword purposes, automatic updating may not be such a good thing. If you find an article with lots of nice keywords, it could be gone tomorrow. Manual inclusion techniques ensure that the article you placed remains in place, and also allow you to, for instance, break up the article into chunks by adding keyword-laden headings. (Although it's hard to say how likely a site owner who uses automatic updating will be to let you use manual inclusion, there is plenty of content out there.)

## Traditional syndication services

Content syndication is nothing new. It's been around for a hundred years. (I just made that up, but it's probably true.) Much of what you read in your local newspapers is not written by the paper's staff; it comes from a syndication service.

Some syndication services will sell content for your site. In general, this material should be better than the free syndicated content. However, much of the free stuff is pretty good, too, so you may not want to pay for syndicated material until you've exhausted your search for free content.

Here are a few places you can find commercial syndicated material:

✔ **AbleStable Syndication:** `ablestable.com/content/syndication.htm`

✔ **Featurewell:** `www.featurewell.com` (articles from $70)

- **MagPortal:** www.magportal.com
- **Moreover:** www.moreover.com
- **The Open Directory Project's List of Content Providers:** dmoz.org/
  Computers/Software/Internet/Site_Management/Content_
  Management/Content_Providers
- **OSKAR Consulting:** www.electroniccontent.com/conFinder.
  cfm?cat=beauty
- **Pages:** www.pagesmag.com ($195 per year for 60–70 new articles each
  month, plus a four-year archive)
- **Thomson Gale:** www.gale.com (kinda pricey; $10,000 for a subscription!)
- **United Media's uclick:** content.uclick.com
- **YellowBrix:** www.yellowbrix.com
- **Yahoo! News and Media Syndicates page:** dir.yahoo.com/
  Business_and_Economy/Business_to_Business/News_
  and_Media/Syndicates

Specialty syndication services provide content for particular industries.
For example, Inman (www.inman.com) provides content for the real estate
industry.

## RSS syndication feeds

RSS is one of those geeky acronyms that nobody can define for certain. Some
say it means *Really Simple Syndication;* others believe it means *Rich Site
Summary* or *RDF Site Summary.* What it stands for doesn't really matter. All
you need to know is that RSS is the new big thing in content syndication.

RSS systems comprise two components:

- An RSS *feed,* a source of content of some kind
- An RSS *aggregator* (also known as a *news aggregator*), a system that takes
  the information from the feed and drops it into a Web page

For example, all the top search engines provide RSS feeds of their news headlines, at least for personal or noncommercial use. You can install an RSS
aggregator on your site and point it to an RSS news feed. The page will then
contain recent searches on news headlines, as you can see in Figure 9-1.

What you need is an aggregator. Aggregators range from fairly simple to very
complicated — and that's assuming you have some technical abilities in the
first place. (If you don't, there's no range; they're all very complicated!)

Before you go to the trouble of getting an aggregator, decide whether there's enough suitable content to make it worthwhile. Although RSS is growing rapidly, still many of the feeds are a little geeky. If your subject area is *macramé and knitting,* I suspect you may find a dearth of material at present (on the other hand, search and you may be surprised). Also, often RSS feeds merely pass a link to material on another site, in which case you won't benefit much. Make sure that you're getting the actual material passed to your site.

Check out these RSS feed sites:

- **Blogdex:** `blogdex.net`
- **Fagan Finder:** `www.faganfinder.com/search/rss.shtml`
- **Feedster:** `www.feedster.com`
- **Lockergnome:** `rss.lockergnome.com`
- **NewsKnowledge:** `www.newsknowledge.com`
- **Syndic8:** `syndic8.com`

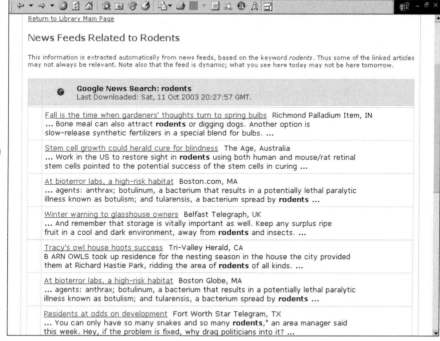

**Figure 9-1:**
A page created using an RSS aggregator, zFeeder. Look at all those lovely bolded keywords!

Unlike the automated syndication techniques I mention earlier, which use JavaScripts and other browser-side systems for inserting content, RSS aggregators often use *server-side* techniques, so the content is inserted into the Web page *before* the search engines see it. That's what they call in the search engine business a *good thing*.

If you decide you want to go ahead with RSS, you need an aggregator. Try searching for *news aggregator* or *rss aggregator,* and either check out the following software directories or ask your favorite geek to do so for you:

- ✔ **freshmeat:** `freshmeat.net`
- ✔ **SourceForge.net:** `sourceforge.net`

If your geek has never heard of freshmeat or SourceForge, it's just possible that he or she isn't quite geeky enough.

I have used an aggregator called zFeeder (formerly zvonFeeds), which was fairly simple to work with. You can find it at `zvonnews.sourceforge.net`.

## Open content and copyleft

Have you heard of *open-source software?* It's software that is created through the contributions of multiple individuals who agree to allow pretty much anyone to use the software, at no charge. Another movement that doesn't get quite the same attention as open-source software is the *open content* movement. Open content is, as explained on the Open Content List Web site, free and available for your use.

Open content relies on what has become known as *copyleft*. Under copyleft, the owner of a copyrighted work doesn't release it into the public domain. Instead, he or she releases the work for public modification, with the understanding that anyone using the work must agree to not claim original authorship and to release all derivative works under the same conditions.

Stacks of information are released under copyleft. Start at these sites:

- ✔ **Creative Commons:** `creativecommons.org`
- ✔ **Open Content List:** `www.opencontentlist.com`
- ✔ **The Open Directory Project's Open Content page:** `dmoz.org/Computers/Open_Source/Open_Content`

You really should check out open content, in particular the open content encyclopedias, which have information on just about anything. You can find these encyclopedias on the Open Directory Project's Open Content page.

Watch for competitors' information. Some companies use open content as a way to get their links out onto the Web.

## Search pages

Flip back to Figure 9-1, the search page I showed you in the "RSS syndication feeds" section, earlier in the chapter. As you can see in the figure, the great thing about such search pages is that they have the exact keywords you define, liberally scattered throughout. When you conduct a search in a search engine — whether you're searching Web sites, a directory of magazine articles, or news headlines — what does the search engine return? Matches for your keywords.

RSS provides one way to insert searches — in particular, searches of news headlines — into your pages. Even though the page's content will change continually, you don't have to worry about the content changing to a page that doesn't contain your keywords, because the content is a reflection of the keywords you provide. You may also be able to find search pages that you can manually copy and paste. Sites that contain large numbers of articles and a search function may be good candidates. Run a search, and then copy the results and paste them into a Web page.

Make sure that the links in the search results still work and that they open the results in a new window. (You don't want to push people away from your site.) You'll probably also want to check with the site owner to make sure that this is okay. In many cases, site owners will be fine with it; again, it's more links to their site!

## Press releases

The nice thing about press releases is that you can use them without permission. The purpose of a press release is to send it out and see who picks it up. You don't need to contact the owner of the press release, because there's already an implied agreement that you can simply take the release and post it wherever you want (unchanged and in its entirety, of course).

You may be able to find press releases that have the keywords you want, are relevant to your site in some way, and are not released by competitors. For instance, if you're in the business of running rodent-racing events, companies selling rodent-racing harnesses and other gear are not direct competitors and may well have press releases you can use.

Where do you find these press releases? Try searching for press releases at a search engine. Combine the search term with some keywords, such as *rodent racing press release.* You can also find them at press release sites, such as these:

- **Hot Product News:** www.hotproductnews.com
- **Internet News Bureau:** www.internetnewsbureau.com
- **M2PressWIRE:** www.presswire.net
- **Online Press Releases:** www.onlinepressreleases.com
- **PR Newswire:** prnewswire.com
- **PR Web:** www.prweb.com
- **USANews:** www.usanews.net

You might even subscribe to some of these press release services so you get relevant press releases sent to you as soon as they are published.

## Q&A areas

After you get sufficient traffic to your site, you may want to set up a Question and Answer (Q&A) or *FAQ (Frequently Asked Questions)* area on your site. Visitors to your site can ask questions — providing you with keyword-laden questions in many cases — and you can answer them.

A number of free and low-cost software tools automate the creation and management of such areas. Search the utility sites, such as resourceindex.com, for these tools, and find a friendly geek if you need help installing a tool.

Make sure the search engines can read pages created by any tool you install on your site, such as the FAQ tool or the BBS and blog tools I tell you about next. Find a tool you like and then find out if Google indexes the pages in the demo or sample sites. If not, ask the software author to point you to a demo that *does* have indexed pages.

## Message boards

Message board areas can be very powerful, in more than one way. Setting up a message board — also known as a *forum* or *Bulletin Board System (BBS)* — allows site visitors to place keywords in your site for you! A message board often draws traffic, bringing people in purely for the conversation.

Own a site about kayaks? As you sleep, visitors will leave messages with the word *kayak* in them, over and over. Does your site sell rodent supplies? While you go about your daily business, your visitors will leave messages containing words such as *rodent, mouse,* and *rat.* Over time, this can build up to hundreds of pages with many thousands of keywords.

BBS systems — even really cool ones with lots of features, such as the ability to post photos — are cheap, often free, in fact. They're relatively easy to set up even for low-level geeks. Don't underestimate this technique; if you have a lot of traffic on your Web site, a BBS can be a great way to build huge amounts of content. Search for terms such as *bbs software* and *forum software.*

## Blogs

*Blogs* are sort of like diaries. (The term is a derivation of *weblog*.) They're systems that allow someone to write any kind of twaddle — er, musings — they want and publish this nonsense — um, literature — directly to a Web site. My cynicism aside, you can find some very interesting blogs out there (or so I'm told).

In fact, over the last couple of years blogs have become important SEO tools. . . the search engines seem to like them, visiting frequently to index them. In fact, Google even owns one of the top blogging-tools companies, Blogger (blogger.com). (What's the bet that blogs hosted by Blogger get indexed by Google?!) In fact, there are actually plenty of blog-hosting sites, such as Blog.com, Blogster.com, and many more. Search for *blog hosting.*

Many blog-hosting services, such as Blogger, provide a way to integrate pages into your Web site, and blogs can be very effective SEO tools, if you can find a way to create enough content. While many people set up blogs, the number that actually maintain them is far lower!

If you use any tool that allows visitors to post messages on your site, you should monitor and delete inappropriate messages. Many search engine marketers use such tools to post messages with links pointing back to their sites (known as *blog spam*).

# Part III

# Adding Your Site to the Indexes and Directories

The 5th Wave          By Rich Tennant

"Look, I've already launched a search for 'reanimated babe cadavers' three times and nothing came up!"

# In this part . . .

**G**etting your Web site indexed by the search engines and directories should be easy. Let them know the URL and wait for them to add it, right? Wrong. Sure, you can submit information about your site to the search engines, but they probably won't index it.

In this part, I explain what you need to do to get your site into the major search engines, including the new Google and Yahoo! sitemap systems. (Hint: You need to make it easy for the search engines to find your site on their own.) I also explain how to work with the two major search directories: Yahoo! (easy, just pay) and the Open Directory Project (easy, and free, but you may have to keep trying).

This part also tells you how to find important but lesser-known systems and how they can help you. (Sure, most searches are carried out through the major systems, but the specialized systems can often provide valuable, highly targeted traffic.)

# Chapter 10

# Finding Traffic via Geo-Targeting

*I*ncreasingly the Internet is being used as a tool for finding local resources. Not just for finding information, or for buying online, you can use it to find homes for sale in your neighborhood, local independent insurance agents, stores close to you that sell the products you need, and so on. And so it's increasingly important to keep *geo-targeting* in mind when optimizing for the search engines — that is, to not only target by a searcher's keyword, but by the searcher's geographic location.

*Wait!* But before you skip this chapter because you have a purely online business, you need to understand the *two* basic reasons you should consider geo-targeting:

✔ Because you have a local business

✔ Because your prospects — your target customers — search locally

Say you are a local business. You sell insurance in your town, or own a local health-food store, or are a personal trainer with clients within a 5-mile radius. Clearly you don't need to rank well on the terms *insurance, health food,* or *personal training.* You need to rank well on the terms *insurance denver, health food waco,* or *personal training paducah.* There's no point competing for general terms against hundreds of thousands of other companies when you're interested in a fraction of the searches.

But say you're not a local shop for local people. You sell to anyone, anywhere. But you may find that the people you want to reach don't search for generic terms. They search for generic terms *in combination with local terms.* This is something you may discover if you do a good keyword analysis, which I describe in Chapter 5. Most people don't search for lawyers, for instance; they search for lawyers *in a particular city.* They don't search for real estate agents; they search for real estate agents *in a particular city.* They don't search for *insurance;* they search for insurance *in a particular state or city.*

---

### Click and mortified

During the last quarter of 2004, the average W2S buyer spent

✔ $250 online (29%)

✔ $400 offline on researched products (47%)

✔ $200 offline on additional purchases (24%)

That's 29% online and 71% *offline!* Furthermore, another recent study found that 25% of all searches made by people researching products are people looking for local merchants.

---

You may find then, that if you want to reach the largest number of people, you *have* to consider the local aspect. Large online businesses targeting home buyers, for instance, often create *geo-targeted* pages designed to reach people in thousands of different locales.

# Understanding Geo-Targeting's Importance

The local aspect of search is hugely important. For instance, 1995 surveys by ShopLocal.com and Forrester Research discovered these gems about Internet users:

✔ Most are *off-channel* or *Web-to-shop (W2S)* buyers.

✔ Almost half spend extra dollars when in the brick-and-mortar store on products they didn't research.

✔ More money is spent *offline* after online research than is spent *online* after online research.

Thus, many businesses are trying to target people in their own areas, to get them to walk into their brick-and-mortar stores. Geo-targeting helps you find those people.

# Looking Through Local Search

There's another aspect to geo-targeting: All four of the major search engines — Google, Yahoo!, MSN, and Ask.com — now have local search features. *Local search* is the generic term given to the ability to search for information related to a particular location — a state, a city, or even a zip code. All four have a <u>Local</u> link immediately above the Search box. You click this link, then tell the search engine what you're looking for and where, and it finds the best matches it can. See Figure 10-1.

**Figure 10-1:**
The four top search engines all provide a local search feature.

Actually, you don't always have to *tell* the search engines the location. The search engines can figure it out. (I explain how in the next section in this chapter.) Although Google, Yahoo!, and Ask.com want you to provide a city or zip code, if you give MSN a word and choose Local Search, MSN figures out where you are and finds local matches. The other search engines have the ability to locate you, but at the time of writing are limiting that to *pay-per-click (PPC)* advertising.

# How Does Local Search Work?

Local search is based on several different methodologies, including the science known as *geolocation,* the science of trying to figure out where the heck a computer actually *is,* geographically speaking. When a computer contacts a search engine and says "Hi, I'm computer 67.176.77.58; can you search for information about *rodent racing* and send me the results?", how does the search engine figure out if that computer is in Colorado and thus wants information about the famous Rocky Mountain prairie-dog racing, or is in Florida, and is interested in the famous African Gambian pouch rat races?

Local search generally works in a few basic ways. Different services will use different combinations of these methods.

## Search terms

If someone types *dentist new york,* the search engine can be pretty sure that they're looking for a dentist in New York, not a dentist in Oklahoma City. Simple, eh?

## Partner sites

Search services can guess at a location based on the Web site someone is using. If someone is searching at www.google.fr, there's a good bet that person is in France; if someone searches at www.yahoo.co.uk, that person is probably in the United Kingdom. In other cases partner sites can be even more specific, and related to a particular region or even city.

## IP numbers

*Internet Protocol (IP)* numbers identify computers on the Internet. Every computer connected to the Internet at any moment has a unique IP number.

With information being sent to and fro — from your computer to Web sites and back — there has to be a way for the information to be "addressed," so the various servers on the Internet know where to deliver the information. Thus every computer connected to the Internet has an *IP number or IP address.*

In some cases two or more computers share an IP number, as in a situation in which a house or apartment is using a cable or *digital subscriber line (DSL)* connection, with several computers connected through a single router; but for the purposes of figuring out location this isn't important, of course.

In some cases computers "own" a particular IP number; turn the computer off now, turn it on next week, and it has the same number. This is known as a *static IP number.* Often, however, computers share IP numbers. Log out of a dial-up account now, and dial back in five minutes, and your computer is assigned a different IP number (known as a *dynamic IP number*). That IP number is shared among many computers, but at any moment only one computer can use the number.

Take a look at this IP number: 67.176.77.58. This number uniquely identifies a particular computer in Colorado. If a server sends a page to that address, the page can only go one place, because at that moment only one computer on the Internet is using that number to identify itself. It's like a telephone number. Every telephone in the entire world has a unique number (when you include the country code). Pick up the phone and dial the full number, and there's only one telephone in the world that you can possibly be connected to.

An IP number is a *hierarchical* system. A block of numbers is assigned to a particular organization or company; that organization or company then assigns blocks of numbers to other organizations or companies, which can then assign their numbers to different organizations or companies, or divisions within a company, and so on.

Consider, again, 67.176.77.58. This number is "owned" by Comcast Cable Communications, a large American cable-TV company. In fact, Comcast has a large block of numbers: 67.160.0.0–67.191.255.255. Within that large block lies another block that Comcast uses in Colorado: 67.176.0.0–67.176.127.255. Clearly, 67.176.77.58 lies within this block.

Want to see this at work? A number of sites will tell you where you are (or at least where they think you are). I just visited IP2Location (www.ip2location. com), and it was able to identify my city (though not my zip code, and it got my latitude and longitude wrong). See Figure 10-2.

**Figure 10-2:** IP2Location can figure out where an IP number is located. It's often more or less correct, though your mileage may vary.

# From coast to coast

There are other cases in which geolocation doesn't work, too. To "mask" your location as an example, follow these directions:

1. Search for **anonymous browsing** at any major search engine.

2. Visit one of the anonymous Web-browsing sites.

3. Use one of these systems, such as `www.ip2location.com`, to visit an IP location site.

4. See where it thinks you're coming from.

Quite likely it thinks you're somewhere the other side of the country or the world.

Now, geo-targeting with IP numbers is not perfect; it's definitely an imprecise science, for a few reasons.

- ✔ **You can't assume that a number assigned to a company in a particular area is being used in that area.** It's possible for two computers using two IP numbers just one digit apart — 67.176.77.58 and 67.176.77.59, for instance — to be thousands of miles apart. An IP number assigned to an organization in one area can be used by many different computers in many different locations. For example, a computer in San Francisco assigned a block of IP numbers may use those numbers for computers in branch offices in San Diego, Oklahoma City, Seattle, and so on.

- ✔ **Dynamic IP numbers are "here today, there tomorrow."** When you dial into a network and are assigned an IP number, you could be in California, while the computer that assigned the number is in Virginia. But when you log off and someone logs on and takes your number, the new computer might be in Wyoming.

Still, geolocation is getting better all the time. While the authorities that assign blocks of IP numbers provide very basic geographic information, this information can then be combined with other clues, such as hostnames. For example, it's possible to trace the path from one computer to another, and get the IP numbers and hostnames of the servers between the start and destination computers. The following path is from a computer in Australia to 67.176.77.58:

```
1   FastEthernet6-0.civ-service1.Canberra.telstra.net
        (203.50.1.65)
2   GigabitEthernet3-0.civ-core2.Canberra.telstra.net
        (203.50.10.129)
3   GigabitEthernet2-2.dkn-core1.Canberra.telstra.net
        (203.50.6.126)
```

```
 4   Pos4-1.ken-core4.Sydney.telstra.net (203.50.6.69)
 5   10GigabitEthernet3-0.pad-core4.Sydney.telstra.net
         (203.50.6.86)
 6   10GigabitEthernet2-2.syd-core01.Sydney.net.reach.com
         (203.50.13.38)
 7   i-6-1.wil-core02.net.reach.com (202.84.249.201)
 8   sl-gw28-ana-10-0.sprintlink.net (144.223.58.221)
 9   sl-bb21-ana-11-0.sprintlink.net (144.232.1.29)
10   sl-bb22-ana-15-0.sprintlink.net (144.232.1.174)
11   sprint-gw.la2ca.ip.att.net (192.205.32.185)
12   tbr1-p014001.la2ca.ip.att.net (12.123.29.2)
13   12.122.10.25 (12.122.10.25)
14   12.122.9.138 (12.122.9.138)
15   12.122.12.134 (12.122.12.134)
16   gar1-p360.dvmco.ip.att.net (12.123.36.73)
17   12.125.159.90 (12.125.159.90)
18   68.86.103.141 (68.86.103.141)
19   68.86.103.2 (68.86.103.2)
20   * * *
21   c-67-176-77-58.hsd1.co.comcast.net (67.176.77.58)
```

A *hostname* is assigned to a computer. The Internet uses IP numbers for addressing, but to make things easier for mere mortals, names can be applied to computers. Notice something about the hostnames in the preceding code? Some of them have geographic information embedded in them: Canberra, Sydney, co (Colorado), la2ca (Los Angeles, California), and so on. Another clue: Some major *Internet service providers (ISPs)* assign blocks of IP numbers geographically, so once you crack the code, you can figure out where people using that ISP actually live. Using clues such as these, it's possible for geolocation engineers at various companies specializing in this science to get pretty accurate about locating IP numbers. Not perfect, but close much of the time.

# *Reaching People Locally*

Let me summarize:

- ✔ People often type location names with their keyword searches.
- ✔ The search engines are providing local search services, encouraging people to search locally.
- ✔ The local search services either require location information or guess where searchers are.

How can your site turn up when people search using these systems? Here are a few things you can do:

- ✔ **Include your full address in your Web pages.** That means street, city, state, and zip code. Although you could put the address in the footer, it's better to put it near the top of the page somewhere. (Know about prominence? No? Then see Chapter 6.)

- ✔ **Find other reasons to mention the city and zip code in the body of your text.** If possible, in <H> tags; use bold font on some of the references, too.

- ✔ **Include the full address in your TITLE and DESCRIPTION meta tags.**

- ✔ **Include city and state names in link text when linking from other sites to yours.** See Chapter 14 for more.

- ✔ **If you use PPC campaigns, use geo-targeting.** I cover this topic in more detail in the magnificent tome _Pay Per Click Search Marketing For Dummies_ (Wiley).

- ✔ **Register for local search with the major search engines.** The next section in this chapter tells you how.

By adding location names in your pages, you increase the chance of being returned in the search results. For instance, say your Chicago health-food store's Web site has your address on the contact page. What happens when someone searches for _vitamins Chicago?_ Your page probably will not be included in the search results, because the search engine is looking for a page containing the word _vitamins_ on the same page as the word _Chicago._ If, however, every page on your site contains the address, you have a chance of being included in the search results.

Consider adding your address to product pages, and adding product keywords to your contact page.

# Registering for Local Search

In Chapter 11 you read about how to get your site listed in the search engines indexes. Let me quickly cover _another_ way here.

Google and Yahoo! let you submit information about your business directly to local search, increasing the likelihood of being found during a local search. The search engines search through the local search index _and_ through the normal Web-page index.

What sort of information do you provide? It depends on which system you are submitting to, of course. Typical information includes the following. See Figure 10-3.

- ✔ Your street address
- ✔ Phone and fax numbers
- ✔ A link to your Web site
- ✔ A business description
- ✔ Payment methods you accept
- ✔ Operating hours
- ✔ Year your business was established
- ✔ Languages spoken by your staff
- ✔ Brands you sell

Table 10-1 summarizes the top four local search systems.

| Table 10-1 | The Big Four Go Local | |
|---|---|---|
| *Site* | *Description* | *URL* |
| **Yahoo! Local Listings** | Free or $9.95/mo for enhanced features. You get a free Web site either way. | `http://listings. local.yahoo.com/` |
| **Google Local Search** | Visit the Local Business Center to add your business. If you have more than ten locations, you can submit a data file. | `http://www.google. com/local/add/` |
| **MSN Local Search** | MSN doesn't currently provide a way to submit data directly to local search, but keep checking. | `http://search.msn. com/local/` |
| **Ask Local** | Ask.com doesn't provide a way to submit data directly to local search, but keep checking. | `http://local.ask. com/local.` |

**Figure 10-3:**
This
business
submitted
information
to Yahoo!
Local
Listings, so
searchers
can read
more
about the
business.

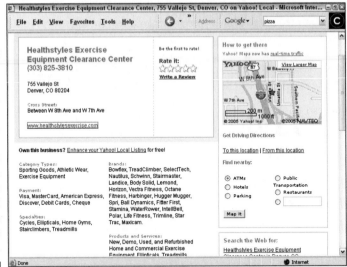

# Chapter 11

# Getting Your Pages into the Search Engines

*Y*ou've built your Web pages. Now, how do you get them into the search systems? That's what this chapter and the next chapter explain. In this chapter, I talk about how to get your pages into the search engines, and in Chapter 12 I explain how to get your site listed with the search directories.

Many site owners are confused about how they get their Web sites into search engines. They assume that to submit or register their sites, they go to a search engine's Web site, provide the URL to one (or all) of their pages, and wait for the search engine to come along and index the pages. The truth is more complicated.

## Why Won't They Index Your Pages?

It's frustrating when you can't seem to get search engines to index your site. The top three search engines — Google, Yahoo!, and MSN — provide a way for you to submit information about your site, but doing so often doesn't seem to make any difference. Your site may not be picked up. As Google says, "We do not add all submitted URLs to our index, and we cannot make any predictions or guarantees about when or if they will appear." MSN is a little more positive, perhaps, but still offers no guarantee: "Submitting your site does not guarantee that your site will be indexed. But it does help us locate your site so that MSNBot can try to crawl it." Ask.com doesn't even provide a way for you to submit.

A search submission system that doesn't seem to work? And a search engine that has no way for you to tell it about your site? What's going on here?

It's all about links. The search engines believe that they can maintain the quality of their indexes by focusing on Web pages that have links pointing to them. If nobody points to your site, the reasoning goes, why would the engines want to index it? If nobody else thinks your site is important, why should the search engine? They would rather find your pages themselves than have you submit the pages.

By the way, when I say that a page is in a search engine's index, it doesn't mean the search engine has read and indexed the entire page. In many cases, the search engine has never even read the page but knows where the page is based on links it has seen in pages that it *has* read. And even if a search engine has read a page, it may not have read the entire page.

# Linking Your Site for Inclusion

In Chapters 14 and 15, I talk about the importance of — and how to get — links pointing from other sites to yours. The more links you have pointing at your site, the more important the search engines will think your pages are.

Links are also important because they provide a way for the search engines to find your site. Without links, you *might* get your site into the search engine's indexes, but chances are you won't. And getting into the most important index — Google's — is much quicker through linking than through registration. I've had sites picked up and indexed by Google within two or three days of having put up a link on another site. If you simply submit your URL to Google, you may have to wait weeks for it to index your site (if it ever does).

But one or two links sometimes aren't enough for some search engines. They often are for Google; if it sees a link to your site on another site that it's already indexing, it will probably visit your site and index that, too. But other systems are far choosier and may not visit your site even if they do see a link to it. So the more links you have pointing to your site, the better. Eventually, the search engines will get sick of tripping over links to your site and come see what the fuss is all about.

Don't think your work is done when you create a site and then submit a page or two to the search engines. Building links from other sites is an essential part of the process. It's frustrating and requires tremendous patience, but that's the way it works!

# Submitting Directly to the Major Systems

The next few sections take a quick look at the major systems and whether you can submit your site directly to them. Remember, the only really important search engines are Google, Yahoo!, MSN, and Ask.com. Chapter 1 details the big four, and you look at directories in Chapter 12.

Just because you submit a site doesn't mean you'll get picked up. But the process of submitting your site is quick and easy, so what do you have to lose?

## Why submitting is safe

Will submitting directly to the search engines, or submitting many pages over and over, harm your search engine position? Will the search engines get annoyed and penalize your pages? Why am I even asking this question? Because there's a myth that registering a Web site can harm your chances of getting into the search engines. It's not true — and here's why.

Imagine that your rodent racing Web site is sitting at the top of page two for a popular search term in a particular search engine. You feel this ranking isn't good enough, so you go to the search engine, run the search, and then grab the URLs of all the pages that turn up on the first results page. You then submit those URLs to the search engine over and over and over again, perhaps using a submission program. You keep doing this for days, until the search engines get so annoyed they remove all those pages, pushing your page to the top! Simple, eh? Too simple, in fact, which is why that tactic doesn't work.

However, you do need to be aware of some potential repercussions. Systems that repeat submissions to an egregious degree may be blocked. The search engine may identify your system's *IP address* (the unique number identifying your computer on the Internet) and then block you from submitting or even using the search engine. If the IP address used by the program submitting URLs is the same as the IP address at which your Web site is hosted, your site could be penalized. These situations are rare, though, because the IP numbers used by such submission programs and the associated Web sites are usually different. It's far more common for the search engines to simply block the submission program from submitting more than a certain number of URLs at a time.

## Submitting for free

The following systems accept free URL submissions. Note that in some cases, they won't accept more than a specific number of submissions: one a day, three a day, or whatever. Also, these systems do not want multiple URLs, just one per Web site.

Here's where you can submit your site for free:

- ✔ **Google:** `www.google.com/addurl.html`
- ✔ **Yahoo:** `http://search.yahoo.com/info/submit.html`
- ✔ **MSN:** `http://search.msn.com/docs/submit.aspx`

How about Ask.com? They currently have no way to submit your Web site. They rely on their searchbots to find pages through links.

If a search engine doesn't provide a way for you to submit a URL, that doesn't mean you can't get into the search engine. You need lots of links pointing to your site so the search engine will find it, and a fair amount of patience, but it definitely can happen. And just because the search engine *does* provide a way for you to submit a URL doesn't mean you *will* get into the search engine. You need lots of links pointing to the site.

## Submitting a Sitemap

In 2005 Google introduced a new submission system and was quickly followed by Yahoo! You read about sitemaps in Chapter 7, of course. In that chapter I recommend creating a sitemap page on your site, and link to it from the home page. The sitemap is a page visitors can see, and that any search engine can use to find its way through your site.

But the Google and Yahoo! sitemaps are different; they are special files placed on your site that contain an index to help the search engine find its way to your pages. You create and place the file, then let the search engine know where it is. These are *invisible* files — visitors can't see them — in a format designed for those search engines. I think it's worth creating these files, because it's not a huge task and *may* help, particularly if your site is large.

There's another reason for using the Google sitemap: Google provides a variety of statistics related to your site, including information on pages that it was not able to find, PageRank, and even search-query statistics. See Chapter 14 for more information about PageRank.

## Sitemap, schmitemap

Don't think that creating a Yahoo! or Google sitemap is a magic trick guaranteed to get your site indexed. I've seen, for example, Yahoo! pick up the sitemap file, put it into the search results, come by and pick up 3 pages from the index, ignore the other 20, and leave a whole bunch of old, nonexistent pages in the index. The sitemap is something that may help, but there's no guarantee if or when the search engines will use it.

# Using Google sitemap

So what's this all about? In Google's words, "Using sitemaps to inform and direct our crawlers, we hope to expand our coverage of the web and speed up the discovery and addition of pages to our index." And if I can help Google by getting them to index my site more quickly, well, that's fine by me.

What does this sitemap file look like? The preferred format is the Google Sitemap Protocol, a form of XML. Here's what the format looks like. Don't worry. I show you later how easy it is to create these.

```
<?xml version="1.0" encoding="UTF-8"?>
<urlset xmlns="http://www.google.com/schemas/sitemap/0.84"
xmlns:xsi="http://www.w3.org/2001/XMLSchema-instance"
xsi:schemaLocation="http://www.google.com/schemas/sitemap/
          0.84
http://www.google.com/schemas/sitemap/0.84/sitemap.xsd">
  <url>
    <loc>http://www.yourdomain.com/</loc>
    <lastmod>2005-12-06T12:51:00-07:00</lastmod>
    <changefreq>monthly</changefreq>
    <priority>0.5</priority>
  </url>
  <url>
    <loc>http://www.yourdomain.com/index.htm</loc>
    <lastmod>2005-12-06T12:51:00-07:00</lastmod>
    <changefreq>monthly</changefreq>
    <priority>0.5</priority>
  </url>
  <url>

        <loc>http://www.yourdomain.com/products/index.h
        tm</loc>
    <lastmod>2005-08-22T12:41:51-07:00</lastmod>
    <changefreq>monthly</changefreq>
    <priority>0.5</priority>
  </url>
```

Google accepts other formats, though, including an RSS feed and even a plain text list of URLs.

There are various ways to create this sitemaps file. Google provides the Sitemap Generator program, which you can install on your Web server; it's a Python script, and if you don't know what that means, perhaps you should consider creating the file in some other way.

### *Setting up*

Here's how you can submit your sitemap to Google:

1. **Set up your Google Sitemap account at** `www.google.com/webmasters/sitemaps/`.

2. **Generate your sitemap file.**

3. **Place your sitemap into the root of your Web site.**

    The root is the same directory in which your home page sits.

4. **Log into your Google Sitemap account.**

5. **Click the Add tab.**

6. **Select the General Web Sitemap option button.**

    You can also create sitemaps for sites intended for mobile devices.

7. **Click the Next button.**

8. **Type the URL of the sitemap file into the text box shown in Figure 11-1.**

9. **Click the Add Web Sitemap button.**

**Figure 11-1:** Telling Google where you placed the Google sitemap.

That's the basic process, but Google recently added something interesting: a reporting function telling you how often Google visits your site and a variety of other statistics.

### Using advanced features

To use the more advanced Google sitemap features, you have to *verify* your sitemap. You do that by creating a verification file, which is an empty text file whose name has a special code provided by Google. For instance, the file-name may look like this:

```
googlea1df974a4b32ecd9.html
```

Follow these steps to "verify" your site:

1. **Find the verification-file code under Site Overview⇨Verify tabs.**

2. **Create the verification file; a text file using the code as the filename.**

3. **Place the file into the same directory as your sitemap.**

4. **Go to your Google sitemaps console and click the Verify button.**

   The button is at the bottom of the Site Overview⇨Verify page.

   Google looks for the file and turns on these advanced features. You should leave the file on your site, because Google periodically checks it.

Once verified, you can find some interesting statistics about your Web site:

✓ **Top search queries:** The top searches queries for which your site was included in the results.

✓ **Top search query clicks:** The top search queries that actually sent traffic to your site.

✓ **Crawl results:** Information about which pages Google was able to crawl and index, and which ones it wasn't (and why).

✓ **PageRank:** Information about the your pages' Google PageRanks; see Chapter 14.

This great information is well worth the trouble of creating a sitemap!

Sitemap files can be up to 10MB, and contain up to 50,000 URLs. If you need to go over either limit, you must create multiple sitemap files and a sitemap index file that refers to the individual sitemap files.

You can point Google to just a small number of pages among millions that have changed recently: List the changed pages in a single sitemap file, then, in the sitemap index file, use the `lastmod` tag to indicate which sitemap files have changed. In effect, you point Google to the files containing the changes. Visit the Google sitemaps site for all the details: www.google.com/webmasters/sitemaps/.

## Using Yahoo! sitemap

Soon after Google released its sitemap system, Yahoo! followed suit and launched its own, simpler sitemap system.

Here's how to submit a sitemap to Yahoo!:

1. **Create a text file with a list of URLs, one for each page in your site.**

2. **Save the text file with the name** urllist.txt.

3. **Save the file in your site's root directory.**

4. **Go to** http://submit.search.yahoo.com/free/request.

    You have to log in or create a Yahoo! account to access this area.

5. **Submit the file's URL.**

Yahoo! also accepts multiple formats; in addition to a plain text file, you can create a compressed *.gz* file (Yahoo! decompresses it before using), or use an RSS or Atom feed.

By the way, before you submit the file to Yahoo!, check carefully what file-name they want. Right now they're stating that it should be *urllist.txt,* but in the past they've requested *sitemap.txt,* and some of the following tools in this chapter create *sitemap.txt* files. (Just change the name to whatever Yahoo! requests.)

## Finding third-party sitemap creators

How, then, to create these sitemaps? As I mentioned earlier, Google provides a tool, but in many cases third-party tools are easier to use. (Very large sites will probably need some kind of custom coding.)

Some of these tools create just the Google *sitemap.xml* file, but others provide both the Google and Yahoo! sitemap formats. But note that many of the tools that call themselves Google sitemap creators also create simple text files that you can submit to Yahoo!

Some of these programs run on your computer, some require installing on your Web server, and some are services run from another Web site. Table 11-1 is by no means an exhaustive list of places to find third parties.

| Table 11-1 | **Finding Third-Party Sitemap Creators** | |
|---|---|---|
| *Creator* | *URL* | *Description* |
| Google | `http://code.` `google.com/sm_` `thirdparty.html` | They're not the biggest for nothing. |
| Tarant IT's Google Sitemap Generator | `www.tarrantit.com/` `GoogleSiteMap/` | Free Web tool actually creates both Google and Yahoo! sitemaps. Reports bad links and page errors to you before creating. Up to 1,000 pages. |
| GSiteCrawler | `http://gsite` `crawler.com/` | Free, Windows-based sitemap generator for both Google and Yahoo! |
| AuditMyPC.com Sitemap Builder | `www.auditmypc.com/` `free-sitemap-` `generator.asp` | A free, Web-based generator that works on sites up to 50,000 pages, and creates sitemaps for both Google and Yahoo! Requires Java running on your computer. |
| George Petrov's Google Generator | `www.dmxzone.com/` `ShowDetail.asp?` `NewsId=10538` | Dreamweaver extension that creates Google sitemaps. |
| Vigos GSitemap | `www.vigos.com/` `products/gsitemap/` | Free, Windows-based Google sitemap generator; doesn't currently create Yahoo! sitemap. |
| Coffee Cup Google Sitemapper | `www.coffeecup.com/` `google-sitemapper/` | $29 Windows program that creates Google and HTML sitemaps, but no Yahoo! sitemap. Try using a word processor's search-and-replace function to pull the list of URLs out of the HTML sitemap file. |
| Sitemaps Pal | `www.sitemaps` `pal.com/` | Free, Web-based generator for Google. |
| Google Sitemap Generator | `www.develop` `sitemap.com/` | $20 Windows-based sitemap generator for Google. |

# Using Paid Inclusion

*Paid-inclusion programs* provide you the privilege of paying to have a search engine index your pages. Happily, such programs have fallen out of favor. Only one of the major systems, Yahoo!, now has a paid-inclusion program: Search Submit Express at `http://searchmarketing.yahoo.com`. Some smaller systems still have them, but they're rarely worthwhile.

Here's the concept: You pay Yahoo! a fee for each page you want indexed, and Yahoo! guarantees to index your pages quickly, promises to come back frequently to reindex (every 48 hours), and guarantees that your pages will remain in the index for the full term of the agreement (usually a year).

I don't like the idea of paid inclusion; it strikes me as a bit of a scam. The Federal Trade Commission doesn't like it much either, and consumer-advocate complaints have targeted paid inclusion based on federal law that "prohibits unfair or deceptive acts or practices in or affecting commerce [such as] a representation, omission, or practice that is likely to mislead the consumer acting reasonably in the circumstances, to the consumer's detriment."

The argument is over whether paid inclusions are, in effect, ads. Yahoo! says they're not; you're simply paying for an improved service in getting your URLs into the index, thereby improving the index. For dynamic sites, this is true because it is nearly impossible to crawl a dynamic site. (See Chapter 7 for more on why this is so.)

But from the consumer's perspective, paid-inclusion ads are misleading. If a search engine has a complex algorithm designed to provide accurate, relevant search results, and if that algorithm includes links pointing to a site as a factor, but then allows sites to partially bypass the algorithm — by getting into the index despite insufficient incoming links to attract the interest of the search engine — how is that not misleading to searchers? The search engines say that the paid-inclusion pages still have to compete on the same terms with all the other pages in the index and are not ranked any higher based on their payment status. That may be true, but paid-inclusion pages definitely *are* going to rank higher than the pages that are *not* in the index because their owners haven't paid! Note, by the way, that the founders of Google *also* find paid inclusion to be misleading and have refused to allow the search engine to use such programs.

Yahoo! charges $49 a year for the first page, $29 a year per page for the second through tenth pages, and $10 a year per page for all additional pages. But Yahoo! added a twist that paid-inclusion systems didn't use to have; not only do they charge to index your pages, but they charge each time someone clicks a link to your page! They have two different site categories: Tier 1 sites (adult, books, sports, and so on) pay 15 cents per click, while Tier 2 sites (apparel, electronics, real estate, and so on) pay 30 cents per click.

## Hasta la Vista, AltaVista et al

The first edition of this book included infor- | Ask.com. Today, all these have gone, with the
mation about four major paid-inclusion sys- | first three being combined into Yahoo!'s system.
tems: Inktomi, AltaVista, FAST/AllTheWeb, and

## *Excluding inclusion*

If you're trying to decide whether to use paid inclusion, consider the following points:

- ✔ **Never-ending fees.** You may get stuck paying fees year after year.

- ✔ **Getting indexed via links.** If you have a really good linking strategy, you may get Yahoo! to index your site without having to pay them. A large number of high-quality links into your site will help ensure you get picked up.

- ✔ **Paying for a no-show.** If you don't have a good linking strategy, your pages probably won't rank well anyway. Paid inclusion gets you into the index, but it doesn't affect your position in the index, so you may be paying to be on a page that few people read.

On the other hand, some people like paid inclusion because of the speedy updates. You can tweak pages and see the results in Yahoo! within a few days.

Here's an interesting conundrum: Most pages are added to the Yahoo! index for free. Its searchbots add pages and you can submit pages directly. If Yahoo!, with billions of pages in its index, limited its index to only paid inclusions, it would quickly go out of business. So, a few important questions about paid inclusion:

- ✔ If you pay to have your pages indexed, what happens when the agreement period expires? Presumably, Yahoo! should remove your pages; otherwise the paid-inclusion program more or less collapses, doesn't it? That would mean that Yahoo!, in effect, holds you hostage, removing pages that might otherwise have been indexed automatically by its searchbots!

- ✔ What's to stop you from indexing a single page using paid inclusion — a page that contains lots of links to your other pages, to make sure the search engines find all your pages? A sitemap page is a good example. Yahoo! wants you to submit multiple pages via the paid-inclusion program, so it would be against their interests to do this. Is Yahoo! disabling the normal algorithm for paid-inclusion pages to ensure they aren't picked up for free?

✔ If, in its normal course of travel, the Yahoo! searchbot runs across pages that you have paid to have included, will it index those pages and flag them as no longer requiring payment? Will Yahoo! refund your money for the rest of the submission period?

## Using trusted feeds

Another form of paid inclusion is known as a *trusted feed* — a sort of en masse paid inclusion. As with paid inclusion, trusted-feed services used to be provided by several large search engines, but now only Yahoo! has this service. (It's known as Search Submit Pro at `http://searchmarketing.yahoo.com/`.) Trusted feeds are sometimes used by companies with dynamic Web sites (see Chapter 7 for more on what makes sites dynamic) and are generally intended for large numbers of pages, 1,000 or more. Yahoo! targets companies that are likely to spend $5,000 or more a month.

With Yahoo!'s trusted-feed program, you don't pay to have your pages included, but you do pay every time a searcher clicks on a link in the search results pointing to your site, $0.25 or more per click.

You provide information about your pages to Yahoo! You can get data into the search engines in a couple of ways: by providing an XML file containing all the information, or some other kind of data feed, such as an Excel spread-sheet. You provide this information:

✔ URL

✔ Page title

✔ DESCRIPTION meta tag

✔ KEYWORDS meta tag

✔ Page content

Providing the data in a trusted feed allows you to submit data to the search engines so they don't have to crawl your Web site to pick it up. It also allows you to submit the relevant data — ignoring irrelevant page content — which raises the question, "Isn't this just a legal form of cloaking?"

*Cloaking* is a technique for showing a searchbot a different page from the one a site visitor would see, and it's frowned upon by the search engines. You can read about cloaking in Chapter 8.

Unlike basic paid inclusion, a trusted feed actually feeds data into the index; the searchbot doesn't have to index the page itself, because you *tell* the searchbot what the page is about. This means that a trusted feed is even closer to being an ad than paid inclusion is.

## Little giant

Some secondary systems are still fairly popular sites. For instance, I've seen Alexa rank ExactSeek as the 1,600th most popular Web site at one point, though recently it dropped to around 2,200.

Yahoo! argues that paid-inclusion programs don't help your site rank higher. But it's hard to argue this for trusted feeds, especially when Yahoo!'s sales staff are telling people that they can help *tweak* the data feed so that the pages rank better, and when their online demo use phrases like "Search Submit Pro helps match your listings more effectively with relevant queries . . ."! Yahoo! even states in the online demo that the data feed "eliminates information that is irrelevant to your content and confusing to search engines." In other words, the trusted feed helps your site rank better. The demo — which you can currently view at `http://searchmarketing.yahoo.com/imgs/as/srchsbp.swf` — makes quite clear that the intention of the trusted feed is to manipulate the search results!

# Submitting to the Secondary Systems

You can also submit your site to smaller systems with perhaps a few hundred million pages in their indexes — sometimes far fewer. The disadvantage with these systems is that they are seldom used, compared to the big systems discussed earlier in the chapter. Many search engine professionals ignore the smaller systems altogether. So if your site is ranked in these systems, you have less competition because they're so small.

These secondary systems are worth submitting to:

- ✔ **ExactSeek:** `www.exactseek.com/add.html`
- ✔ **Gigablast:** `www.gigablast.com/addurl`

I've provided a list of additional search engines at my site, `www.SearchEngineBulletin.com`, and you can find more, including regional sites, listed on the following pages:

- ✔ `www.searchenginewatch.com/links/article.php/2156161`
- ✔ `www.dir-search.com`
- ✔ `www.allsearchengines.com`

- ✔ www.searchengines.com/generalKids.html
- ✔ www.searchengines.com/worldUSCan.html
- ✔ http://dmoz.org/Computers/Internet/Searching/ Search_Engines/
- ✔ dir.yahoo.com/Computers_and_Internet/Internet/ World_Wide_Web/Searching_the_Web/Search_ Engines_and_Directories/

Some of the smaller search engines encourage you to pay for a submission. Don't. Unless you know for sure otherwise, you can safely assume that the amount of traffic you are likely to get is probably not worth the payment.

Many smaller search sites don't have their own searchbots; they get the data from other systems such as the Open Directory Project (which feeds around 350 different systems). So, sometimes you'll run across search sites to which you can't submit directly.

If you plan to submit your site to many search engines, you may want to use a programmable keyboard or a text-replacement utility or macro program such as ShortKeys (www.shortkeys.com), which can make entering repetitive data much quicker:

- ✔ With a programmable keyboard, you can assign a string of text — URL, e-mail address, and so on — to a single key. Then all you need to do is (for instance) press F11 to enter your e-mail address.

- ✔ A text-replacement utility replaces a short string of text with something longer. To enter your e-mail address, for instance, you might just type *em*.

A few sites require that you submit your site with a username and password. Most sites require at least an e-mail address, and some also require that you respond to a confirmation e-mail before they add your site to the list. *Don't use your regular e-mail address!* Use a throwaway address, because you'll receive a lot of spam.

# Using Registration Services and Software Programs

You can also submit your pages to hundreds of search engines by using a submission service or program. Many free services are available, but some of them are outdated, running automatically for a few years now, not having kept up with changes in the search engine scene.

Many of the free services are definitely on the *lite* side. They're provided by companies that hope you'll spring for a fee-based full service. For example, one well-known service, AdPro (`www.addpro.com`), provides free submission to the following search engines:

- ✔ ABACHO (German search engine)
- ✔ Acoon (German search engine)
- ✔ Aeiwi
- ✔ Cipinet
- ✔ Entireweb
- ✔ ExactSeek
- ✔ FindOnce
- ✔ Fybersearch
- ✔ Google (Automated submission programs no longer work with Google.)
- ✔ Jayde
- ✔ Towsersearch
- ✔ ScrubTheWeb
- ✔ SplatSearch
- ✔ Subjex
- ✔ SurfGopher
- ✔ Walhello
- ✔ WotBox
- ✔ Searchit

AdPro also has a paid service that submits to 120 search engines. For $29.95 a year, it manually submits your site to "the top search engines" and uses a submission program to submit to 120 other services.

Another popular submission system is provided by ineedhits (`www.ineedhits.com`), which submits a URL to 300 search engines for as little as $2.50. Submitter.com (`www.submitter.com`) submits to over 200 search engines for $50. There are many, many submission services; search for *search engine submission service,* and you'll find a gazillion of them.

Will you get much traffic from these 300 search engines? Probably not, but submitting to them can't hurt. Note also that some submission services increase their submit count by including all the services that are fed by the systems they submit to. For instance, if a service submits to Yahoo!, it counts it as multiple submissions, because Yahoo! feeds AlltheWeb, Lycos, Terra.com, HotBot, Overture, InfoSpace, Excite, and more.

Many software programs are available, as well. Here are a few of the more popular ones:

- ✔ **Dynamic Submission**, which you can find at `www.dynamicsubmission.com` and see in Figure 11-2. I like this program because it's easy and quick to use.
- ✔ **SubmitWolf** at `www.submitwolf.com`.
- ✔ **WebPosition Gold** at `www.webposition.com`. Okay, this program does have some limited submission tools, but it's really more useful for checking search engine positions. See Chapter 20 for more on that score.

The big advantage of these software programs is that you only pay once rather than paying every time you use a service.

Although automated tools are handy, submitting a URL by hand is the best option for the three major systems, if only because (despite what some automated tools may tell you) automated submission tools no longer work with the major search engines. But if you're submitting to 300 little-used search engines, by all means use an automated tool!

There are actually a couple of reasons to use these automated tools. You may get a little traffic out of these small search engines, though don't bank on getting much. But in many cases the systems being submitted to are not really search engines, they're search *directories,* and being listed in a directory may mean the major search engines pick up a link pointing to your site. (Several of the systems in the preceding AddPro list are directories.) I talk more about submitting to search directories in Chapter 12, and you discover the power of linking in Chapters 14 and 15.

**Figure 11-2:**
The Dynamic Submission mass-registration tool.

# Chapter 12

# Submitting to the Directories

*I*n Chapter 11, you look at getting your site into the search engines. In this chapter, you look at getting your site into the directories. The major directories are very important to a search strategy, although they can be rather frustrating to work with. Compared to search engines, the overall process of working with directories is very different — and in some ways it's simpler, but in other ways not.

## Pitting Search Directories against Search Engines

Before you starting working with directories, it's helpful to know a few basics about what directories are — and are *not:*

✔ The directories don't send *searchbots* out onto the Web looking for sites to add.

✔ The directories don't read and store information from Web pages within a site.

✔ Because the directories don't read and store information, they don't base search results on the contents of the Web pages.

✔ The directories don't index Web *pages;* they index Web *sites.* Each site is assigned to a particular *category.* Within the categories, the directory's index contains just a little information about each site — not much more than a URL, a title, and a description. The result is categorized lists of Web sites — and that's really what the search directories are all about.

Not too long ago, Yahoo! was based around its directory. In fact, look at Figure 12-1 for an example of what Yahoo! looked like early in 1998 (courtesy of a wonderful service called the WayBackMachine, which you can find at `www.archive.org`). The idea behind Yahoo! was a categorized directory of Web sites that people could browse. You could click links to drill down through the directory and find what you needed, similar to flipping through a Yellow Pages directory. Although you could use the Search box to peruse categories, site titles, and site descriptions, the tool was nothing like the Yahoo! search tool of today, which can hunt for your term in over 15 billion Web pages.

But Yahoo! made an enormous mistake. In fact, the image in Figure 12-1 is from a time at which Yahoo! was at its peak, a time when most of the world's Web searches were carried out through its site . . . just a few months before Google began operations. Yahoo! evidently hadn't fully realized the weaknesses of the directory system until it was too late. These weaknesses include the following:

✔ **Directories provide no way for someone to search individual pages within a site.** The perfect fit for your information needs may be sitting somewhere on a site that is included in a directory, but you won't know it because the directory doesn't index individual pages.

**Figure 12-1:** The main Yahoo! page, when Yahoo! Directory was what it was all about.

✔ **Categorization is necessarily limited.** Sites are rarely about a single topic; even if they appear to be, single topics can be broken down into smaller subtopics. By forcing people to find a site by category and keyword in a very limited amount of text — a description and title — the directories are obviously very restrictive.

✔ **Hand-built directories are necessarily limited in size.** *Hand-built* directories, such as Yahoo! Directory and the Open Directory, add a site to their directories only after a real live human editor has reviewed the site. With hundreds of millions of Web sites, there's no way a human-powered system could keep up.

✔ **Hand-built directories get very dated.** Yahoo! Directory contains some extremely old and out-of-date information that simply wouldn't be present in an index that is automatically reindexed every few days or weeks. (Yahoo! *spiders* the sites — that is, sends out searchbots to look through the sites — in its index for broken links and dead sites, but if the site's purpose has changed, Yahoo! may not realize that fact.)

The proof of directories' weaknesses is in the pudding: Google took over and now is the dominant search system on the Web. (To be fair, Yahoo! helped Google by integrating Google results into Yahoo! searches, although, in the summer of 2004 it dropped Google and began using its own index.)

The old Yahoo! site directory is still there, but it's virtually hidden to many visitors. Just a couple of years ago the directory was still on the home page, but so low you had to scroll to see it; now the directory is not even on the home page. You can still find it by going to `dir.Yahoo.com` or by clicking the Directory link at the top of the Yahoo.com home page.

# Why Are Directories So Significant?

If the Yahoo! directory is hidden away, and if most people have never heard of the world's second most important directory (the Open Directory Project, at `www.dmoz.org`), why do you care about them? They're still very significant, for a number of reasons:

✔ Yahoo! Directory is part of the Yahoo! search system, one of the world's most popular search sites. As such, it still gets a lot of traffic. You can access it directly at `dir.yahoo.com`, and some people do access it from the Yahoo! main page. In addition, when you use the Search the Web box at the top, Yahoo! produces search engine results as well as a tab at the top of the page that takes you to matching directory results. Yahoo! claims that 230 million *unique users* visit Yahoo! Directory each month (though Yahoo! probably actually means 230 million *unique visits,* which is a very different thing).

✔ The Open Directory Project feeds results to Google Directory, which is part of the world's *most popular* search site.

✔ The Open Directory Project feeds results to literally hundreds of other sites, large and small; many of these sites are crawled by the major search engines (such as Google), so a link from the Open Directory Project can show up as links from many other sites, too.

✔ Google and Yahoo! often use directory entries for the blurb below a page title in Web search results — the search-results page shown when someone searches their indexes. Google often grabs the site description from the Open Directory Project, and Yahoo! pulls the description from Yahoo! Directory, so having a directory entry allows you to control the text that appears on the search-results pages for your site.

✔ Links in the major directories help provide context to the search engines. If your site is in the Recreation: Pets: Rodents category in the Open Directory Project, for instance, the search engines know the site is related to playing with rodents. The directory presence helps search engines index your site and may help your site rank higher for some search terms.

By the way, don't underestimate the Open Directory Project just because you've never heard of it or because the submission forms are often broken or unreliable. Data from this system is widely spread across the Internet, and has often been used to kick-start major search systems. Yahoo!, for instance, once used data from the Open Directory Project (which, incidentally, is owned by AOL/Netscape).

# Submitting to the Search Directories

The previous chapter has what some may find an unusual message: "Sure, you can submit to the search engines, but it may not do you any good." Search engines really like links to your site, and having links to your site is often the best way to get into the search engines.

But the search directories don't care about links, and the only way to get into search directories is to *submit* to them. And you can forget automated submission programs for the major directories — there's no way to use them. Submissions must be entered into Yahoo! and the Open Directory Project "by hand."

## Submitting to Yahoo! Directory

Once free, submissions to Yahoo! Directory used to be very difficult. Surveys showed that people who had managed to get their sites listed in the directory had to try multiple times over a matter of months. Well, I've got good news and bad.

✔ The good news: You can get your site listed in Yahoo! Directory within about a week. Of all the major search systems, getting into Yahoo! Directory is easiest; Yahoo! guarantees to review your site within seven business days. They're not guaranteeing to include your site, by the way — only to review and add it if it's appropriate. In general, most people don't have many problems. Yahoo! will almost certainly accept your site if it is

- Functioning without a lot of broken links

- In the correct language for the particular Yahoo! directory to which you are submitting (Yahoo! has directories in several languages)

- Designed for multiple browser types; they expressly exclude Java-only sites

- In an appropriate category

✔ The bad news: It's probably going to cost you $299 a year for the privilege ($600 for adult sites). It's free if you have a noncommercial site — though it may take some time for your site to be accepted, if it is at all — but for any kind of commercial venture, you have to cough up the cash. (Note, however, that Yahoo! Directory still contains many sites that predate the paid-listing policy and do not require payment.)

Is listing in Yahoo! Directory worth $299? Hard to say, but there are some good reasons to do so:

✔ It seems likely that getting into its directory ensures that you get into the Yahoo! Web Search, and may even improve your indexing in Yahoo! Web Search. The company actually states that it "can increase the likelihood," but doesn't guarantee inclusion. I've seen a site get fully indexed fairly soon after submitting to the directory, though that could be coincidence.

✔ It's crawled by other search engines, such as Google, so having a link in the directory helps the search engines find your site and may encourage them to index it.

✔ The search engines use the directory to help them categorize your site.

✔ Many people, as I mention earlier, *do* use the directory.

✔ If your site is in the directory, you may be able to place a cheap ad at the top of your category. Some category sponsors are paying as little as $25 per month.

### The 1-2-3s of getting listed

Here's how to get listed:

1. **Find a credit card.**

   Preferably the card is yours or that of someone who has given you permission to spend $299 (or is it $600?).

2. **Open your browser and go to** `dir.yahoo.com.`

   You're going to make sure that your site isn't already included.

3. **After the page has loaded, type your domain name into the Search box and click Search.**

   If you have total control over your site, this step isn't necessary. Of course, you'll know if your site is already listed. But if, for example, you inherited it from another department in the company you work for, who knows — it may already be there.

4. **Return to the Yahoo! Directory main page and browse through the categories looking for the best match for your site.**

   You can find tips on choosing a category in the next section, "Picking a category."

5. **Look for a link that says something like** _Suggest a Site,_ **or perhaps a promotional box of some kind.**

   The link is probably somewhere in the top right of the page.

6. **Click the link and follow the instructions.**

   You have to enter a site description, contact and billing information, and so on.

### Picking a category

Because of the sheer volume of categories, picking a category is not as simple as it might seem. Yahoo! Directory has 14 major categories, and many thousands of subcategories. But understanding a few points about hunting for and submitting to a category can make the process a little smoother.

You need to choose a fairly specific category. You can't submit to a category or subcategory if it only holds other subcategories. For instance, you can't submit a site to the Business & Economy category. It's just too broad. Rather, you have to drill down further into the subcategories and find a category that's specific enough to contain actual Web sites.

You'll probably find that your site could perhaps fit into several categories, so you're going to have to dig around for a while and pick the most appropriate. Although discouraged, you can put a single site into multiple categories, but of course you have to pay for each category. (And Yahoo! doesn't like doing this, anyway; it can take time and effort to persuade them.)

One good strategy is to look for your competitors: What categories are they assigned to? If you find a category with a whole bunch of companies similar to yours, you've probably found the right one.

Note, by the way, that as you move through Yahoo! Directory, you'll see that some category names have an @ sign at the end, such as Graduate Programs@, Booksellers@, Intranet@, and so on. These cross-references are to categories under different branches of the directory. For instance, if you browse down the directory to Recreation & Sports > Travel, you see a link to Tour Operators@; click this link, and you jump over to Business and Economy > Shopping and Services > Travel and Transportation > Tour Operators. In fact, virtually all Web sites that sell or promote a product end up somewhere under Business and Economy, even if they are linked from other parts of the directory.

Note also that you have to actually be *inside* a category before you can add a page. This is a little confusing perhaps. When you first search in the directory, Yahoo! displays a page that contains a list of categories and a whole bunch of Web sites that match your search, but from various different categories; see Figure 12-2. Thus, you are not actually inside a category at this point, so can't add a page here, but you will see links that take you into specific categories.

After searching, you see links to categories.

**Figure 12-2:** After searching at Yahoo! Directory, you see links to directory categories.

By the way, Yahoo! may not take your advice; it may put your site into a different category. If you are convinced your choice is best, ask them to change. I've successfully requested a change, by pointing out not that the category is best for my client, but that the placement was misleading to searchers, because people visiting that category would not expect to see my client's type of Web site.

## Submitting to the Open Directory Project

Yes, the Open Directory Project is free, and yes, you can submit much more quickly. But the problem is there's no guarantee that your site will be listed. I've seen sites get into the Open Directory Project within a week or two of submission, and I've seen others that waited months without ever getting in. In addition, the submission forms sometimes don't seem to work!

But don't give up. As I make abundantly clear, both earlier in this chapter and in Chapter 1, the Open Directory Project is very important. Here's how to submit:

1. **Read the editor's guidelines at** `dmoz.org/guidelines/describing.html`.

   If you know what guidelines the editors use, you may be able to avoid problems. It's hard to get into the directory, so you might as well give yourself the best chance of getting in.

2. **Go to** `www.dmoz.org`.

   The Open Directory Project home page appears.

3. **Find a suitable category for your site.**

   See "Picking a category," earlier in this chapter.

4. **Click the <u>Suggest URL</u> link at the top of the page.**

5. **Follow the (fairly simple) directions.**

Submitting to the Open Directory Project is much easier than doing so to Yahoo! Directory. You simply enter your home page's URL, a short title, a 25–30-word description for the site, and your e-mail address. That's it. Then you wait.

But understand that the editors at DMOZ don't care about your site, they care about the directory; in fact, read the DMOZ forums at `www.resource-zone.com` and you'll find that the attitude tends to be "tells us about your site, then go away and forget about it." There are all sorts of factors working against you:

- There are 8,000 editors managing over 700,000 categories.
- Many small directories may only be reviewed by an editor every six months . . . or far less frequently.

> ✔ The editors regard a six-month wait, or longer, not particularly excessive.
>
> ✔ In some cases editors may even ignore submissions. As one editor explained, "there is no obligation to review them in any order nor is there a requirement to review them as a priority . . . some editors find it more productive to seek out sites on their own and rarely visit the suggested sites."

As another DMOZ editor succinctly explained it, DMOZ is "very much like a lottery." The fact is, as important as DMOZ is, you may never get into this directory!

## Understanding different link types

A link from Yahoo! looks something like this:

```
http://rds.yahoo.com/_ylt=A9htfTeuNtRDAVsBGtyEzbkF;_ylu=
        X3oDMTB2bmc5YWltBGNvbG8DZQRwb3MDMQRzZWMDc3IEdnR
        pZANERlgwXzM-/SIG=1165et4rd/EXP=1138067502/**
        http%3a//abc.go.com/
```

A link from the Open Directory Project, and from many other search engines, looks like this:

```
http://abcnews.go.com/
```

In other words, links from the Open Directory Project, and many secondary directories, count as a link directly to your site for the purposes of PageRank (see Chapter 14 for an explanation of this essential concept) — these links not only help search engines find your site and categorize it, but can also help ranking by acting as a "vote" for your site.

# Submitting to Second-Tier Directories

*Second-tier* directories are smallish directories with nowhere near the significance of Yahoo! Directory or the Open Directory Project. They can help you a little if you're willing to spend a few hours registering your site with them.

Unlike search engines, directories can be *crawled* by a searchbot. Directories, remember, are categorized collections of sites that you can browse. If you can browse by clicking links to drill down through the directory, then so can a searchbot. In fact, the major search engines index many small directories. If you have a link in one of these directories and one of the major systems sees it, that can help your rank in that search engine, as explained in Chapter 14.

## Finding second-tier directories

There are hundreds of directories, though you don't want to spend much time with most of them. Many of the directories you find are using data from the Open Directory Project, so you have, in effect, already submitted to them. (You did submit, didn't you?) Often these sites have a little Open Directory Project box, like the one shown in Figure 12-3, near the bottom of the page. This box will soon become familiar as you dig around looking for directories. But sometimes a site's relationship to the Open Directory Project isn't so clear.

**Figure 12-3:**
This box
means the
data comes
from the
Open
Directory
Project.

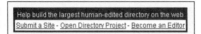

Help build the largest human-edited directory on the web.
Submit a Site - Open Directory Project - Become an Editor

## Avoiding payment — most of the time

Don't bother paying to register with these second-tier systems. As with search engines, the directory owners are also trying to get site owners to pay for indexing. For example, JoeAnt wants a $39.99 one-time fee to take your information. In most cases, the listing simply isn't worth the fee. Regard being listed in these directories as cheap additional links, not as something you need to spend a lot of money on.

On the other hand, you may run across directories that you feel really *are* of value. Business.com (www.business.com) is a great example of a very important second-tier directory, integrated into busy sites such as BusinessWeek Online (www.businessweek.com, the online companion to *Business Week* magazine).

Note, however, that to be included in the partner sites you must be using their pay-per-click service — see Chapter 17 for pay-per-click information. And Microsoft's Small Business Directory (http://sbd.bcentral.com/) is an example of a low-cost ($49) directory that is quite popular. Both provide links that are readable by the search engines. Being in such directories may bring sufficient traffic to your site to make payment worthwhile, and may help boost your position in the search engines.

# Chapter 13

# Buried Treasure — More Great Places to Submit Your Site

## In This Chapter

▶ Keeping track of what you find online
▶ Searching for specialized directories
▶ Browsing for specialized directories
▶ Getting listed in the Yellow Pages Web sites

*I*n Chapters 11 and 12, you find out about the places where you can register your site — the major search systems such as Google and the Open Directory Project, and secondary systems such as ExactSeek (www.exact seek.com) and Business.com (www.business.com). Some of the sites you find out about in this chapter are more important than the secondary systems and, in some cases, even more important than the major search systems. That's right: Some companies do more business from the sites I discuss in this chapter than from the major search engines.

Don't forget the Yellow Pages sites, which handle billions of searches each year. Although most businesses probably won't want to pay for an ad on a Yellow Pages site (if you have a business phone line, you've already got a free listing), many businesses use these search systems very profitably. In general, if you've found the paper Yellow Pages to be worthwhile, you may find online Yellow Pages useful, too. And in fact, if you're buying a Yellow Pages ad, your sales rep is probably trying to upsell you on Internet features these days, such as links to your Web site and additional information posted about your business on the Yellow Page search site.

## Keeping a Landscape Log

I recommend keeping track of what you discover during your online research. You'll come across small directories related to your area of business, news-groups, Web-based forums, mailing-list discussion groups, private sites created by interested individuals, competitors — all sorts of things that can help promote your site.

In effect, you're mapping the Internet landscape, the area of the Internet in which your business operates. You need to keep the information you gather so you can use it after your research is complete. Maybe you find some directories that you want to register with. Or you discover some e-mail newsletters that you want to work with when you have the time. For instance, you may want to contact newsletters to see if they will do a review of your site or your products. (There's more to promoting a site than just working with the search engines!)

Your landscape log doesn't have to be complicated. It can be a Microsoft Word document or maybe an Excel spreadsheet. If you want to get really organized, you can use an ACT or Access database. I suggest that you keep the following information:

- ✔ Site name.
- ✔ Company name, if different from the site name.
- ✔ URL.
- ✔ PageRank. I explain PageRank in Google Chapter 14. It's a good indication of the value of any link you might get from the site. In general, the higher the rank, the more valuable the link.
- ✔ Alexa traffic rank. When you visit a site, look at the traffic ranking noted on the Alexa toolbar. (I suggest that you load this toolbar in Chapter 1.) This ranking provides a good indication of how much traffic the site gets so you can decide if some kind of cooperative venture is worthwhile.
- ✔ Contact name. If you can find a contact name, it's useful to have.
- ✔ Contact e-mail address.
- ✔ Notes. Write a quick description of your impression of the site and how it might help you.
- ✔ Actions. Keep track of when you contact the site (to ask for a link, for example).

I'm not just talking about the research you do while looking for specialized directories. Whenever you work online and uncover competitors, potential partners, useful resources, and so on, you should store that information somewhere for later use.

# Finding the Specialized Directories

For just about every subject you can imagine, someone is running a specialized search directory. Although specialized directories get very little traffic when compared to the big guys, the traffic they do get is highly targeted — just the people you want to attract. And such directories are often very popular with your target audience.

Here's an example of how to search for a specialized directory. Suppose that you're promoting your rodent-racing Web site. Go to Google and type *rodent racing directory*. Hmmm, for some reason Google doesn't find any directories related to rodent racing. Strange. Okay, try *rodent directory*. Now you're getting somewhere! I did this search and found several useful sites:

- ✔ **PetsSquare:** This site has a variety of directories related to pets, including rodents. The Rodent page has a PageRank of 4 — pretty good — and an Alexa traffic rank of 66,762. I don't regard rodents as pets (race rodents are working animals), but I could probably register them here.

- ✔ **NetVet's Electronic Zoo:** This is a big list of links to rodent-related sites, though mostly related to research (the Digital Atlas of Mouse Embryology and the Cybermouse Project, for instance). But with a PageRank of 6 and an Alexa traffic rank of under 5,600, it might be worth your trying to get listed. Perhaps you can suggest that your site is related to research into cardiovascular performance of rodents under stress.

- ✔ **Rodent Resources at the National Center for Research Resources:** Hmm, this is another rodent-research site, but with an Alexa traffic rank of 284 and a PageRank of 9. Getting listed in this directory would be very useful. (Maybe it's time to apply for a research grant.)

- ✔ **The Rodent Breeders List:** This directory strikes me as one of those "not very pleasant, but somebody's got to do it" things. Still, if you breed rodents for your races, you may want to get onto this list.

When you do a search for a specialty directory, your search results will include the specialty directories you need, but mixed in with them, you'll also find results from the Yahoo! Directory, Google Directory, and the Open Directory Project. If you want, you can clear out the clutter by searching like this:

```
rodent directory -inurl:yahoo.com -inurl:google.com -
        inurl:dmoz.org
```

This search phrase tells Google to look for pages with the words *rodent* and *directory,* but to ignore any pages that have `yahoo.com`, `google.com`, or `dmoz.org` (the Open Directory Project) in their URLs.

Note that some of the specialty directories you find actually *pull* data from the Open Directory Project. For instance, I found the Rodents Directory, which is part of Directory.NET (`www.directory.net/Recreation/Pets/Rodents`). This directory looked very large and professional, but upon further investigation, I discovered it was using the Open Directory Project data. You certainly want to be listed in this rodent directory, but in order to get into the directory, you need to get into the Open Directory Project itself, as I explain in Chapter 12.

Hundreds of sites use the Open Directory Project information, so you're bound to run into them now and then. How can you tell when a site is pulling data from the Open Directory Project? Here are a few signs to look for:

✔ Although it's a little-known site, it seems to have a lot of data, covering a huge range of subjects.

✔ The directory seems to be structured in the familiar table of categories and subcategories.

✔ The real giveaway is usually at the bottom of the page, where you'll find a box with links to the Open Directory Project, along with a note crediting that organization. See Figure 13-1.

You may also want to search for these directories by using the term *index*. Although this term is not used as commonly as *directory,* some sites do use it. For instance, when I searched for *photography index,* I found the Nature Photo Index (`http://nature.photoarticles.com/`), which includes a directory of Web sites related to nature photography.

With a traffic rank of almost 18,000, Directory.net is definitely not a top-level search system . . .

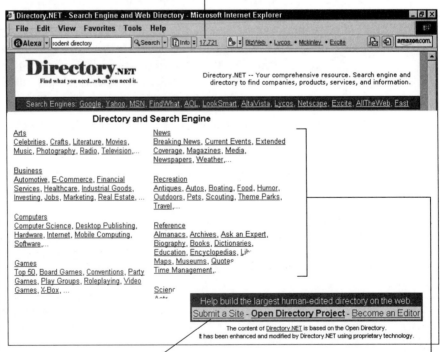

**Figure 13-1:** Identifying data pulled from the Open Directory Project.

Here's what gives it away — the attribution to the Open Directory Project.

. . . but still, it has a huge amount of information.

# *Finding directories other ways*

You can use other methods to track down specialty directories. In fact, as you get to know the Internet landscape around your business, you'll run into these directories eventually. People mention them in discussion groups, for instance, or you'll find links to them on other Web sites.

I also like browsing for these directories in the major directories, Yahoo! and the Open Directory Project. Yahoo! Directory (`dir.yahoo.com`) has many subcategories for directories. It doesn't have one for rodent racing, which apparently gets no respect, but it certainly has directories for many other topics, such as the following:

- ✔ Snowboarding > Web Directories
- ✔ Photography > Web Directories
- ✔ Radio Stations > Web Directories
- ✔ Arts > Web Directories
- ✔ Transgendered > Web Directories
- ✔ Comics and Animations > Web Directories

For some reason, Yahoo! Directory also has subcategories simply called Directories. (No, I don't know the difference between a Web Directories sub-category and a Directories subcategory.) Here's a sampling of the Directories subcategory:

- ✔ Travel and Transportation > Directories
- ✔ Business and Economy > Directories
- ✔ Reference > Directories
- ✔ Haunted Houses > Directories
- ✔ Ethnic Studies > Directories

Pay attention while you're working in Yahoo!, or you may find yourself in the Yahoo! Search results area rather than the Yahoo! Directory. Note the tab at the top of the page. When the Web tab is highlighted, you're in Yahoo! Search; when the Directory tab is highlighted, you're in the Yahoo! Directory.

The best way to find the Web Directories or Directories subcategories is simply to go to the Yahoo! Directory and browse for suitable categories for your Web site. Each time you find a suitable category, search the page for the word *directory* to see if the page includes a link to a Web Directory or Directory subcategory. (You can also use the Search box; search for *haunted houses directory,* and one of the resulting links will be to *Haunted Houses > Directories.*)

The Open Directory Project also lists thousands of directories. Again, browse through the directory (at `www.dmoz.org`) looking for appropriate categories, and then search the page for the word *directories.* Or search for an appropriate directory: *golf directories, golf directory, rodent directories, rodent directory, transgender directories, transgender directory,* and so on. (Yes, searching on *directories* and *directory* will provide different results.)

When you find a directory, see what's in it. Don't just ask for a link and move on. Dig around, see what you can find, and add information to your landscape log. The directory will contain links to other sites that may also have their own directories.

## Local directories

You can also find *local directories* — directories of businesses in your area. These local directories are often good places to get listed. They are easy to get into and can provide more site categorization clues for the search engines, and they often have high PageRanks.

It's easy to find such directories:

 ✔ Search for a place name and the term *directory.* (For instance, look for *colorado directory* or *denver directory.*)
 ✔ Look in Yahoo!'s and the Open Directory Project's regional categories.

---

### Unscientific subcategories

Yahoo! currently has around 1,400 directory sub-categories, representing many thousands of directory Web sites. I found links to 13 directories of haunted houses (a number that one might almost imagine is intentional); 13 directories of humor sites; 9 directories of sites related to transgendering; 7 directories of sites that provide electronic greeting cards; and 6 directories of fitness Web sites. This grossly unscientific survey suggests to me that probably almost 14,000 directory sites are listed in Yahoo! So chances are good that several may be good candidates for listing your site.

## Bothering with directories

Why should you care about these directories? Here are a few reasons:

- **They provide another channel to your site from the search engines.** When someone searches on, say, *fitness,* your Rodent Chasing for Cardiovascular Health site may not appear, but Buzzle.com and AtoZfitness.com might. If you're listed in those directories, maybe the searcher will find you.

- **Some of the pages at these directory sites have very good PageRanks.** Links from pages with high PageRanks pass on part of the PageRank to *your* site, helping you rise in the search engines. For instance, one of the directory pages I looked at on the AtoZfitness.com site had a PageRank of 5, which is very good. (For the lowdown on PageRank, check out Chapter 14.)

- **As a general principle, links are good.** Almost all links help boost your PageRank, but in addition, links increase the chances of search engines finding you. The more links to your site, the more often searchbots will stumble across your site and index it.

- **Some of these directory sites get a lot of traffic.** Buzzle.com, for instance, is more or less the world's 1,700th most popular Web site. I know that sounds like a low rank, but with hundreds of millions of users online, and millions of Web sites, that's not bad. Some of these directories may be able to send you some really good traffic.

## Getting the link

After you've found a directory, you want to get the link. In some cases, you have to e-mail someone at the directory and ask. Many of these little directories are run by individuals and are often pretty crudely built. The problem you may run into is that it may take some time for the owner to get around to adding the link — the directory is just a hobby in many cases, after all.

Some directories have automated systems. Look for a Submit Your Site link, or maybe Add URL, Add Your Site, or something similar. The site may provide a form in which you enter your information. Some directories review the information before adding it to the directory, and in other, less common, situations, your information may post directly to the site.

By the way, some of these directories may ask you to pay to be added to the directory or give you preferential treatment if you pay.

### Should you pay?

Generally, no.

### Why not?

Look, it sometimes seems like everyone's trying to get you to pay these days. Every time you try to get a link somewhere, someone's asking for money. Buzzle.com, for example, a portal with all sorts of directories, wants you to pay $59 ("regularly" $99, though I'm not sure what or when regular is). That gets you into the index within seven days and gets you preferential placement.

The term *portal* is an Internet-geek term that, roughly translated, means "We've got all sorts of stuff on our site like news, and weather, and you know, *communities,* and, like, stuff, and we still have some of our dotcom cash left, which should keep us going a few more months while we try to figure out how to make money, and heck, if we don't, Uncle Joe still wants me to come work for him in his furniture store."

Of course that means Buzzle.com must have listings over which you can have preferential placement; in other words, you *can* get in for free. Scroll down the page a little, and you'll find the free Basic Submission.

I recommend that you do *not* pay for these placements, at least to begin with. In *most* cases, they simply aren't worth spending $60, $100, or more for the link. It's worth spending a few moments getting a free link, though. If a site asks you to pay, dig around and see if you can find a free-placement link. If not, just move on. (If the site can guarantee that you'll be on a page with a PageRank of 6 or 7 or more, the fee may be worth it. See Chapter 14 for more information about PageRank.)

At some point, it might, perhaps, be worthwhile to *consider* thinking about paying for such placements, but generally only if you know the site is capable of sending you valuable traffic.

### You don't have to pay

Luckily, you may find that some of the best directories are free. Take, for instance, the model rocket business. Hundreds of model rocket sites, often run by individuals or families, are on the Web. (See the site shown in Figure 13-2.) Many of these sites have link pages. Although these sites don't get huge numbers of visitors, they *do* get the right visitors (people interested in model rockets) and often have pretty good PageRanks. Most of these sites will give you a free listing, just for the asking. Look for a contact e-mail address somewhere.

**Figure 13-2:**
It's ugly and doesn't get much traffic, but it does have a reasonable PageRank, and if you ask nicely, the site may give you a link. (It probably won't give me a link now, but maybe you'll get one.)

# *Working with the Yellow Pages*

The Yellow Pages companies don't know what's about to hit them. Yellow Pages are incredibly profitable. The biggest Yellow Pages companies make billions of dollars each year, with profits of many hundreds of millions. They're real cash cows, but they're about to get steamrollered.

It won't happen this year, or next year. But pretty soon the shakeup will begin. Millions of computer-literate, Internet-loving people no longer pick up a Yellow Pages book or, perhaps, pick one up once or twice a year, compared with several times a month in the pre-Internet days. Five or ten years from now, the number of people using the book will be declining precipitously, and businesses will realize it. Google is already experimenting with geographic searches, and in a few years, online searches for local businesses will be as convenient for searchers as using the paper Yellow Pages — better, actually. (I'm not suggesting that the Yellow Page companies will disappear, though, because they have one huge advantage: "Feet on the street." They have huge armies of salespeople talking to businesses every day.)

The Yellow Pages have, however, started their foray into the Internet. In fact, several Yellow Pages sites are incredibly important already. It may make sense for you to list your Web site with the Yellow Pages sites — especially if your business already buys Yellow Pages ads.

You rarely hear much about the Yellow Pages sites in discussions about search engines, but they *are* search engines. Directories, anyway. And they're incredibly important ones, too. Billions of searches are carried out every year through the Yellow Pages sites.

Table 13-1 has the largest Yellow Pages sites and their Alexa traffic ranks, indicating the sites' overall popularity.

### Table 13-1: Largest Yellow Pages Sites

| Site | URL | Alexa Rank |
| --- | --- | --- |
| Yahoo! Yellow Pages | yp.yahoo.com | 1 |
| InfoSpace | www.infospace.com | 184 |
| WorldPages.com | www.worldpages.com | 424 |
| SBC SMARTPages | www.yellowpages.com | 646 |
| BellSouth RealPages.com | www.yellowpages.com | 1,210 |
| Yell.com | http://yell.com | 1,296 |
| YellowPages.com | www.yellowpages.com | 1,595 |
| DexOnline.com | www.dexonline.com | 1,651 |
| Verizon SuperPages | http://superpages.com | 18,797 |
| Yellowbook.com | www.yellowbook.com | 22,002 |
| Yellow.com | www.yellow.com | 28,944 |

The advantage to using Yellow Pages sites? They generate lots of local searches. If you own a shoe shop, for example, potential customers are more likely to find you through a Yellow Pages site than through a search engine.

The disadvantages? They're expensive. Basic listings are free because the basic listings come from the paper Yellow Pages, and all business phone customers get a free basic listing. But these basic listings don't have links to your Web site, so however useful they are for generating phone calls, they won't generate clicks. For that, you'll have to pay. An ad like the one shown in Figure 13-3, for instance, will cost you $300 a year on YellowPages.com. On the real Yellow Pages sites, the ones owned by the companies publishing Yellow Pages directories, ads can often be much more.

**Figure 13-3:**
Is it worth
$300 a year?
Sorry, I
really don't
know!

**Eddy Rentals**
1234 North Grassy Lane
Anytown, USA
Phone: (555) 555-1234
Fax: (555) 555-4321

Call us today for an immediate quote. We are available 24
hours a day, with years of experience to better serve you!

Email  Website  Map

# Getting into the Yellow Pages

You can get your business into a Yellow Pages site three ways:

- ✔ **Get a business phone line.** You get your free listing in the local Yellow Pages book, which also gets your listing in the online Yellow Pages. As with the book, this is just a simple listing, with no extras.

- ✔ **Buy a listing or ad through your local Yellow Pages rep.** This is the same guy selling you space in the paper book.

- ✔ **Sign up directly through the Web site.** Some Yellow Page sites allow businesses to buy an ad directly through their Web sites; look for an Advertise With Us link or similar.

The Yellow Pages companies share listings. If you have a business phone in Colorado, your listing is in a QwestDex paper book, ends up on Dex Online.com, and also ends up in the Verizon SuperPages.com site, as shown in Figure 13-4.

I recommend that if your company already buys Yellow Pages ads and your business is *geo-specific* — that is, you're trying to attract buyers in a particular area — you should look into using the Yellow Pages. Talk to your rep. The rep should be able to tell you how many searches are carried out in the company's online Yellow Pages, in a particular category and a particular region, each month. From that information, you may be able to decide if purchasing an ad makes sense.

The online Yellow Pages companies sell a variety of services, such as the following. You can see some of these in Figure 13-5.

- ✔ A link from the listing in the online Yellow Pages to your Web site. The search engines probably will not recognize it as a link to your site; rather, you get a *servlet link* that forwards people to your site through the Yellow Page's server.

- ✔ An e-mail link.

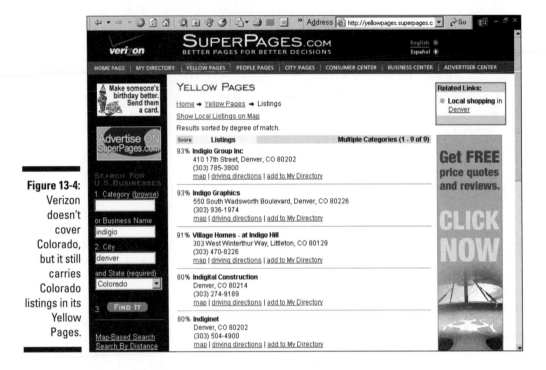

✔ A page with detailed information, such as a map to your location, information about your products and services, payment options, and so on.

✔ A link to a picture of your ad that appears in the paper Yellow Pages.

✔ A pop-up promo box that appears when someone points at an icon, and that can be modified through an online-management system.

✔ A link to a coupon that customers can print.

## Buy online

You can sign up online for ads at, for instance, YellowPages.com. But this isn't a *real* Yellow Pages site. It's not owned or operated by a company that makes Yellow Page books. It's also ugly and hard to use. (I'm shy, and don't like to upset anyone, so I won't tell you what I really think about the site.) On the other hand, some of the bigger sites, owned by major Yellow Pages companies have recently begun allowing businesses to buy advertising online. In some cases you can request a quote online, but your information is probably sent to a real-live rep who then calls you. (Traditional Yellow Pages companies often have agreements with the sales-reps unions that make direct online sales impossible.)

Click here to view an image of the ad in the Yellow Pages book.

Click here to go to
a company's Web site.

Click here to view details
about this company.

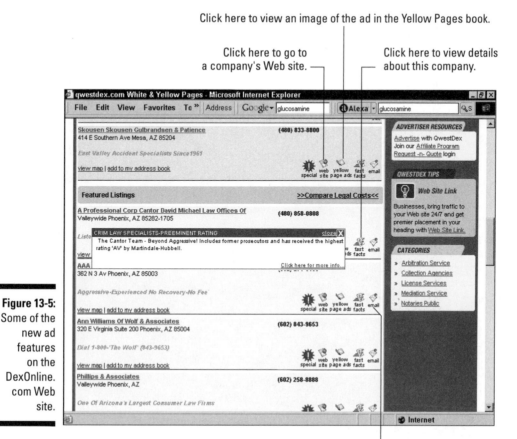

**Figure 13-5:**
Some of the
new ad
features
on the
DexOnline.
com Web
site.

Click here to send an e-mail to the company.

As I've already mentioned, these ads can be pricey. You pay by the month
for each component — maybe $30 a month for a link to your Web site, $30
for a detailed information page, $20 for an e-mail link, and so on. (Rates vary
among companies.) Such advertising probably makes sense if you are a
dedicated advertiser in the paper Yellow Pages and find it works for you.
The online version may work, too. Dedicated users of the Yellow Pages are
moving online, and the Yellow Pages companies are spending millions of
dollars in an effort to encourage people to use their sites.

# Part IV
# After You've Submitted Your Site

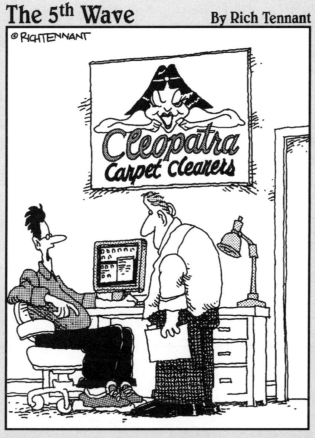

The 5th Wave      By Rich Tennant

Cleopatra Carpet Cleaners

"So far our web presence has been pretty good. We've gotten some orders, a few inquiries, and nine guys who want to date our logo."

# In this part . . .

Submitting your site to the search engines isn't enough. It doesn't guarantee that they'll include your site, and it doesn't guarantee that your site will rank well. So this part of the book is essential to your success. In particular, you must understand the value of links pointing to your Web site.

Search engines use links to find your site, to figure out what your site is about, and to estimate how valuable your site is. Search engine optimization without a link campaign is like looking for a job without a résumé: You may make contact, but you won't close the deal. In this part, you discover the different ways search engines use links, and then you find out how to get those all-important incoming links.

But this part of the book has more. You find out about the shopping directories, specialized systems that index commercial products (and, in a few cases, services) — from Froogle and Google Catalogs, to Shopping.com and Yahoo! Shopping. If you're selling online, you must know about these systems.

Finally, this part provides information that helps you make the most of a pay-per-click (PPC) advertising campaign. Billions of dollars are being spent on paid placement search results. Many companies use these ads very successfully, while others lose money. Read this part to find out how to be part of the right group!

# Chapter 14

# Using Link Popularity to Boost Your Position

. . . . . . . . . . . . . . . . . . . . . . . . . . . . . . . . . . . . . . . . . .

. . . . . . . . . . . . . . . . . . . . . . . . . . . . . . . . . . . . . . . . . .

*T*housands of site owners have experienced the frustration of not being able to get search engines to index their sites. You build a Web site, you do your best to optimize it for the search engines, you register in the search engines, and then nothing much happens. Little or no traffic turns up at your site, your pages don't rank well in the search engines, and in some cases, you can't even find your pages in the search engines. What's going on?

Here's the opposite scenario: You have an existing site and find a few other sites to link to it. You make no changes to the pages themselves, yet all of a sudden you notice your pages jump up in the search engines.

There's a lot of confusion about links and their relationship to Web sites. Most site owners don't even realize that links have a bearing on their search engine positions. Surely all you need to do is register your page in a search engine and it will be indexed, right? Maybe, maybe not. This chapter takes the confusion out of links by showing you the ways they can help, and the things you need to know to make them work.

# Why Search Engines Like Links

A few years ago, pretty much all you had to do to get your site listed in a search engine — and maybe even ranked well — was register with the search engine. Then along came Google in 1998, and that all changed. Google decided to use the links from other Web sites as another factor in determining if the site was a good match for a search. Each link to a site was a vote for the site, and the more votes the site received, the better a site was regarded by Google.

To rank well today, you probably need to use links to *vote* the site up in the search engines. Links pointing to a Web page do several things:

- ✔ **Links make it easier for search engines to find the page.** As the searchbots travel around the Web, they follow links. They index a page, follow the links on that page to other pages, index those pages, follow the links on those pages, and so on. The more links to a page, the more likely the page is picked up and indexed by the search engines, and the more quickly it happens.

- ✔ **Search engines use the number of links pointing to a page as an indication of the page's value.** If lots of pages link to your page, the search engines place a greater value on your page than pages with few links pointing to them. If you have lots of links from sites that are themselves linked to by many other sites, search engines conclude that your site must *really* be important. (Google calls this value the page's *PageRank*, but Google is not the only search engine to use links as an indication of value; Yahoo!, for instance, has something called *Web Rank*.)

- ✔ **Links provide information to the search engines about the page they're pointing to.** The link text often contains keywords that search engines can use to glean additional information about your page. The theme of the site pointing to your site also gives search engines an indication of your site's theme. For example, if you have links from hundreds of rodent-related Web sites, it's a good bet that your site has something to do with rodents.

- ✔ **Links not only bring searchbots to a page, but may also bring *people* to the page.** The whole purpose of your search engine campaign is to bring people to your site, right? Sometimes people will actually click the links and arrive at your site.

Links are very important. Sometimes they mean the difference between being indexed by a search engine and not being indexed, and between being ranked well in a search engine and not being ranked well. In this chapter, I delve into this subject, a topic often broadly known as *link popularity,* to give you a good understanding of what links are all about. In Chapter 15, you discover *how* to get other sites to link to yours.

Backlinks are an integral part of the optimization of your Web site. A *back-link* — this may surprise you — is a link back to your site. Search engines look at backlinks to figure out what your site is about and how important it is. Links aren't something detached from your site; they're an integral part *of* your site.

Think of your Web site in terms of a regional map: Your site is the major city, and backlinks are the roads bringing traffic into the city. A geographer looking at the map wouldn't regard the city and roads as separate entities; they are all part of the same economic and social system. So don't think of the links pointing to your site as something "out there"; they are a critical part of your site. Here's an indication of just how important Google considers links to be: The original name of the Google search engine, before it was officially launched, was *BackRub,* so named for its ability to analyze backlinks. (Fortunately, the founders changed the name.)

The search engines are trying to figure out what site or page is the best match for a search. As you discover later in this chapter, search engines use links as one way to determine this. As with content though (discussed in Chapter 9), using the number of links to and from a site to measure significance is an imperfect method. A page can conceivably be the best page on a particular subject, yet have few links to it. Just because I publish a page today doesn't mean it's worse than a page that was published five years ago and now has many links to it. However, search engines have difficulty figuring out what the searcher needs, so they have to use what information is available to them. Using links is a way of recruiting Web site owners to help point out useful sites and pages. The strategy is imperfect, but that's the search engine world we're living in.

# Understanding Page Value and PageRank

Search engines assign a value to your site based on the links pointing to it. The most popular term for this kind of ranking is *PageRank,* which Google uses. The *PageRank* is a value that Google gives to a page, based on the number and type of links into the page.

PageRank is used frequently in the search engine optimization field for several reasons.

- ✔ Google is the world's most important search engine, and will remain so for the foreseeable future.
- ✔ You don't need a PhD to figure out a page's PageRank. The Google toolbar — the handy little tool I show you how to download in Chapter 1 — shows you the currently loaded page's PageRank. (Okay, strictly speaking that's not true, but it does provide an *indication* of the PageRank.)

✔ We also have a good idea of how PageRank is calculated. Sergey Brin and Lawrence Page, founders of Google, published a paper about the algorithm while at Stanford University. It's unclear whether the algorithm used by Google is exactly the same as the one they published, but it's likely to be similar.

Although this section focuses on PageRank, other search engines use similar rankings, and the things you do with links that boost your PageRank also help boost your site with other search engines.

## *PageRank — One part of the equation*

Keep in mind that the PageRank value is just one part of how Google determines which pages to show you when you search for something. I want to stress that point because so many people get really hung up on PageRank. A low PageRank is often an indicator of problems, and a high PageRank is an indicator that you're doing something right, but PageRank itself is just a small part of how Google ranks your pages.

When you type a search term into Google and click Search, Google starts looking through its database for pages with the words you've typed. Then it examines each page to decide which pages are most relevant to your search. Google considers many characteristics: what the <TITLE> tag says, how the keywords are treated (are they bold or italic or in bulleted lists?), where the keywords sit on the page, and so on. It *also* considers PageRank. Clearly it's possible for a page with a low PageRank to rank higher than one with a high PageRank in some searches. When that happens, it simply means that the value provided by the high PageRank isn't enough to outweigh the value of all the other characteristics of the page that Google considered.

I like to think of PageRank as a tiebreaker. Imagine a situation in which you have a page that, using all other forms of measurement, ranks as equally well as a competitor's page. Google has looked at both pages, found the same number of keywords in the same sorts of positions, and thinks both pages are equally good matches for a particular keyword search. However, your competitor's page has a higher PageRank than yours. Which page will rank higher in a Google search for that keyword? Your competitor's.

Many people claim PageRank isn't important, and that site owners often focus too much on PageRank (that may be true). But PageRank, or something similar, definitely *is* a factor. As Google has said:

> "The heart of our software is PageRank(tm), a system for ranking web pages developed by our founders Larry Page and Sergey Brin at Stanford University. And while we have dozens of engineers working to improve every aspect of Google on a daily basis, PageRank continues to provide the basis for all of our web search tools."

---

### Pulling rank

By the way, you could be forgiven for thinking that the term *PageRank* comes from the idea of, well, ranking pages. Google claims, however, that it comes from the name of one of the founders of Google and authors of the original PageRank document, Larry Page. (The other founder is Sergey Brin.) The truth is probably somewhere in between. Otherwise, why isn't it the PageBrinRank?

---

So Google claims that PageRank *is* in use and *is* important. (It's likely that the current algorithm is not quite the same as the original, but it's probably similar.) But you need to keep its significance in perspective. It's still only part of the story.

Remember that it all comes down to what the searcher is searching for. A page that ranks well for one keyword or phrase may rank poorly for another.

## *The PageRank algorithm*

I want to quickly show you the PageRank algorithm; but don't worry, I'm not going to get hung up on it. In fact, you really don't need to be able to read and follow it, as I explain in a moment. Here it is:

PR (A) = (1 − d) + d (PR (t1) / C (t1) + ... + PR (tn) / C (tn))

Where:

PR = PageRank
A = Web page A
d = A damping factor, usually set to 0.85
t1...tn = Pages linking to Web page A
C = The number of outbound links from page tn

I could explain all this to you, honestly I could. But I don't want to. And furthermore, I don't have to because you don't need to be able to read the algorithm. For instance, do you recognize this equation?

$$F_{ij} = G \frac{M_i M_j}{D_{ii}^2}$$

Don't think you can kid me. I know you don't know what this is. (Well, okay, maybe you do, but I'll bet over 95 percent of my readers don't.) It is the Law of Universal Gravitation, which explains how gravity works. I can't explain this equation to you, but I really don't care, because I've been using gravity for some time now without the benefit of understanding the jumble of letters. The other day, for instance, while walking down the street, someone shoved a flyer into my hand. After walking on, glancing at the flyer, and realizing that I didn't want it in my hand, I held it over a trash can, opened my hand, and used gravity to remove it from my hand and deposit it into the trash can. Simple.

Rather than take you through the PageRank algorithm step by step, here are a few key points that explain more or less how it works:

- ✔ **As soon as a page enters the Google index, it has an intrinsic PageRank.** Admittedly, the PageRank is very small, but it's there.

- ✔ **A page has a PageRank only if it's indexed by Google.** Links to your site from pages that have not yet been indexed are effectively worthless, as far as PageRank goes.

- ✔ **When you place a link on a page, pointing to another page, the page with the link is voting for the page it's pointing to.** These votes are how PageRank increases. As a page gets more and more links into it, its PageRank grows.

- ✔ **Linking to another page doesn't reduce the PageRank of the origin page, but it does increase the PageRank of the receiving page.** It's sort of like a company's shareholders meeting, at which people with more shares have more votes. They don't lose their shares when they vote. But the more shares they have, the more votes they can place.

- ✔ **Pages with no links out of them are wasting PageRank; they don't get to vote for other pages.** Because a page's inherent PageRank is not terribly high, this isn't normally a problem. It becomes a problem if you have a large number of links to dangling pages of this kind. Or it can be a problem if you have a dangling page with a high PageRank. Though rare, this could happen if you have a page that many external sites link to that then links directly to an area of your site that won't benefit from PageRank, such as a complex e-commerce catalog system that Google can't index or an external e-commerce system hosted on another site. Unless the page links to other pages inside your Web site, it won't be voting for those pages and thus won't be able to raise their PageRank.

- ✔ **A single link from a dangling page can channel that PageRank back into your site.** Make sure that all your pages have at least one link back into the site. This usually isn't a problem because most sites are built with common navigation bars and often text links at the bottom of the page.

✔ **You can increase a site's overall PageRank two ways:**

- Increase the number of pages in the site, although it's a small increase because the inherent PageRank of a new page is low.

- Get links to the site from outside.

✔ **The page receiving the inbound link gets the greatest gain.** Thus, ideally, you want links into your most important pages — pages you want ranked in the search engines. PageRank is then spread through links to other pages in the site, but these secondary pages get less of the boost.

It's important to understand that Web sites don't have PageRanks, Web *pages* have PageRanks. It's possible for a site's home page to have a high PageRank, while internal pages have very low ranks.

Here are a couple of important implications from this:

✔ **You can vote large amounts of PageRank through your site with a single link.** A page with a PageRank of 5 can pass that on to another page as long as it doesn't split the vote by linking to other pages.

When I use the term *pass*, I use it in the sense of passing on a virus, not passing a baton. You can pass PageRank from page to page. Linking from page A to page B passes PageRank from A to B in the same way that person A may pass a cold to person B. Person A doesn't get rid of the cold when he passes it to B; he's still got it. And page A still has its PageRank when it passes PageRank on to page B.

✔ **You can ensure PageRank is well distributed around your Web site by including lots of links.** Linking every page to every other page is the most efficient way to ensure even PageRank around the site.

## Getting details

If you want all the nasty, complicated details about PageRank, you can find a number of sources of information online. One description of PageRank that I like is at the WebWorkshop site (www.webworkshop.net/pagerank.html). This site also provides a calculator that shows you the effect on PageRank of linking between pages in your site. Or you can get the lowdown on PageRank from the horse's mouth: Read *The PageRank Citation Ranking: Bringing Order to the Web* by Sergey Brin and Lawrence Page, the founders of Google. Search on the document's title at Google.

## Huge sites equal greater PageRank

Because every page is born with a PageRank (as soon as Google finds it, anyway), the more pages in your site, the greater the site's intrinsic PageRank. If you create a linking structure that links all your pages well, you'll be providing your pages with a high PageRank simply because you have many pages.

However, don't think of creating pages as a search engine strategy. You'd need a huge number of pages to make a difference. If you own or manage a site that already has hundreds of thousands of pages just because that's *what you do,* consider yourself lucky. But don't build hundreds of thousands of pages just to boost PageRank.

This fact does provide another reason for Web sites to retain old pages, perhaps in archives. A news site, for instance, should probably keep all news articles, even very old ones. Of course, massive repositories of data often have high PageRanks for another reason: because many other sites link to the data. Remove pages and you lose the links.

## Measuring PageRank

How can you discover a page's PageRank? You can use the Google toolbar. (I explain in a moment why you can never find out the *true* PageRank.) As I mention in Chapter 1, you should install the Google toolbar, which is available for download at `toolbar.google.com`. Each time you open a page in Internet Explorer 5.0 or later, you see the page's PageRank in a bar, as shown in Figure 14-1. If the bar is all white, the PageRank is 0. If it's all green, the PageRank is 10. You can estimate PageRank simply by looking at the position of the green bar, or you can mouse over the bar, and a pop-up appears with the PageRank number.

If the PageRank component isn't on your toolbar, click the Options button to open the Toolbar Options dialog box, select the PageRank checkbox, and click OK.

If you don't have the Google toolbar, you can still check PageRank. Search for the term **pagerank tool** to find various sites that allow you to enter a URL and get the PageRank. Mozilla's FireFox browser also has *extensions* that display the page rank in the status bar of every page.

**Figure 14-1:**
The
PageRank
bar on the
Google
toolbar
shows
PageRank.

Here are a few things to understand about this toolbar:

- **Sometimes the bar is gray.** Sometimes when you look at the bar, it's grayed out. Some people believe that this means Google is somehow penalizing the site by withholding PageRank. I've never seen this happen, though. I believe the bar is simply buggy, and that PageRank is just not being passed to the bar for some reason. Every time I've seen the bar grayed out, I've been able to open the Web page in another browser window (you may have to try two or three) and view the PageRank.

- **Sometimes the toolbar guesses.** Sometimes the toolbar guesses a PageRank. You may occasionally find it being reported for a page that isn't even in the Google index. It seems that Google may be coming up with a PageRank for a page on the fly, based on the PageRank of other pages in the site that have already been indexed.

  Also, note that Google has various data centers around the world, and because they're not all in sync, with data varying among them, it's possible for one person looking at a page's PageRank to see one number, while someone else sees another number.

- **A white bar is not a penalty.** Another common PageRank myth is that Google penalizes pages by giving them PageRanks of 0. That is, if you see a page with a PageRank of 0, something is wrong with the page, and if you link to the page, your Web page may be penalized, too. This is simply not true. Most of the world's Web pages show a PageRank of 0. That's not to say that Google won't take away PageRank if it wants to penalize a page or site for some reason. I'm just saying you can't know if it's a penalty or if it's simply a page with few valuable links pointing in.

- **Zero is not zero, and ten is not ten.** Although commonly referred to as *PageRank,* and even labeled as such, the number you see in the Google toolbar is not the page's actual PageRank. It's simply a number indicating the approximate position of the page on the PageRank range. Therefore, pages never have a PageRank of 0, even though most pages show 0 on the toolbar, and a page with a rank of, say, 2 might actually have a PageRank of 25 or 100.

The true PageRank scale is probably a logarithmic scale. Thus, the distance between PageRank 5 and 6 is much greater than the difference between 2 and 3. The consensus of opinion among people who like to discuss these things is that the PageRank shown on the toolbar is probably on a logarithmic scale with a base of around 5 or 6, or perhaps even lower.

Suppose, for a moment, that the base is actually 5. That means that a page with a PageRank of 0 shown on the toolbar may have an actual PageRank somewhere between a fraction of 1 and just under 5. If the PageRank shown is 1, the page may have a rank between 5 and just under 25; if 2 is shown, the number may be between 25 and just under 125, and so on. A page with a rank of 9 or 10 shown on the toolbar most likely has a true PageRank in the millions. With base 5, for instance, the toolbar PageRank numbers would represent true PageRanks, as shown in Table 14-1.

| Table 14-1 | Pure Conjecture — What Toolbar PageRanks Would Represent if PageRank Were a Logarithmic Scale Using Base 5 |
|---|---|
| *Toolbar PageRank* | *True PageRank* |
| 0 | 0–5 |
| 1 | 5–25 |
| 2 | 25–125 |
| 3 | 125–625 |
| 4 | 625–3,125 |
| 5 | 3,125–15,625 |
| 6 | 15,625–78,125 |
| 7 | 78,125–390,625 |
| 8 | 390,625–1,953,125 |
| 9 | 1,953,125–9,765,625 |
| 10 | 9,765,625–48,828,125 |

The maximum possible PageRank, and thus this scale, continually changes as Google recalculates PageRank. As pages are added to the index, the PageRank has to go up.

How can you be sure that the numbers on the toolbar are not the true PageRank? The PageRank algorithm simply doesn't work on a scale of 1 to 10 on a Web that contains billions of Web pages. And, perhaps more practically, it's not logical to assume that sites such as Yahoo! and Google have PageRanks just slightly above small, privately owned sites. I have pages with ranks of 6 or 7, for instance, whereas the BBC Web site, the world's 25th most popular Web site according to Alexa, has a PageRank of 9. It's not reasonable to assume that its true PageRank is just 50 percent greater than pages on one of my little sites.

Here are two important points to remember about the PageRank shown on the Google toolbar:

- Two pages with the same PageRank shown on the toolbar may actually have very different true PageRanks. One may have a PageRank of a fifth or sixth, or maybe a quarter, of the other.

- It gets progressively harder to push a page to the next PageRank level on the toolbar. Getting a page to 1 or 2 is pretty easy, but to push it to 3 or 4 is much harder (though certainly possible), and to push it to the higher levels is very difficult indeed. To get to 8 or above is rare.

## Leaking PageRank

It's possible for PageRank to *leak* out of a site, despite the fact that pages don't lose PageRank when they link to other pages. Here's how: Each time you link from one page to another, the origin page is voting for the recipient page. Thus, a link from one page in your site to another page in your site is a vote for that other page. If you link to a page on another site, you're voting for another site's page rather than your site's page.

Suppose that you have a page with a PageRank of 10,000 and it has 40 links on it. Each link is getting a PageRank vote of 250 ($250 \times 40 = 10,000$). Now suppose that half the links on the page are external. In that case, you're taking 5,000 votes and pointing to pages out of your site rather than inside your site. So PageRank leaks in the sense that your overall site PageRank is lower.

As a general rule, you should worry more about getting backlinks to your site from appropriate Web sites than about how much PageRank is leaking through your outgoing links. You can build PageRank quickly by using the techniques in Chapter 15, and in most cases, worrying about outgoing links won't save you much PageRank. Still, you can do two simple things to help reduce *rank leak:*

- If you have a page with lots of outgoing links, make sure it also has links to the other pages in your site. You'll be splitting the vote that way between outgoing and internal links, instead of passing all of it on through outgoing links.

- Ideally, you want the page with the external links to be one with a low PageRank, reducing the outgoing votes. You can do that by minimizing the number of links from other pages on your site into the link page.

By the way, it's possible to create links that the search engines won't follow; use the `rel` attribute, like this:

```
<a href=http://www.domainname.com/page.html rel="nofollow">
          Link Text</a>
```

Tell the search engines not to follow the link, and what exactly will they do? They ignore the link. It will be as if the link were never there. They won't bother following the link to the referenced page, and they won't use the information to index the page in any way. No PageRank, Web Rank, or equivalent benefit, and no benefit from the keywords in the link.

## Page relevance

*Page relevance* is harder to measure. The idea is that a link from a page that is related in some way to your page is more valuable than a link from a page that is entirely unrelated. A link to your rodent-racing site from a Web site that is also related to rodent racing is more valuable than, say, a link from your Aunt Edna's personal Web site.

The problem with PageRank is that it's independent of keywords. The value is a number derived from links pointing at a page, but it has no relation whatsoever to a specific keyword. Just because a page has a high PageRank doesn't mean it's the type of page you're looking for when you search for a particular keyword.

Thus, the search engines add something else to the mix: *relevance* or *context*. The major search engines are attempting to do this sort of analysis by matching keywords. In effect, the search engines are trying to create what have been termed *context-sensitive PageRanks* or *topic-sensitive PageRanks*. A topic-sensitive PageRank is dependent on a particular topic. Rather than counting any and all links, only links from relevant Web sites are included.

One way the search engines are probably trying to do this sort of thing is by using the Open Directory Project directory to provide some context. Because Web sites listed in the directory have been put into categories, it gives the search engines a starting point to figure out what keywords and sites relate to what categories.

Because the search engines use the Open Directory Project and Yahoo! Directory to help figure out what category you're related to, this is yet another reason it's important to be in these two directories.

This discussion is getting complicated now, and you really don't need to know the details. But if you want to read a little geek stuff related to relevance or context, search for a paper titled "Topic-Sensitive PageRank" by Taher Haveliwala of Stanford University.

My feeling is that this sort of technology isn't as advanced as many believe or as advanced as the search engines want you to believe. Still, people in the search engine business swear that links from related sites are more valuable than links from unrelated sites. Or, to be more precise, links from sites that a search engine *thinks* are related are more valuable than those from sites that a search engine *thinks* are unrelated. Because the technology is imprecise, search engines don't always get it right. The fact is that no search engine really knows for sure if one site is related to another; it can only guess. As with everything else, relevance is just one ingredient in the mix.

Don't let anyone tell you that links from unrelated sites have no value. A link from an unrelated site helps search engines find your pages, boosts PageRank, and may even bring visitors to your site. These links just won't have the extra boost provided by relevance.

As I discuss in more detail in Chapter 15, the ideal link is one from a related Web site, not just any old Web site you can convince to link to you. The most powerful *link hubs* — networks of interlinked Web sites — are those that are tightly focused on a particular topic. The search engines respect that, want to uncover such situations and rank the target sites more highly, and are probably getting better every day at doing so.

# Hubs and Neighborhoods

Search engines are also looking for what may be thought of as Web *neighborhoods* or *communities* or *hubs* — groups of Web sites related to a particular subject, and the sites that appear to be most central. If you're positioned in the middle of a cloud or web of Web sites related to a particular subject, that's a good thing.

Imagine a chart showing the world's rodent-racing Web sites and how they're connected. In this chart, little boxes represent all the Web sites and lines connect the boxes to show links between the sites. (Figure 14-2 gives an example of such a chart.) Some of the boxes seem to be sitting by themselves — very few links are going out, and very few are coming in. Other boxes have lots of links going out of them, but few other boxes are linking back to them. Now imagine your rodent-racing site. It seems to be the hub; your box has lots of links going out, and lots of links coming in. That would look pretty important on a chart. Wouldn't you think the search engines would find that interesting? In fact, search engines are trying to figure out this sort of thing all the time, so if you can build links to turn your site into a hub, that's a great thing!

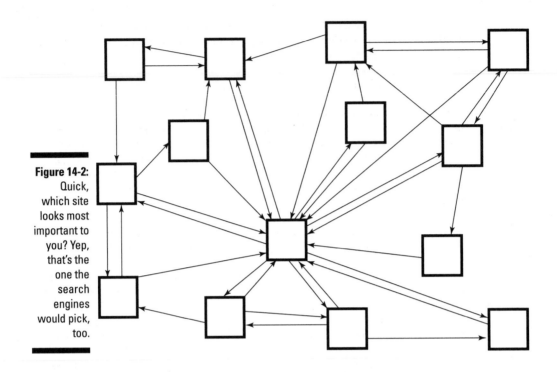

**Figure 14-2:**
Quick,
which site
looks most
important to
you? Yep,
that's the
one the
search
engines
would pick,
too.

# *Recognizing Links with No Value*

Some links have no value:

- ✔ If a page isn't in Google, the links from the page have no value. Google doesn't know about them, after all. (On the other hand, those pages may be in *other* search engines, so the links do have value on those engine's rankings.)

- ✔ If a page is what Google regards as a *link farm* (described in a moment), Google may know about the page but decide to exclude it from the index.

When site owners figured out that links were valuable, they started playing tricks to boost incoming links to their sites. Some tricks were so egregious that the search engines decided they were totally unacceptable. The trick you hear about most often is the *link farm,* an automated system that allows site owners to very quickly create thousands of incoming links by joining with thousands of other site owners to exchange links. Another trick is to create multiple *shadow domains* — small, well-optimized Web sites that redirect traffic into a single site — and link them all into one. The search engines don't like link farms and will exclude link-farm pages if they identify them.

However, as with much in the search-engine-optimization business, another myth has arisen over this subject. You may hear that if a link is found to your site from a link farm, you will be penalized.

Let me set the record straight: Search engines do not penalize sites for incoming links. They can't, or it would encourage dirty tricks. Want to push a competitor's site down so your site can beat it? Then link to it from as many link farms as you can. Obviously it wouldn't make sense for the search engines to encourage this sort of thing, so links from such pages won't hurt your site — though they won't help it, either. On the other hand, links *to* such sites may hurt you. Because you do have control over links from your site to others, if a search engine decides that you are linking to a bad neighborhood, it may penalize you.

The bottom line is that you should avoid working with link farms because they could potentially harm you, and they won't help you anyway.

Do search engines ever penalize? Sure. But with billions of Web pages in the large indexes, these penalties have to be automated (though you can report cheating to the search engines, and the offending site may be reviewed). In order to automate penalties, search engines have to create a very loose system that penalizes only the very worst offenses, or they risk penalizing innocent people. The proof is that if you spend time searching through the major search engines, you will find many pages that clearly break the rules, yet which are still included in the indexes.

## *Identifying links that aren't links*

I've seen this happen many times. Someone gets a link to his site from another site with a high PageRank, perhaps a perfectly related site, and is excited: That's a great vote for his site, isn't it? Then some jerk, perhaps me, has to burst his bubble and point out that, actually, no, it's not going to have the slightest effect on his site because it turns out the link is not a link.

When is a link not a link? In cases such as these:

- ✔ The link has been created such that the search engines can't read it.
- ✔ The link points somewhere else, perhaps to a program on someone else's Web site, which then forwards the browser to your site.

Here is an example:

```
http://ad.doubleclick.net/clk;6523085;7971444;q?http://
         www.yoursite.com
```

This link passes through an ad server hosted by an advertising company called DoubleClick. When someone clicks this link, which may be placed on a banner ad, for instance, a message goes to a program on the `ad.doubleclick.net` ad server, which logs the click and then forwards the browser to `www.your domain.com`. You may think this is a link to `www.yourdomain.com`, and it may work like one, but as far as the search engine is concerned, it's really a link to `ad.doubleclick.net`.

Here's another example: Suppose the person creating a link to your site doesn't want the search engine to be able to read the link. This person may be trying to get as many incoming links as possible while avoiding outgoing links, so he does something like this:

```
<SCRIPT LANGUAGE="JavaScript">
<!--
document.write("Visit <A HREF='http://www.yourdomain.com/'>
Joe's Rodent Racing site here</A>.")
//-->
</SCRIPT>
```

The author is using a JavaScript to write the link onto the page. You can see the link, other visitors can see it, and the link works when clicked upon. But search engines won't read the JavaScript, and they won't know there's a link there. What appears to be a perfectly normal link on a Web page is invisible to the search engines. So it does your site no good as far as PageRank or any other link-popularity algorithm goes.

Here's another form of link that the search engines can't read:

```
<A HREF="#" class=results
         onclick="window.open('searchresult-
temp1.php?CS=cddzdzdrzfzpzpdc&SRCH=134893378&YD=0.88&RK=
3&PID=16&URL=yourdomain.com','merch','Height=' +
screen.availHeight + ',Width=' + screen.availWidth +
',left=0,top=0,scrollbars=yes,status=yes,toolbar=yes,
directories=yes,menubar=yes,location=yes,resizable=yes',
false)";>Everything About Rodent Racing!</A>
```

This is a real <A> link tag. However, it doesn't use the HREF= *attribute* to point to a Web page. Rather, it uses a JavaScript onclick event handler to make it work. The JavaScript runs a program that, in this case, loads the page into another window. Again, the link works in most browsers, but search engines won't see it.

Incidentally, it's also possible to do the reverse: to make links appear to the search engines to be links to your site when actually they're links to another site. For instance, look at the following link, created by a system called Links4Trade.com, which you find out about in Chapter 15:

```
<A HREF="http://www.yourdomain.com?cid=33003&refid=
139782&link=www%2Eyourdomain%2Ecom" onClick="return
rewrite(this);" class="">Joe's Rodent Racing</A>
```

This link starts off well, showing `yourdomain.com` as the page being linked
to. In fact, if you took the URL from the `HREF=` and pasted it into a browser, it
would work properly. However, when someone clicks the link, the JavaScript
`onClick` event handler runs, taking the domain and passing it through to a
JavaScript function called `rewrite`. Because the search engines don't read
JavaScripts, they don't see what really happens when someone clicks the link.
(In this example, the click runs through a program on the Links4Trade.com
site, which tracks how many people use the link.) The search engines think it's
a link to your site, and I guess it is in a sense, but it has to pass through a program on a different site first.

## Pinpointing more valuable links

It seems likely that search engines — and Google in particular — regard
some links as more valuable than others. And it seems very likely to me that
they — and Google in particular — will tighten up the way they regard links.
Because the search engines keep their techniques secret, the following practices may already be in use or could be soon:

- ✔ Links inside paragraphs of text are likely regarded as more valuable than
  links in large lists or links set apart from text.

- ✔ The search engines could compare incoming links with outgoing links,
  and downgrade a page or site if it appears to do a lot of reciprocal linking from link pages.

- ✔ Links pointing to a page inside a site might be valued more highly than
  links to the home page.

- ✔ Outgoing links concentrated on a few pages might be valued less than
  links spread around a site.

# Inserting Keywords into Links

As Chapter 5 makes abundantly clear, keywords in your pages are very
important. But keywords *outside* your pages can also affect the page results.
That is, the keywords in *links* pointing to your site are very important.

---

# From the horses' mouths

Read this, from Sergey Brin and Lawrence Page, founders of Google:

"... anchors often provide more accurate descriptions of web pages than the pages themselves ... This idea of propagating anchor text to the page it refers to was implemented in the World Wide Web Worm [a search engine that pre-dates Google]

especially because it helps search non-text information, and expands the search coverage with fewer downloaded documents. We use anchor propagation mostly because anchor text can help provide better quality results."

*The Anatomy of a Large-Scale Hypertextual Web Search Engine,* 1998

---

If hundreds of links around the world point to one of your pages and all these links contain the words *rodent racing,* then search engines will get the idea that your pages are somehow related to rodent racing. It actually makes a lot of sense if you think about it. If hundreds of site owners create links pointing to your site, and, in effect, say, "This site I'm pointing to is about rodent racing," then Google is being given a darn good clue regarding what your site is about! In effect, Google has recruited site owners to tell it what other owners' sites are about.

Link text, in geek terminology, is known as *anchor text.* The link tag is an <A> tag, and the *A* stands for *anchor.* Thus, you may, if you hang around in geek company, hear links referred to as *anchors.*

In other words, Google and other search engines use links to get an idea of what the pages are about. Links can even help search engines figure out what a document is about if they can't read it for some reason (though that's not really our primary concern here).

Now, wait a second. This is important. If a link pointing to your site can describe to a search engine what your site is about, you'd better do all you can to make sure the link says what you want it to say! Even if you don't own the site pointing to the one you're trying to optimize (or are trying to get another site owner or site manager to link to your site), it's in your interest to try to get the right keywords into the link!

## Looks like success

Just how powerful is putting keywords in links? I'm going to show you a couple of pages that rank very well for keywords that don't even appear in the pages. How could that be possible? It's all in the power of linking

First, search Google, Yahoo!, or MSN for the term *miserable failure*. The page that appears first, in all three cases, is www.white house.gov/president/gwbbio.html George Bush's bio page. This was done by a small group of people using links in blog pages. Despite the fact that this page contains neither the word *miserable,* nor the word *failure,* and certainly not the term *miserable failure,* a few dozen links with the words *miserable failure* in

the link text were enough to trick the major search engines.

This became big news, so the President's supporters tried to deflect attention from his page; thus you may also find links to Hilary Clinton's, Michael Moore's, and Jimmy Carter's pages.

Here's another example: Type the word *liar* into Google, and what comes up first? Tony Blair's bio (www.number-10.gov.uk/output/ Page4.asp). This doesn't work at Yahoo! or MSN, unless you search their British sites (www.yahoo.co.uk and www.msn.co. uk). Again, the word isn't in the page, it's all done with links.

As you browse the Web, take a close look at links on the sites you visit. Now that you know how critical it is to add keywords to links, you'll see that many links provide relatively little value to the sites they're pointing to. Sure, a link is better than no link, but a bad link could be better. Here are some of the problems you'll see:

- ✓ **Image links, including buttons or banners linking to sites:** Search engines can't read images, so they're not getting keywords from them. (You should add keywords to the ALT attributes to the image, but ALT text isn't weighted by the search engines as highly as link text.)

- ✓ **One- or two-word links, such as company names:** In most cases, company names don't help you in the search engines. Use the keywords your potential visitors and clients are using.

- ✓ **Combinations of descriptions and *click-here* links:** For instance: *For more information on rodent racing — rats, mice, gerbils, and any other kind of rodent racing — click here.* Wow, what a waste! All the keywords are there, they just have no link! Remember, click-here links are a total waste of hyperlink space.

# Recalling a Few Basic Rules about Links

**REMEMBER**

You know that links are valuable and can help boost your position in the search engines. But what sorts of links? Let me quickly summarize:

- ✔ Links from sites related to yours are often more valuable than links from unrelated sites. (Because the relevancy software is almost certainly imprecise, this is not always the case.)

- ✔ Links from pages with high PageRanks are much more valuable than from pages with low PageRanks.

- ✔ Virtually all incoming links to your site have some kind of value, even if the pages have a very low PageRank or are not contextual. It may not be much of a value, but it's there.

- ✔ The more outgoing links on a page that has a link pointing to your site, the lower the value of the link to your site. This is because the vote is being shared. Thus, in some cases, a link from a low-PageRank page with no other links may actually be more valuable than a link from a high-PageRank page with many links.

- ✔ Links are even more valuable when they include keywords because keywords tell the search engines what the referenced site is about.

- ✔ A link strategy that positions your site as an authority, or a *hub,* in a Web community or neighborhood can be a powerful way to get the attention of the search engines.

# Chapter 15

# Finding Sites to Link to Yours

· · · · · · · · · · · · · · · · · · · · · · · · · · · · · · · · · · · · · · · · · · · · · ·

· · · · · · · · · · · · · · · · · · · · · · · · · · · · · · · · · · · · · · · · · · · · · ·

*I*n Chapter 14, I explain the value of linking — why your site needs to have *backlinks,* links from other sites pointing to it. Now you have the problem of finding those sites.

Chapter 14 gives you some basic criteria. You need links from pages that are already indexed by the search engines. Pages with high PageRanks are more valuable than those with low PageRanks. Links from related sites may be more valuable, and so on. However, when searching for links, you probably don't want to be too fussy to start with. A link is a link. Contrary to popular opinion, links bring value, even links from unrelated sites.

It's common in the SEO business to say that only links from "relevant" sites have value, but I don't believe that's true. How do the search engines know which sites are relevant, and which are not? They don't. Sure, they can guess to some degree. But they can't be quite sure. So my philosophy is that every link from a page that is indexed by the search engines has some kind of value. Some will have a higher value than others, but don't get too hung up on relevance. And don't worry too much about PageRank; sure, if you can go after sites with high PageRanks first, do it, but often it makes sense to simply *go get links* and not worry too much about the rank of the linking page.

Use this chapter to go get links, and things will start happening. Your site will get more traffic, the search engines will pick it up, and you may find your pages rising in the search engine ranks.

# Controlling Your Links

Before you run off to look for links, think about what you want those links to *say*. In Chapter 14, I talk about how keywords in links are tremendously important. The position of a page in the search engines depends not only on the text within that page, but also on text on other pages that refer to that page — that is, the text in the links.

For instance, suppose your rodent-racing company is called Robertson Ellington. (These were the names of your first two racing rats, and they still have a special place in your heart. And you've always felt that the name has a distinguished ring to it.) You could ask people to give you links like this:

### Robertson Ellington
Everything you ever wanted to know about rodent racing — rodent-racing schedules, directions to rodent-racing tracks, rodent-racing clubs, and anything else you can imagine related to rodent racing

You got a few useful keywords into the description, but the link — Robertson Ellington — is the problem. The link text contains no keywords that count — are people searching for `Robertson Ellington`, or are they searching for `rodent racing`?

A better strategy is to change the link to include keywords. Keep the blurb below the link, but change the link to something like this:

### Rodent Racing — rats, stoats, mice, and all sorts of other rodent racing

Here are some strategies for creating link text:

- Start the link with the primary keyword or keyword phrase.
- Add a few other keywords if you want.
- Try to repeat the primary keyword or keyword phrase once in the link.
- Mix in a few other words.

You need to control the links as much as possible. You can do this a number of ways, but you won't always be successful:

- Provide a *Link to Us* page at your Web site. On this page, provide suggested links to your site — include the entire HTML tag so people can grab the information and drop it into their sites.

Remember that although links on logos and image buttons may be pretty, they don't help you in the search engines as much as text links do. You can add ALT text to the image, but ALT text is not as valuable as link text. Some site owners now distribute HTML code that creates not only image links but also small text links right below the images.

✔ When you contact people and ask them for links, provide them with the actual link you'd like to use.

✔ As soon as someone tells you he or she has placed a link, check it to see if the link says what you want. Immediately contact that person if it doesn't. He or she is more likely to change the link at that point than weeks or months later.

✔ Occasionally use a link-checking tool to find out who is linking to you and to see how the link appears. If necessary, contact the other party and ask if the link can be changed. (I mention some link-checking tools later in this chapter.)

Whenever possible, *you* should define what a link pointing to your site looks like, rather than leave it up to the person who owns the other site. Of course, you can't force someone to create links the way you want them, but sometimes if you ask nicely . . . .

Always use the www. portion of your URL when creating links to your site: http://www.yourdomain.com and not just http://yourdomain.com. Search engines regard the two addresses as different, even though in most cases they are actually pointing to the same page. So if you use both URLs, you are, in effect, splitting the vote for your Web site. The search engines will see a lower link popularity. (See Chapter 14 for a discussion of how links are votes.)

# Generating Links, Step by Step

Here is a quick summary of additional ways to get links; I describe them in detail next:

✔ **Register with search directories.** The Open Directory Project, and specialty directories, are not only important in their own right, but often also provide links that other search engines read.

✔ **Ask friends and family.** Get everyone you know to add a link.

✔ **Ask employees.** Ask employees to mention you.

✔ **Contact association sites.** Contact any professional or business association of which you're a member and ask for a link.

✔ **Contact manufacturers' Web sites.** Ask the manufacturers of any products you sell to place a link on their sites.

✔ **Contact companies you do business with.** Get on their client lists.

✔ **Ask to be a featured client.** I've seen sites get high PageRanks by being linked to from sites that feature them.

- ✓ **Submit to announcement sites and newsletters.** This includes sites such as URLwire (www.urlwire.com).

- ✓ **Send out press releases.** Sending out press releases, even if distributed through the free systems, can sometimes get you links.

- ✓ **Promote something on your site.** If you have something really useful, let people know about it!

- ✓ **Find sites linking to your competition.** If other sites link to your competition, they may link to you, too.

- ✓ **Ask other sites for links.** During your online travels, you may stumble across sites that really should mention your site, as a benefit to their visitors.

- ✓ **Make reciprocal link requests.** Ask other site owners to link to you, in exchange for a link to them.

- ✓ **Respond to reciprocal link requests.** Eventually, other people will start asking you to link swap.

- ✓ **Search for** keyword add url**.** You can find sites with links pages this way.

- ✓ **Use link-building software and services.** Try using a link-exchange program or service to speed up the process.

- ✓ **Contact e-mail newsletters.** Find appropriate e-mail newsletters and send them information about your site.

- ✓ **Mention your site in discussion groups.** Leave messages about your site in appropriate forums, with links to the site.

- ✓ **Respond to blogs**. Blog sites are often well indexed by search engines.

- ✓ **Pursue offline PR.** Getting mentioned in print often translates into being mentioned on the Web.

- ✓ **Give away content.** If you have lots of content, syndicate it.

- ✓ **Apply for online awards.** Sign up for site awards.

- ✓ **Advertise.** Sometimes ads provide useful links.

- ✓ **Use a service or buy links.** Some services sell links from high-PageRank sites.

- ✓ **Just wait.** Eventually links will appear, but you must prime the pump first.

These link-building strategies are ranked by priority in a very general way. One of the first things you should do is to ask friends and family for links, and one of the last is just wait. However, in between these first and last strategies, the priority will vary from business to business, person to person. You may feel that a strategy lower down on this list is important to do right away.

The next sections look at each of these link-generation methods.

# Register with search directories

In Chapter 12, I discuss getting links from directories, the Yahoo! Directory and the Open Directory Project. And in Chapter 13, I tell you about getting links from specialty directories. Links from directories are important not only because people will find you when searching at the various directories, but also because search engines often spider these directories.

Google, for instance, spiders both Yahoo! and the Open Directory Project. And the Open Directory Project results are syndicated to hundreds of smaller search engines, many of which Google reads. These links are also highly relevant because they're categorized within the directories; as you find out in Chapter 14, the search engines like relevant links. So if you haven't registered with the directories, you should probably consider that the first step in your link campaign.

# Ask friends and family

Ask everyone you know to give you a link. Many people now have their own Web sites or blogs — *Weblogs,* which I discuss in more detail in Chapter 9 and later in this chapter. Ask everyone you can think of to mention your site. Send them a short e-mail detailing what you'd like them to say. You may want to create a little bit of HTML that they can paste straight into their pages, perhaps with a link to a logo stored on your Web site so the logo appears in their pages. If you do this, you get to control the link text to ensure that it has keywords in it: *The best damn rodent racing site on the Web,* for instance, rather than *Click here to visit my friend's site.*

# Ask employees

Employees often provide a significant number of links back to their employer's Web site, often by accident. In particular, employees often mention their employer in discussion groups that get picked up by the search engines. So why not send an e-mail to all your employees, asking them to link to the company's site from their Web sites and blogs and to mention you in discussion groups? Again, you might give them a piece of HTML including an embedded logo.

You can also ask them to include a link to your site in the signature of their e-mails. The signature is the blurb you see at the bottom of e-mail messages, often containing contact information. (Ask them to add a full link — not just www.domainname.com, but http://www.domainname.com.) That way, whenever they post messages via e-mail to discussion groups, search engines may pick up the link. And you can also ask them to always use a signature with the link when posting via non-e-mail methods, such as posting to Web-based discussion groups.

Of course, some employers don't want their employees talking about them in discussion groups because they're scared what the employees will say. If that's your situation, I can't do much to help you, except suggest that you read *Figuring Out Why Your Employees Hate You For Dummies* by I. M. N. Ogre.

## Contact association sites

Association sites are a much-overlooked source of free and useful links. Contact any professional or business association of which you're a member and ask for a link. Are you in the local Better Business Bureau? The Lions Club or Rotary Club? How about the Rodent Lovers Association of America, or the Association for Professional Rodent Competitions? Many such sites have member directories and may even have special links pages for their members' Web sites.

## Contact manufacturers' Web sites

Another overlooked source of links are manufacturers' Web sites. If you sell products, ask the manufacturer to place a link from its site to yours. I know one business that sells several million dollar's worth of a particular toy that it gets from a single retailer. The link from the retailer, which does not sell directly to consumers, brings the company *most* of its business. This is a valuable link in itself, but because the manufacturer is a well-known national company that gets plenty of traffic, the manufacturer's Web site has a PageRank of 6 on its main page. (See Chapter 14 to see why that's impressive.) The link to the retailer is on the manufacturer's home page, so not only does the link bring plenty of business, but it also gets plenty of attention from the search engines.

## Contact companies you do business with

Many companies maintain client lists. Check with all the firms you do business with and make sure that you're on their lists.

## Ask to be a featured client

While looking at a competitor's Web site for a client, I noticed that the competing site had a surprisingly high PageRank even though it was a small site that appeared to be linked to from only one place, www.inman.com, which is a site that syndicates content to real-estate sites. It turned out that the competitor was linked to directly from one of Inman's highest PageRanked pages. Inman was using the client as an example of one of its customers.

If you're using someone's services — for Web hosting, e-mail services, syndication services, or whatever — you may want to contact the site and ask if *you* can be the featured client. Hey, someone's going to be, so it might as well be you.

## Submit to announcement sites and newsletters

Though not as popular as they used to be, a number of site-announcement Web sites and e-mail newsletters still exist. (The newsletters usually end up published on the Web, too.) Some of these services are *very* influential because they are either very popular (USAToday.com's Hot Sites, for instance) or are read by many journalists.

Check out URLwire (www.urlwire.com), for instance. This service claims to have over 125,000 readers, of whom 6,500 are journalists and site reviewers who get the e-mail newsletter. You have to pay for this service, from $300 to $1,000 to get into one of the announcements, but other announcement services are generally free.

Unfortunately, getting your site into the announcements can be difficult because of stiff competition! In fact, some announcement sites don't accept submissions — Yahoo! Picks, for instance, doesn't take suggestions. Sometimes to get picked up by these sites, you need to be mentioned in another influential announcement service, such as URLwire. However, if you *can* get in, the effect can be huge. Not only do you get a link from a site that is undoubtedly well indexed, but you probably also get picked up by many other sites and newsletters. URLwire in particular (no, I'm not getting a kickback!) is incredibly influential.

Here are a few announcement services to try:

- ✔ **USAToday.com's Hot Sites:** www.usatoday.com/tech/webguide/front.htm
- ✔ **URLwire:** www.urlwire.com
- ✔ **Yahoo! Picks:** picks.yahoo.com/picks

These announcement services used to be abundant, but unfortunately, most have died off.

# Send out press releases

Does your company publish press releases? You should distribute these as widely as possible. Even if you submit press releases through a large service such as PR Newswire (`prnewswire.com`), you should also distribute them through the free and low-cost distribution services, which will quite likely get them placed onto other Web sites. You may want to write a few quick press releases and send them out through the free-distribution services, just to see if you can generate some links.

These are the free and low-cost services that I know of:

- **PR Web:** `www.prweb.com/`
- **24-7 Press Release:** `www.24-7pressrelease.com/`
- **Free-Press-Release.com:** `www.free-press-release.com/`
- **Press World:** `www.press-world.com/`
- **Click2newsites.com:** `www.click2newsites.com/press.htm`
- **US News:** `www.usanews.net/`
- **PR Leap:** `www.prleap.com/`
- **eWorldWire:** `www.eworldwire.com/`
- **pressbox:** `www.pressbox.co.uk`

You may want to create your own list of press-release distribution e-mail addresses and Web pages. For instance, look for industry journals in your field that accept press releases.

Make sure that the press release includes your URL at least twice, preferably three or four times. For instance, include it once in the header, once in the contact information at the bottom, and a couple of times in the text. And use a full link: `http://www.yourdomainname.com` rather than just `your domainname.com`.

The URL should be clickable. That is, it should appear in a Web page as a real link that can be clicked. You don't have a lot of control over this with a free distribution service, though you should experiment to see if the service automatically converts URLs to links, or whether you can enter an HTML link (`<a href=" http://www.yourdomainname.com">Your link text </a>`). Just create a full URL and hope for the best. (If you're working with fee-based press-release services, talk to them to find out how to make sure your URLs are clickable links.)

# Promote something on your site

One of the most powerful link-building techniques is to place something very useful on your site and then make sure everyone knows about it. I've included a little story in the sidebar "How links build links," at the end of this chapter. It shows how links can accumulate — how, in the right conditions, one link leads to another, which leads to another, and so on. In this true story, the site had something that many people really liked — a directory of glossaries and technical dictionaries. Over 2,000 sites link to this site, all because the site owner provided something people really wanted and appreciated.

# Find sites linking to your competition

If a site links to your competition, it may be willing to link to you, too. Find out who links to competing sites and then ask them if they'll link to yours. In some cases, the links will be link-exchange links, which I look at in the section "Respond to reciprocal link requests," but in many cases, they'll just be sites providing useful information to their readers. If your competitors' sites are useful, and (I'm assuming) yours is too, you've got a good chance of being listed.

So how do you find out who links to your competitors? You can do this a number of ways, as described in the next few sections. I list the methods in order of the number of links that you're likely to find, from the least to the most.

### Google toolbar

The Google toolbar — the one I show you how to download in Chapter 1 — has a Backward Links command. Open your competitor's home page, click the little blue i button on the toolbar, and then select Backward Links from the drop-down menu. This feature generally shows pages with a PageRank of 4 or more; it doesn't show all the links in Google's index. (Sometimes lower-ranked pages seem to sneak through.) It also shows links to that page, not links to all the pages on the site.

If you don't see the i button on the toolbar, click the Options button, and check the Page Info Menu checkbox on the Options tab of the Toolbar Options dialog box.

### Google search

Search for `link:domainname.com` in Google or in the search box in the Google Toolbar.

### Alexa toolbar

The Alexa toolbar has a similar tool. Select a page at a competitor's site (which doesn't have to be the home page), click the little downward-pointing triangle on the Info button, and an information box opens. At the bottom of the box, you see a line that says something like `See 7,419 sites that link here`. Click this link to open a page on the Alexa site listing all the links.

### Link popularity sites

Online tools, such as LinkPopularity.com, can help you find links. Enter the competitor's URL and click the search button, and LinkPopularity.com searches Google, AltaVista, and HotBot for you.

Another service I like is the tool at Marketleap (`www.marketleap.com/publinkpop`), which searches for links at AlltheWeb, Google, AltaVista, HotBot, and MSN.

Many such tools are available. Search for **link popularity tools**, and you'll find them.

### Link-popularity software

A number of link-popularity software tools are available to run on your computer. My current favorite is SEO Elite (`www.SEOElite.com/`, see Figure 15-1), a $167 program that looks for links to a site in various search engines, then visits each of the pages containing the links and returns with a plethora of information:

- The URL of the page linking to the site
- The *Internet protocol (IP)* number of the site on which the page is held
- Whether the link that the search engine *thinks* is on the page is still there
- The PageRank of the page
- The Alexa rank of the page
- The `<title>` text from the page
- The *anchor* text — that is, the link text
- The number of outbound links on the page
- The total number of links on the page (outbound plus internal site links)
- *Whois* information — data about who owns the site on which the page sits
- The link value, and estimate of the value of the link, based on the PageRank divided by the number of links on the page
- A contact e-mail address pulled from the page

This is a great little program, with nifty tools such as the ability to find potential link partners and e-mail them, and a way to search for potential link-submission pages and quickly submit information to them. You can export your results to an Excel spreadsheet.

Another program I've used is LinkSurvey, which you can find at `www.ants soft.com`. This little tool lets you enter all your competitors' URLs and have it run link checks on them all at once. You can define whether you want to find links to any page in the domain or links only to the specified page, and then search up to ten search engines. It even has a built-in Web browser, so in its list of pages linking to your competitors you can click a link to quickly see what that page looks like. The program even highlights the link within the page. However, it doesn't include the critical link text, just a list of pages containing links.

**Figure 15-1:**
The SEO Elite link-popularity tool in action.

### Asking for the link

Once you've found sites linking to your competitors, you'll discover that some of them may be appropriate for a link to yours; directories of products or sites, for instance, may want to include you. So how do you ask for the link? Nicely. Send an informal, chatty message. Don't make it sound like some kind of form letter that half a billion other people have received. This should be a personal contact between a real person (you) and another real person (the other site's owner or manager). Give this person a reason to link to your site. Explain what your site does and why it would be of use to the other site's visitors.

## Ask other sites for links

During your travels online, you'll run across sites that provide lists of links for visitors, and maybe your site should be listed, too. For instance, while working for a client that had a site related to a particular disease, I found sites that had short lists of links to sites about that disease; obviously my client should also have been in those lists.

Approach these sites the same way you would approach the sites linking to your competitors: Send an informal note asking for a link.

## Make reciprocal link requests

A *reciprocal link* is one that you obtain in exchange for another. You ask site owners and managers to link to your site, and you in turn promise to link to theirs.

Reciprocal linking, if done right, can help you in two ways:

- ✔ The search engines see nice, keyworded links coming into your site from appropriate, relevant sites.
- ✔ You link to appropriate, relevant sites too. (In Chapter 14, I discuss the concept of hubs or value networks.)

Reciprocal linking is different from asking to be added to a list, although plenty of overlap exists. With the latter, you don't need to offer a link in exchange because the link list is a service to the other site's visitors. However, sometimes (often?) site owners respond with, "Sure, but will you link to us, too?" In this case, you've just found yourself in a reciprocal linking position.

Relevant or contextual links are more valuable than irrelevant, noncontextual links. Links to your rodent-racing sites from *other* rodent-racing sites are more valuable than links from sites about Satan worship or *Star Trek*. If you get links from any site you can, without regard to whether the sites are of use to your visitors or whether your site is of use to theirs, search engines won't regard them as relevant links. However, I'm not saying, as many in the business would, that irrelevant links have no value; they clearly do, though perhaps not as much value as relevant links. As the search engines really don't know for sure what's a relevant link and what isn't, even irrelevant links will have some value.

Reciprocal linking is a popular method for obtaining links to your site. Find a site that appears to be in an area similar to yours — that is, attracts the same sort of people you want to attract and involves a related subject area — and then contact the owner and ask for a link.

### Making the contact

Before you contact others to ask for reciprocal links, link from your site to their sites. Find a page from which it would make sense to link. If possible, avoid the use of *links pages* (which I discuss next). Rather, find a spot on your site where a link to the other site would *fit,* a position in which it would make sense from a visitor's point of view. Keyword the link nicely. (Do unto others as you would have them do unto you.)

Then contact the site owner. Let the site owner know that you've added the link *and* that you've keyworded it. In fact, why not explain keyworded links and their purpose? Doing so will probably make it easier to persuade the site owner to give you the type of keyworded link you want. Provide the URL to the page on which the link sits. You might even explain why you try to avoid the use of links pages.

Then ask for a reciprocal link and suggest a page on which it would make sense. You're better off *not* being on a links page if you can avoid it.

### Should you use links pages?

You've undoubtedly seen links pages all over the place — pages with titles such as *Useful Links, Useful Resources, Visit Our Friends,* and so on. To be honest (I say that when I'm about to upset people), these pages don't generate much traffic to your Web site. How often do you find useful links useful, or useful resources particularly, er, resourceful? Not very often, I bet. People simply don't use them. And having tested link-exchange software that measures the amount of traffic going through the links pages, I can tell you that they don't generate much traffic to Web sites. (I discuss link-exchange software later in this chapter.)

You may hear the term *link exchange.* In many quarters, this practice is frowned upon because it implies that the site owners simply want to accumulate as many links as possible and don't really care about the type of sites they're working with. It also implies the use of a links page. On the other hand, *reciprocal linking* implies to many people a more circumspect methodology, in which links are carefully considered and placed throughout the site.

However, as I explain at the beginning of Chapter 14, you have three reasons to get links to a Web site. One is to get traffic through the links, and I've pretty much killed that idea for the typical *links page.* The other reasons are to help search engines find your site and to push up your PageRank; links pages *can* do that, the proof being that it's possible to find sites that have a decent PageRank, perhaps 4 or 5, that have very few links apart from reciprocal links.

However, you are far better off *not* using links pages because of the following problems:

🔸 **Search engines may already downgrade links from such pages.** A link from an ordinary page is likely to be more valuable than a link from a links page.

🔸 **Links pages often have dozens or even hundreds of links on them.** Remember that the more links on a page, the lower the vote for each outgoing link.

🔸 **Links pages may be further downgraded in the future.** If someone at Google or Yahoo! decides that removing the effect of links pages from their algorithms will improve search results — and there's good reason to think that it would have this effect — you could one day wake up and discover that all the links to your site from links pages no longer have *any* value.

I'm not saying that you should never use links pages. Life is an exercise in compromise, and, to be honest, a really good reciprocal-link campaign can be incredibly time consuming. However, the ideal situation would be to do the following:

🔸 Scatter links to other sites around your site, in locations that make sense.

🔸 Encourage site owners linking back to you to do the same. Start educating the other sites you work with! (In fact, tell them to run out and buy this book; better still, tell them to buy ten copies of this book, for colleagues, friends, and family.)

🔸 Avoid having large numbers of links on one page.

🔸 Avoid calling a page a *links* page. You might try using *resource* page, although I suspect this title is also overused.

Some people claim that search engines don't index these links pages. This simply is not true. They often (usually?) do, and the proof is in the pudding:

🔸 Go to Google and search for these terms, making sure to include the quotation marks:

- **"visit our friends"** (I found 1,030,000000 pages)

- **"link exchange"** (almost 34 million)

- **"links page"** (almost 26 million)

Sure, not all the pages you find are links pages, but many are.

✔ Go to links pages and check to see if they're in the Google cache, or go to Google and search for the URLs of the pages to see if they're in the Google index. They often are.

✔ When you visit links pages, look at the Google toolbar. You'll often see that they have a PageRank. However, I should reiterate: Links from links pages probably do not have the value of links from normal pages.

### Finding high-PageRank links

Ideally, you want links from pages with high PageRanks. Now, you may hear that you should focus on links from sites that are related to you, not from sites with high PageRanks. That's partially true. Although relatively little traffic goes through link exchanges, remember that links from related sites are more valuable than links from unrelated sites. Links to your rodent-racing site from other rodent-related sites will probably be more valuable, in terms of PageRank, than links from unrelated sites about music or Viagra. (On the other hand, I wouldn't be surprised if links from sites about horse racing or car racing are more valuable.)

The best strategy is to get links that are related to you *from pages with high PageRanks!* Thems the facts, ma'am, and it doesn't matter how many politically correct statements people want to make about not worrying about PageRank. The fact is, PageRank *does* matter.

I'm not implying that you should turn down links from pages with low Page-Ranks, but what if you could search for pages with a high PageRank, and then go after them? If you're looking for reciprocal-link partners anyway, you might as well use a search technique that uncovers sites with high PageRanks, for several reasons:

✔ If a page has a high PageRank, it either has lots of links to it or a small number of links from other pages with high PageRanks (or both). This means that search engines are more likely to find and reindex the page, thus are more likely to find and follow the link to *your* page.

✔ For obvious reasons, people are more likely to follow the links to your page, too.

✔ The vote from the high-PageRank page counts for more than the vote from a low-PageRank page.

Here are some ways to find pages with high PageRanks:

✔ **Use the Backward Links command on the Google Toolbar or the**
   `links:domainname.com` **search syntax.** (Both techniques are discussed in "Find sites linking to your competition," earlier in this chapter.) These techniques find only high-PageRank pages, 4 or above. So you can look for pages linking to a competitor and know that the pages have a decent PageRank.

 ✔ **Use a link-analysis tool such as SEO Elite.** This program, and some others, report the PageRank of the linking pages, so you can target high PageRank pages first.

 ✔ **Look in the Google Directory.** Go to `directory.google.com` and browse through the directory until you find an appropriate category. Notice that each entry near the top of the category is shown with a green and gray bar in the left column. The longer the green part of the bar, the higher the PageRank.

## A to B to C to A Links

A more complicated form of reciprocal linking is one that many people are using these days. The idea is that rather than linking from site A to site B, and back from site B to site A, you do a three- or four-way link, as shown in Figure 15-2.

It's easy for the search engines to recognize reciprocal linking, which is why I, and many others in the business, believe that the value of such linking has been downgraded. (Unlike some others, I do not believe that reciprocal linking has no value whatsoever.) If a search engine sees a link from one site to another, and then sees a link coming *back,* well, there's a good chance it's a reciprocal link. (I'm sure it's more complicated than this — does the site have lots of outgoing links, to sites that link back, on the same page, for instance? — but the basic principle remains.) So it's pretty easy for search engines to recognize reciprocal linking, and as they are aware that such linking is used as an artificial way to boost ranking, they can lower the value of these links.

---

## High PR Link Club

Using the techniques described in this chapter will help you find sites with high PageRanks, but that doesn't necessarily mean the pages on which your links will be placed will have high PageRanks. However, I ran across a PageRank club: the High PR Link Club (`www.highprlink club.com`). The owner, Rick Katz, spends hours searching for sites that have link-exchange pages that have PageRanks of 4 or above. Club members have access to a categorized directory of these sites, containing the site title, the URL, a description, the PageRank of the link-exchange page, and the site-owner contact information.

Yes, links pages are not ideal, but perhaps you can convince the site owner to place a link elsewhere.

I tried this service (it's $97 a year), and within ten minutes I found 45 sites that seemed to be appropriate for one of the sites I was currently working on. Nineteen of them had a PR of 5, three had a PR of 6, and 23 had a PR of 4. It's better to spend your time trying to get links from 45 pages with high PageRanks of 4, 5, and 6, than from a couple of hundred pages with PageRanks of 0.

---

Say, however, you have a large collection of sites that want to trade links. Rather than have every site link to every other, you might try a more complicated structure, where site A links to B, while B links to C, and C links back to A; see Figure 15-2. Rather than getting two incoming links, each site only gets one, but it's probably of more value, because it's not so obviously a reciprocal link. Or maybe you link site A to B, B to C, C to D, and D to A; in this case each site gets one link rather than three, but again, the links are likely to be more valuable than simple A-to-B-to-A reciprocal links. Some companies that do SEO work for large numbers of clients use this technique, or even combine traditional reciprocal links with three-way or four-way linking.

**Figure 15-2:**
Traditional
reciprocal
linking has
site A
linking to B,
and site B
linking back
to A (top
left). But
three- and
four-way
linking are
probably
more
beneficial.

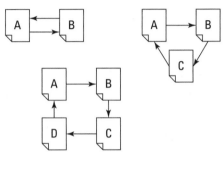

## Respond to reciprocal link requests

Eventually, other sites will start asking *you* to link swap. Remember, ideally you should treat your outgoing links like gold and link only to relevant sites that will be of use to your visitors . . . but also remember, all links have *some* value.

## Search for keyword add url

Go to Google and search for something like this:

```
"rodent racing" + "add url"
```

Google searches for all the pages with the term *rodent racing* and the term *add url*. You'll find sites that are related to your subject and have pages on which you can add links, as shown in Figure 15-3. (For some inexplicable reason, you won't find much with `"rodent racing" + "add url"`, but you will find plenty with, for instance, `"boating" + "add url"` or `"psychology" + "add url"`.)

You can also try these searches:

```
"rodent racing" + "add a url"
"rodent racing" + "add link"
"rodent racing" + "add a link"
"rodent racing" + "add site"
"rodent racing" + "add a site"
"rodent racing" + "suggest url"
"rodent racing" + "suggest a url"
"rodent racing" + "suggest link"
"rodent racing" + "suggest a link"
"rodent racing" + "suggest site"
"rodent racing" + "suggest a site"
```

However, these are not always high-quality links. In general, the search engines don't really like this sort of linking, and the word on the street is that links from such pages probably don't have the same value that you'd get from links that are personally placed. On the other hand, they may be easy to get . . . it's a trade-off.

**Figure 15-3:**
Searching for a keyword or keyword phrase along with `+"add url"` uncovers sites that are just waiting for you to add a link to your site.

Incidentally, SEO Elite, which I mention earlier, includes a tool to carry out one of these types of link campaigns, searching for pages with submission forms related to whatever keywords you define, and then helping you submit these forms; see Figure 15-4.

**Figure 15-4:**
SEO Elite
has a tool
that helps
you submit
information
on add
URL pages.

## Use link-building software and services

Link-building campaigns are LTT: laborious, tedious, and time consuming. (I love making up acronyms; I'm just hoping this one takes off.) You have to find sites, add links on your site to the sites you want to exchange with, contact the owners, wait to see if they respond, try again when they don't, check to see if they actually add the links, and so on. It's a helluva lot of work.

Some programs and online services can help you automate the process. They usually help you search for appropriate sites to work with, assist you in contacting the owners, and even create your links pages for you. A number of computer programs are available; perhaps the best known are Zeus (www.cyber-robotics.com) and ARELIS (www.axandra.com/). Some people find the online services easier to work with, but you have to pay a monthly fee to use them (in some cases a few hundred bucks a year).

Link-building programs and services can be used or misused. You can easily use these systems to amass a large number of links in a hurry, without regard to relevance or context. Or you can use them to assist you in a careful campaign to garner links from sites that really make sense.

One free service is LinkPartners (www.linkpartners.com), a huge directory of people who want to exchange links. This service is associated with a pay service called LinksManager (www.linksmanager.com), which automates the process of contacting the site owners and verifying that the link-exchange partners have actually placed links on their pages. If you get a request for a link through LinksManager and accept the exchange, LinksManager does the work for you, adding the links to both your pages and the link-exchange partner's pages. It even automatically uploads the links pages to your Web site.

Another service I've used is Links4Trade (links4trade.com), which is similar to LinksManager, but it currently creates only a single page. (LinksManager creates a series of categorized pages.)

Some purists feel that using link-exchange programs is cheating, and indeed these services are walking a fine line between valid linking that the search engines accept and automated link-generation systems that the search engines hate. I've spoken with the owners of both LinksManager and Links4Trade, and they both tell me they have spoken with Google and been told that the way the programs are managed is acceptable. Because the programs are not totally automated and require some manual oversight and management, they're okay. Again, the proof is that these pages *are* indexed by Google.

## Contact e-mail newsletters

E-mail newsletters can be an incredibly powerful method for getting the word out. The first step is to find all the appropriate e-mail newsletters, newsletters that write about the area in which you operate. After you've identified some newsletters, here are some ways you can work with them:

- ✔ **Send the newsletters a short announcement introducing your site.** I like to send informal messages to the editors to ask if they'll mention the site and then give them a reason to do so. What makes your site interesting or useful to the newsletter readers?

- ✔ **Consider buying small ads in the newsletters.** Some ads are cheap, and if the newsletter is highly targeted, buying an ad may be worthwhile. Make sure that you know how many people subscribe to the newsletter. Lots of little newsletters with very few subscribers may charge pricey ad rates!

- ✔ **Offer some kind of cooperative campaign.** For example, provide a special offer for newsletter readers or put together a contest to give away your products.

- ✔ **Write articles for the newsletters.** I cover this topic in more detail in "Got Content? Syndicate It!" later in this chapter.

## Mention your site in discussion groups

Many discussion groups are indexed by the search engines. You need to find a discussion group that publishes messages on the Web, so an e-mail–based discussion group that does not archive the messages in Web pages won't help you.

Whenever you leave a message in the discussion group, make sure that you use a message signature that has a link to your site and also include the link in the message itself.

Sometimes URLs in messages and signatures are read as links, and sometimes they aren't. If you type `http://www.yourdomain.com/` in a message, the software processing the message can handle the URL in one of two ways:

- ✔ It can enter the URL into the page as simple text.
- ✔ It can convert the URL to a true HTML link (`<A HREF=" http://www. yourdomain.com"> http://www.yourdomain.com/ </A>`).

If the URL is *not* converted to a true link, it won't be regarded as a link by the search engines.

## Respond to blogs

Literally billions of blog pages are around the Internet, and some of them have to be related to the subject served by your Web site. Many blogs allow visitors to respond; you might want to respond to messages and include a link to your site. However, two things to consider:

- ✔ **Avoid blog spamming:** If you have nothing valid to say in response to a blog, don't bother. Responses placed on blogs for the sole purpose of garnering links are known as *blog spam,* an obnoxious vandalism of the blogosphere.
- ✔ **Links in blogs are dropping in value:** As a response to blog spam, the search engines introduced a new link-tag attribute, `rel="nofollow"`. For instance, look at this link: `<a href="http://www.domain.com/" rel="nofollow">Visit My Cool Site</a>`. When a search engine sees the `nofollow` attribute, it ignores the link. As more blogging systems begin coding all links in responses in this manner, the less valuable responding to blogs becomes.

## Pursue offline PR

Getting mentioned in print often translates into being mentioned on the Web. If you can get publications to write about and review your site, not only do many people see the link in print — and perhaps visit your site — but often your link ends up online in a Web version of the article.

## Give away content

Many companies have vast quantities of content on their Web sites. It's just sitting there, available to anyone who visits. So why not take the content *to* the visitors before they reach your site? Placing the content on other Web sites is a powerful way not only to build links back to your site but also to get your name out there — to "brand" yourself or your company.

I cover this topic in more detail a little later in this chapter, in the section "Got Content? Syndicate It!" because you need to be aware of several technical issues.

## Apply for online awards

Getting someone to give an award to your site used to be a popular technique for getting links. But it reached the point at which it was possible to get an award for just about any complete-piece-of-junk Web site because the sites giving out the awards were more interested in getting links *back to their sites*. Those who win awards place the award images on their Web sites, so the images are linked back to the sites giving the awards.

Award sites are less common now, but a few still exist, such as www. favouritewebsiteawards.com. Awards with some real heft behind them are probably harder to get these days, but if you think your site is well designed or has some kind of unusual or special function, you may have a chance to get one.

## Advertise

You may want to consider advertising in order to get links to your site. However, you need to consider a couple of issues first:

✔ Advertising is often grossly overpriced. It may be much too expensive to justify just for a link.

> ✔ Advertising links often don't count as links to your site. Rather, they're links to the advertising company, which runs a program that forwards the visitor's browser to your site. Search engines won't see the link as a link to your site. (See Chapter 14 for more information.)

In some cases, buying ads on a site to get a link does make sense. For instance, if many of your clients visit a particular Web site, and it's possible to get a low-cost ad on that site, it may be worthwhile to buy an ad to both brand your company and get a link that will be read by the search engines. And remember, it's a very relevant link, coming from a site important to your business.

## *Use a service or buy links*

I can't stress enough that link campaigns can be very laborious, tedious, and time consuming. You may be better off paying someone to do the work for you. Some of these services simply run the link-acquisition campaign for you. Others already have an inventory of ad space on thousands of sites and charge you to place a link on a set number.

OneWay TextLinks sells 100 links for $18.95 per month. Another company I've seen claims it will put links on 250 sites for $99. Some companies sell links from pages of specific PageRank, too. One company, for instance, claims to be able to sell you a link on a PageRank 8 site for $799. (A PageRank 4 page is just $29.) I have no idea how legitimate such services are.

However, remember that the vote from a page is shared among all the pages it links to, so the more ads that are sold, the less the value of each ad. You should know exactly what page the link will be placed on, and you should be able to view the page. Consider buying links as a form of advertising that should be evaluated as such. How much of an impact will the ad have on bringing more visitors to your site?

Many companies do this sort of work, such as these:

> ✔ **Web Link Alliance:** www.weblinkalliance.com
>
> ✔ **Linking Matters:** www.linkingmatters.com
>
> ✔ **Text Link Ads:** www.text-link-ads.com
>
> ✔ **TextLinkBrokers.com:** www.textlinkbrokers.com
>
> ✔ **OneWay TextLinks:** www.onewaytextlinks.com

I'm not endorsing any of the companies I'm mentioning here. I'm just providing them as examples so you can see the types of services available.

If you're interested in such a service, search for **buy links**, **purchase links**, **link popularity**, and **link building** at a major search engine. Make sure that you understand what you're getting into. As you have seen, you can use many methods to get links to a site, but they don't all provide the same value. Are you working with a company that will find really good links from popular sites that are relevant to yours? Or a company that will use an automated link-exchange tool to gather links from anywhere it can? There's a real difference!

When you buy links, make sure you buy the right type. You won't want links dropped onto a page using JavaScript, or ads that are served through an ad server. In the first case, the search engine probably won't read the link at all; in the second case, the link probably points at the ad server, not at your Web site. For instance, AdBrite (`www.adbrite.com`) sells text ads on a wide range of Web sites; but the link points to AdBrite, not to your site.

Here's an example showing you how to figure out if the link points to your site. Here's an ad I found on one of their advertising site:

```
Gastric Bypass Pill
Approved! FREE Samples
```

Now, pointing to a link will display one of two things in the browser's status bar:

- ✔ The URL the link points to
- ✔ A "fake" URL, which can be placed there using JavaScript in the Web page

In this case, when I point at the link and look at the status bar in my browser, I see this URL:

```
http://www.zetacap.com/
```

However, when I *right-click* the link, I see the real URL in the status bar:

```
http://click.adbrite.com/mb/click.php?sid=19822&banner_id=
       10235529&cpc=302e3030303030303030&ssc=08862a24b
       01e87aa1498dbcafcda01de
```

That's also the URL that I see when I click the link, at least for a second or two, before the ad server forwards me to the zetacap.com Web site. As you can see, the link doesn't point to the advertiser's site — `www.zetacap.com` — it points to the `click.adbrite.com` ad server. I'm in no way suggesting that AdBrite is misleading people, by the way; they don't claim their links will help you with the search engines, they are simply selling ads. But when you go looking for pages on which to place links, you must be aware of this issue.

Remember, a link campaign can be incredibly LTT — you know, *Laborious, Tedious, and Time Consuming* — so don't be surprised if a firm quotes, say, $2,000 to get you 30 links. It may be a reasonable price, assuming the firm is doing it the right way. On the other hand, many firms, particularly in India, are doing link work for as little as 25 cents per link. (This is generally through reciprocal linking programs.)

## Just wait

I'm not really recommending that you sit and wait as a way to build links, but the fact is that if you're doing lots of other things — sending out press releases, getting mentioned in papers and magazines, contacting e-mail newsletters to do product giveaways, and so on — you'll gather links anyway. You've got to prime the pump first; then things seem to just take off.

Consider having a Link to Us page on your site to provide logos and suggest HTML text that people can drop onto their sites.

## Fuggetaboutit

Don't bother getting links in guest books, *Free For All (FFA)* pages, and link farms, for the following reasons:

✔ Many Web sites contain guest book pages, and one early link-building technique was to add a link to your Web site in every guest book you could find. The search engines know all about this technique, so although many guest books are indexed, links from them probably have very little value in most search engines.

✔ FFA pages are automated directories to which you can add a link. They bring virtually no traffic to your site, are a great way to generate a lot of spam (when you register you have to provide an e-mail address), and don't help you in the search engines.

✔ Link farms are highly automated link-exchange systems designed to generate thousands of links very quickly. Don't get involved with link farms. Not only will they not help you, but if you link to one or host one on your site, you may get penalized in the search engines.

The search engines don't like these kinds of things, so save your time, energy, and money.

# Got Content? Syndicate It!

I discuss one aspect of syndication in Chapter 9: using syndicated content to bulk up your Web site. Now, it's time to look at the flip side: taking your content and syndicating it to other Web sites and e-mail newsletters.

E-mail newsletters don't help your search engine position because search engines don't read them (although that could change at any time). However, most e-mail newsletters are placed into Web archives — that is, they become Web pages — which often *are* indexed by search engines. Furthermore, newsletter readers sometimes post articles from the newsletters on their sites or come directly to your site.

Suppose that you're trying to compare load and no-load mutual funds. Go to Google and search for the term **load vs. no load**. When I tried this search, I saw the search results shown in Figure 15-5. The four entries I've pointed to in the figure are actually the same article, written by the same man, promoting the same Web site . . . but appearing on *different* Web sites (none of them his, by the way). He also turns up several times for the term **load vs. no load mutual fund**.

**Figure 15-5:** The four entries I've pointed to are articles written by the same man, syndicated to different Web sites.

What has this man, Ulli Niemann, done? He hasn't managed to get his own Web site onto the first page for this search, but he has managed to get his work onto the first page. People clicking one of the entries have a very good chance of seeing his name, his work, and a link to his site at www.successful-investment.com. See how well this campaign has worked? Now he's got a link in a book, too.

At the end of the day, it's not all about search engines, it's about getting the word out about your Web site, through whatever method that works.

Some site owners use this form of syndication as the *only* type of promotion they do, and it can work incredibly well. They write articles and distribute them as widely as possible. But many sites already have a lot of content. Why not give it away and use it as a technique to grab more search engine positions, generate links to your site, and brand your site and company?

Another huge advantage to using syndication is that the links you get back to your site are from relevant sites. Remember, the search engines like *relevant*. Ulli Niemann is an investment advisor, so what sorts of sites do you think are carrying his articles? Finance and investment sites!

## *Four ways to syndicate*

You can syndicate content four ways. The trick, however, is that some of the methods don't help you one lick in terms of getting your site noticed by search engines! In some cases, it's possible to syndicate content and *not* benefit from those links pointing to your site, depending on how the content is distributed. The following list details the four main syndication categories:

- ✔ **Browser-side inclusion:** Many syndicators employ browser-side content inclusion through the use of JavaScripts; a *JavaScript* in a Web page pulls the article off the syndicating site. The problem is that JavaScripts are run by the Web browser itself. The page loads, and then the browser runs the JavaScripts. Searchbots, however, don't run JavaScripts. Googlebot, when indexing the page, will ignore the JavaScript and thus won't see the content and won't see the link to your site in the content. Although site visitors will see the links, and some will click them, you won't get the benefit of the link popularity in the search engines.

- ✔ **Hosted content:** Some content syndicators, generally those *selling* content, host the content on their own servers, and the sites using the content link to it. The problem with this method is that if you host content for, say, 50 sites, you don't get the benefit of 50 links in the search engines. Google sees that you have the same article 50 times, and ignores 49 of them.

✔ **Manual inclusion:** This method works well for the search engines; they see the content and the links to your site. But the problem is that you're relying on the other site's owner to manually place the content into the page.

✔ **Server-side inclusion:** You can do server-side inclusions a number of ways, such as by using INCLUDE commands, running PHP or ASP scripts (*server-side scripts*), and using a relatively new method, RSS feeds. The advantage is that the search engines *will* see your content and the links back to your site. The disadvantage is that the methods are more complicated to use than either manual or browser-side inclusion.

To ensure that the search engines see links to your Web site, you simply can't use the first or second methods. That leaves the last two, of which the third, manual inclusion, is easiest and by far the most common.

If you want to syndicate your content, prepare the articles carefully. I suggest that you produce each article in two forms: in plain text for text newsletters, and in HTML for HTML newsletters and Web sites. Make the HTML version simple so it can be taken and dropped into any other Web page.

It is possible to make a JavaScript-style syndication give you at least one link that is readable by the search engines. Typically, syndicators ask users to drop a piece of JavaScript into their pages. Of course, you can ask them to drop a piece of HTML that includes a JavaScript inside it. For instance, instead of using this:

```
<SCRIPT LANGUAGE="JavaScript" src="http://www.
        ronaldsrodents.com/content/article.js"></SCRIPT
        >
```

you can use this:

```
<SCRIPT LANGUAGE="JavaScript" src="http://www.
        ronaldsrodents.com/content/article.js"></SCRIPT
        ><P><STRONG>Article provided by <A
        HREF="http://ronaldsrodents.com>Ronald's
        Rodents</A>. Visit us for more great articles
        on rodent racing.</P>
```

## Getting the most out of syndication

If you're going to syndicate your work, you should consider the following points when creating your articles:

✔ Every article should contain your site name near the top of the article. Put a site logo near the top and include a link on the logo back to your site.

✔ If you can find a way to work a link to your site into the article, all the better. You can do it a couple of times maybe, but don't overdo it. Perhaps link to another article on your site for more information. Make sure the link text has useful keywords.

✔ At the bottom of the article, include an attribution or bio box, including a keyworded link back to your site and a logo with a link on it. (Don't forget to use ALT text in the <IMG> tag.)

You'll want to set up a library area on your Web site where people can access the articles. In the library, you should post certain conditions:

✔ Consider putting limits on the number of articles that can be used without contacting you first. For example, site owners can use up to five articles, and if they want more, they must get permission.

✔ State clearly that you retain copyright of the article and make clear the following conditions:

- The user cannot change the content.

- All logos, attributions, copyright notices, and links must remain.

- Links must remain standard HTML <A> tags and cannot be converted to another form of link.

## *Getting the word out*

When you have your articles ready, you need to get them into the hands of people who can use them. First, you need to register with as many syndication directories as possible. Here's a huge list, partially compiled with the help of Ulli Niemann:

✔ www.allnetarticles.com

✔ www.amazines.com

✔ www.articlecity.com

✔ www.authorconnection.com

✔ www.boazepublishing.biz

✔ www.certificate.net

✔ www.clickforcontent.com

✔ www.connectionteam.com/sources.htm

✔ www.content-wire.com/Online/
Syndication.cfm?ccs=111&cs=1696

✔ www.debt-consolidation-directory.com

✔ www.electroniccontent.com/conFinder.cfm

- www.ezinearticles.com
- www.ezine-writer.com.au
- www.family-content.com
- www.freesticky.com/stickyweb
- www.freesticky.com/stickyweb/submitselfsyndicate.asp
- www.goarticles.com
- www.gold-investor.com
- www.greekshares.com
- www.ideamarketers.com
- www.investnewz.com
- www.jogena.com
- www.magportal.com
- www.makingprofit.com
- www.marketing-seek.com
- www.netterweb.com
- www.shoppingwithwomen.com
- www.stickysauce.com/dcd
- www.teenanalyst.com
- www.top7business.com/submit
- www.ultimateprofits.com
- www.usanews.net/todays_releases.htm
- www.vectorcentral.com
- www.webpronews.com
- www.web-source.net/syndicator.htm
- www.windstormcomputing.com/pubs/free-ezine-content
- www.womans-net.com
- www.writers-and-publishers.com

Here are a few more ideas for getting the articles out:

- Make sure that visitors to your site know the library is available.
- Directly contact sites and e-mail newsletters that may benefit from your content.
- Include information about available materials in any e-mails you send and in your printed materials.

## Syndicating utilities

A number of companies have done a tremendous job at building truly huge numbers of incoming links by giving away Web site utilities. One that comes to mind is the Atomz Express Search free search component from Atomz (now owned by WebSideStory). Every site using this program has at least one link, probably several, back to the Atomz.com site. I used a link analysis tool some time ago, and found about 6,000 links to Atomz.com. Another company with a huge number of incoming links is MapQuest (www.mapquest.com). Because it distributes maps, both paid and free, and because all those maps include links back to the home site, thousands of links around the Web point to MapQuest.

This technique has worked incredibly well for many technology companies but can also work for others with a little imagination. Whatever you give away, whether it's clip art, videos, flash animations, or PDF documents, make sure you include links back to your site. For instance, your rodent-racing site could distribute a utility for handicapping mice and rats. (I don't mean to physically damage them; I mean to calculate the race handicap.) The utility would have a link back to your site — nicely keyworded — providing you with lots of great backlinks for search engines to read.

## Using RSS

Grabbing content from RSS feeds, as I explain in Chapter 9, is relatively easy. Creating content is a bit more complicated. Is it currently worthwhile for syndication purposes? Perhaps, but probably not quite yet for most Web sites. (Keep watching, though, things are going to change quickly.) RSS has become very popular, but not so much for placing content into Web sites; rather, people are using RSS readers to pull in RSS content. I suggest that you use the manual form of syndication first.

As I mention in Chapter 9, RSS is one of those geeky acronyms whose real meaning no one has really nailed down. Some stump for *Really Simple Syndication,* while others swear it means *Rich Site Summary* or *RDF Site Summary.*

If you really want to syndicate using RSS, you have some research to do. A good place to start is Lockergnome's RSS Resource (channels.locker gnome.com/rss/), which contains several articles to help you get started. Good luck. Better still, have your company geek or geek friend do all this for you, if you're not a geek yourself.

After you have set up your RSS feeds (do you like the way I jumped?), register the RSS feeds with as many RSS directories as you can, such as the following:

- **Blog Universe:** www.bloguniverse.com
- **blogarama:** blogarama.com
- **Blogdex:** blogdex.com
- **Blogdigger:** www.blogdigger.com
- **BlogSearchEngine.com:** www.blogsearchengine.com
- **BlogShares:** www.blogshares.com
- **BlogStreet:** www.blogstreet.com
- **Blogwise:** www.blogwise.com
- **Bloogz:** www.bloogz.com
- **DayPop:** www.daypop.com
- **Feedster:** feedster.com
- **Lockergnome's RSS Resource Site:** rss.lockergnome.com
- **NewsIsFree:** newsisfree.com
- **SearchEngineBlog.com:** www.searchengineblog.com
- **Syndic8:** syndic8.com
- **Waypath:** www.waypath.com

# Who's Going to Do All This Work?!

Wow, finding sites to link to yours is a lot of work. As I said before, it's very LTT. It's also not, shall we say, high-rent work. How do you get all this done? Assuming you're not using a link-acquisition firm, here are some options:

- Do you have kids? If not, get some. It's a little drastic, but after you've spent a week or two doing this stuff, it may not seem so bad.
- Do your neighbors or employees have kids?
- Do your siblings have kids?
- Local schools and colleges definitely have kids, so you may want to find one or two who will do a few hours of work each evening.

# How links build links

I want to share a story that provides a wonderful illustration of how a link campaign can work. It shows how you can build links, PageRank, and traffic, all at the same time, the old-fashioned way. I found this story in one of WebmasterWorld's discussion groups. As the author of the story puts it, you should remember how the "Internet started and what it was supposed to be all about: sharing information." The search engines want you to remember this, too.

The story is from an Aussie called Woz. Once upon a time, Woz had a site called Glossarist (www.glossarist.com), a directory of glossaries and topical dictionaries. This was a hobby for Woz, and he had done little to promote the site. But one sunny day — July 26, 2003 — he noticed a 4,000-percent increase in traffic. (For the math challenged among you, traffic on that day was 40 times greater than the day before!) It appears that the site was mentioned in the ResearchBuzz e-mail newsletter and Web site (www.researchbuzz.com), by the fairy godmother, Tara Calishain. Not surprisingly, ResearchBuzz is a resource for people interested in research. It's the sort of site that would be interested in a directory of glossaries and topical dictionaries.

The very next day, a wonderfully bright and sunny day, Glossarist was picked up by The Scout Report (scout.wisc.edu/Reports/Scout Report/2001/scout-010727.html), which, perhaps a little more surprisingly, is a "weekly publication offering a selection of new and newly discovered Internet resources of interest to researchers and educators."

Then on August 9, a *really* sunny day, the site was mentioned in USAToday.com's Hot Sites (www.usatoday.com/tech/2001-08-0 9-hotsites.htm). I've had one of my sites mentioned in *USA Today,* and believe me, your traffic really spikes when that happens!

By the middle of August, Woz wuz able to identify links from over 200 sites — "libraries and student-resource pages from schools and universities, translation sites, business reference sites, writers sites, information architecture sites, and so on." He also got a lot of traffic from newsletters that had been forwarded from subscribers to friends and colleagues. (Both *ResearchBuzz* and *The Scout Report* are very popular e-mail newsletters.) Not only did site owners find out about him through these e-mails, but many visitors also came to his site through the e-mail links.

All this publicity was great, providing his site with a lot of traffic through those links and also making it more likely that his site would be found and indexed by the search engines. But it also boosted his site's PageRank. By mid-August, the Glossarist PageRank had reached 3; by the end of August, it was 8, which is an excellent PageRank for what is really a hobby site, created by a single person without a marketing budget! (I just checked, and it's currently showing a PageRank of 7, which is still very good.)

By the end of August, he had around 300 links. I recently checked and found 2,409 links to this site! (Over the last couple of years the number of links seems to have been growing at the rate of two a week.) And, as Woz claims, he didn't request a single one of these links.

Don't underestimate the power of this kind of grass-roots promotion. It can be tremendously powerful. One link can set off a chain reaction, in the way that a single link in ResearchBuzz did.

# Chapter 16

# Using Shopping Directories and Retailers

*I*f your Web site is an e-commerce site, you have more places at which you can register. There's a whole 'nother category of search engines — shopping directories. These are giant catalogs of products. Search for *digital camera,* for instance, and you see a page with pictures of cameras, their prices, links to the appropriate Web sites, and so on. (A few of these services, such as NexTag, list services as well as products.)

Most of these directories expect you to pay, but not all of them do. Froogle, Google's product directory, is completely free, for example. In general, the ones that *do* expect you to pay charge only when someone clicks a link to visit your site, so these directories may be worth experimenting with.

I begin this chapter by talking about the different systems that are available and end by providing you with a little help on preparing your data for the directories.

## Finding the Shopping Directories

The following directories are probably the most important shopping directories to research. Go to each one and try to find information about signing up and uploading your data. In some cases, that process is simple — the directory wants you to join, so you find a link that says something like <u>Sell on Our Site</u> or <u>Merchant Info</u>. Sometimes you have to dig a little deeper because the information is not clearly visible; you may need to use the <u>Contact Us</u> link and ask someone about signing up.

- ✔ **Google Catalogs:** catalogs.google.com
- ✔ **Froogle:** www.froogle.com
- ✔ **Yahoo! Shopping:** shopping.yahoo.com
- ✔ **Shopping.com:** www.shopping.com
- ✔ **BizRate & Shopzilla:** www.shopzilla.com
- ✔ **PriceGrabber.com:** www.pricegrabber.com
- ✔ **NexTag:** www.nextag.com
- ✔ **Price Watch:** www.pricewatch.com
- ✔ **PriceSCAN:** www.pricescan.com

Most of these systems expect you to pay if you want to play — generally you pay each time someone clicks a link to your site. Some let you list your products, and receive traffic, at no cost. Here is a rundown of the three types of systems:

- ✔ **Free:** You have no direct control over your position, but you don't have to pay for any traffic you get from the site. Google Catalogs and Froogle are of this type.
- ✔ **Pay-per-click, fixed fee:** Yahoo! Shopping is of this type. You don't have any control over position because there's no bidding (as there is with the following type); you pay a fixed fee per click.
- ✔ **Pay-per-click bidding:** Most of the other systems charge per click, but have bidding systems that help determine your position on search-results pages. (As you may expect, merchants with the highest bids are listed first on the page.)

What will you pay for the *pay-per-click (PPC)* systems?

- ✔ In most cases, PPC systems don't charge a listing fee.
- ✔ You have to begin by funding your account — typically $50 to $250, which goes toward paying for your clicks.
- ✔ You pay each time someone clicks your link. Clicks vary in price, generally from ten cents up.
- ✔ In systems that accept bids, there's a minimum click rate, but the actual rate is dependant on how many people are bidding and their pain threshold; in some cases, clicks could even cost several dollars.
- ✔ You may be charged other fees, such as a fee to place a store logo next to your listing. (Some of the PPC systems give these logos to the highest bidders free.)

# Google Catalogs

Here's a simple one. A *very* simple one. If your company publishes a catalog of some kind (pretty much any kind), get it to Google Catalogs right away.

1. **Visit** `catalogs.google.com`.

2. **Click the <u>Info For Catalog Vendors</u> link.**

   The page that appears provides the address to which you should send your catalog.

3. **Add the provided address to your subscriber list.**

   This ensures that Google Catalogs gets the next edition (and makes sure it never drops off the list).

4. **Drop a copy of the current edition in the mail.**

5. **E-mail Google letting it know you've done so.**

Google claims to scan every catalog it receives within a few days. It also *OCRs* them; that's a new verb derived from *Optical Character Recognition*. This means the text in the catalog is converted from images to computer text that can be searched.

Take a look at Figure 16-1. This is the beginning of the Consumer Electronics category. The figure shows images of catalog covers. Under each cover is the catalog name, a short description of the contents, the edition, and a link to the company's Web site. Of course, you should always make sure your catalog includes your site's URL in a prominent position, but this is one more good reason to do so.

Click a catalog, and you're inside that catalog, as shown in Figure 16-2. One more click, and you're reading a catalog page, as shown in Figure 16-3. The controls at the top let you move through the catalog page by page, or you can search for a particular word.

At the time of writing, Google Catalogs is in *beta,* and has been for years. It's not on the main Google site, though for a while in the summer of 2003 it was incorporated into Amazon.com. Eventually, you may see more of Google Catalogs — certainly on the main Google site and perhaps elsewhere. However, one theory for why Google Catalogs has been in beta for years is that it may be merely a way for Google to test OCR on a large scale for various other purposes. Also, I should state that there's some question about the future of this service. Many of the catalogs are very out of date. However, Google does still appear to be working on the service, and early in 2006 it was still up and collecting catalogs. And getting into Google Catalogs is so cheap and easy that you might as well do it.

**Figure 16-1:**
The Google
Catalogs
Consumer
Electronics
page.

**Figure 16-2:**
Inside a
catalog.

**Figure 16-3:**
Viewing a
catalog
page.

# Froogle

Froogle (www.froogle.com) is Google's product directory. It's been incorporated into the main Google site for around three years, and has hundreds of millions of products in the index, despite the fact that Google presents it as a beta service. They have added a <u>Shopping? Try Froogle</u> link onto the main page and are also experimenting with providing Froogle results and links to Froogle results on some search-results pages.

Getting into Froogle is easy. Although the instructions (look for the Information for Merchants link at the bottom) say that Froogle will take five to ten days to respond, it will probably send you instructions within minutes of signing up.

The system is entirely free. Froogle displays products in search results and channels traffic to your site at no cost whatsoever. (If you want to advertise on Froogle's search-results pages, you have to use Google AdWords; see Chapter 17 for details.)

Working with Froogle is also simple. You have to submit a *datafeed* file — a simple text file containing the product data, which I discuss later in this chapter. But because Froogle doesn't display a lot of information about each product (see Figure 16-4), it doesn't require much information from you: a link to the information page on your site, a link to an image of the product, the name and description, a price, and a category.

**Figure 16-4:**
Search at Froogle, and you'll find pictures, a little information, and links to retailers' Web sites.

# Yahoo! Shopping

Yahoo! Shopping (`shopping.yahoo.com`) charges you each time someone clicks a link to your site. Yahoo! finds the product you're looking for (see Figure 16-5) and then, when you click the link to the product page, finds merchants that sell the product; see Figure 16-6.

So how much is all this going to cost? That depends on the product category. Unlike some systems, Yahoo! charges a fixed fee per click that varies among categories; other systems charge a fee that is dependent on bidding, like the PPC systems. (See Chapter 17 for more on PPC systems.)

For instance, here are a few click prices:

| | |
|---|---|
| Apparel | $0.19 |
| Beauty | $0.25 |
| Books | $0.19 |
| Computers and Software | $0.38 |

| | |
|---|---|
| Computers and Software > Desktop | $0.44 |
| Computers and Software > Software | $0.38 |
| DVD and Video | $0.25 |
| Electronics | $0.38 |
| Electronics > Digital Cameras | $0.50 |
| Flowers, Gifts and Registry | $0.25 |
| Flowers, Gifts and Registry > Flowers | $1.25 |
| Toys and Baby Equipment | $0.25 |
| Video Games | $0.25 |

This link takes you to a product page, not a merchant.

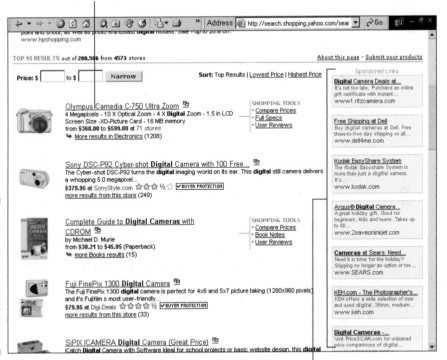

**Figure 16-5:**
Yahoo!
Shopping is
product-
centric,
taking you
to product
pages, not
merchants.

These are ads from Overture.

**Figure 16-6:**
You can find
links to
merchants
on the
product
page.

# Shopping.com

Shopping.com (found on the Web at shopping.com, of all places) is also a pretty important (that is, popular) shopping directory. It also charges by the click, and each category has a minimum rate. For instance, the following list shows a few minimum *cost per clicks (CPCs):*

| | |
|---|---|
| Books | $0.05 |
| Cables and Connectors | $0.10 |
| Computers | $0.30 |
| Drive Cases | $0.10 |
| Furniture | $0.05 |
| Graphics and Publishing Software | $0.05 |
| Kitchen | $0.05 |

Figure 16-7 shows the Digital Cameras page, a subcategory of Electronics.

**Figure 16-7:**
The
Shopping.
com
directory.

Remember, these are *minimums;* your mileage may vary (and almost certainly will). Unlike with Froogle and Yahoo! Shopping, the higher your bid in a system such as Shopping.com, the higher you'll initially appear on the product page. However, at Shopping.com, a site visitor can sort the product page by price, store name, and store rating, so as soon as a visitor sorts the page, most of the benefit of the higher bid price is lost. Bids are placed per category, by the way, not per product.

As with most shopping directories, you can provide a datafeed file to Shopping.com. But it also has another service, by which it grabs the information from your Web site for you. This costs $75 to set up and $50 monthly, but the directory will crawl your Web site every day.

## PriceGrabber and PrecioMania

PriceGrabber (www.pricegrabber.com) and its Spanish-language *hermano* PrecioMania (www.preciomania.com) claim to send over a billion dollars in customer referrals each month. True or not (how do you measure a referral, anyway?), PriceGrabber is a significant shopping directory in its own right, because it feeds data to various other shopping directories.

## Mergers

Shopping.com was formed by a merger of DealTime and Epinions, the most popular product-comparison sites on the Web. Two separate sites, Shopping.com and Epinions.com, now exist; getting into Shopping.com gets you into both sites. It's worth noting that Epinions listings often rank well in search engines.

This system works two ways. You can pay per click for traffic sent to your Web site, as with most other shopping directories, or you can use the PriceGrabber Storefronts system and let PriceGrabber take the order and send the information to you to ship the product. (It charges 7.5 percent.)

## BizRate & Shopzilla

BizRate & Shopzilla (www.shopzilla.com) are two popular per-click sites with common ownership. As with Shopping.com, these services charge a minimum fee per category, typically $0.10 to $0.30, with the actual rate dependent on bidding. Again, merchants with the highest bid are listed first, until the visitor re-sorts the list. Figure 16-8 gives the BizRate take on digital cameras — and, no, I'm not necessarily dropping any hints here, although my birthday *is* coming up.

## NexTag

NexTag (www.nextag.com), yet another popular site, is also a PPC site with a category minimum and bidding for position. You don't pay a setup fee, but you do have to fund your account before you can get started. That's the norm with all these PPC shopping directories, but NexTag's $250 minimum to start is a little high.

NexTag is one of the few shopping systems that lists not only tangible products but also services. If your business sells auto insurance or long-distance telephone service, for instance, you can be listed at NexTag.

You can load data into a Web-form system if you have only a few products. If you have more, you'll want to use a datafeed file. NexTag will take any datafeed file; if you create one for Yahoo! Shopping, for instance, you can use the same one for NexTag. Just send the Yahoo! one to your NexTag account manager, and he or she will handle it.

Figure 16-8:
The BizRate
shopping
directory.

# Price Watch

Price Watch (www.pricewatch.com) isn't well known outside of geek circles. Many people in the computer business use Price Watch to buy their hardware after checking pricing at the site; the site is limited to computers, peripherals, and accessories. This is a crude system (as shown in Figure 16-9) that appeals to UNIX geeks in particular. It's fast and has no graphics on the search page (or even on the results pages in most cases).

The Price Watch folks claim to serve over 200 million pages each month, so if you have products in their categories, you may want to look into working with them. However, they don't necessarily make that easy. Contact them (you can find a contact page somewhere in the About area) and see if they get back to you!

# PriceSCAN

PriceSCAN (www.pricescan.com) got off to a good start — it was one of the earliest shopping or price-comparison directories — but it seems to have been superseded by the other systems I've mentioned. However, PriceSCAN has one great advantage over most of them: As with Froogle, you can list your products for free. The directory does sell advertising, but the price comparisons are intended to be unbiased by fees or PPCs. E-mail the site at vendors@pricescan.com, and who knows, someone might even respond.

**Figure 16-9:**
Price
Watch, a
UNIX geek's
dream
shopping
directory.

# More Shopping Services

Yep, there's more, plenty more. Table 16-1 offers a quick rundown of some other places you can list your products.

**Table 16-1: Shopping Services**

| Service Name | URL | Description |
|---|---|---|
| Shop.com | www.shop.com | Originally CatalogCity.com and designed for catalog companies to sell their wares online, this site is looking for merchants with over 100 consumer-oriented products. |
| StreetPrices.com | www.streetprices.com | A PPC site that claims to get 200,000 visitors each month, generating $90 million per month in "sales leads" (whatever that means). It charges from $0.45 to $0.55 per click. |

| Service Name | URL | Description |
|---|---|---|
| iBuyernet.com | `www.ibuyernet.com` | Is there anyone home? Who knows? This site doesn't seem very interested in signing up new merchants. |
| Ask Jeeves Shopping, Dogpile, MetaCrawler, and Pricing Central.com | `ask.pricegrabber.com, dogpile.price grabber.com, meta crawler.price grabber.com, pricing central.com` | All these systems use PriceGrabber; get in there, and you're in here, too. |
| Lycos Shopping | `shop.lycos.com` | Uses BizRate. |
| mySimon and Shopper.com | `www.mysimon.com www.Shopper.com` | Combined, these are very important sites, but because they don't make it easy for the average store owner to work with them, I've put them in the "more stuff" category. Owned by CNET, these systems don't have automated feeds set up for merchants. Contact them directly about how you can work with them; they may take a couple of months to get back to you. They have a variety of programs, from simple PPC text links (generally from $0.15 to $0.50 per click) to featured advertising positions. |
| AOL Shopping | `webcenter.shop.aol.com` | A very exclusive property; if you want to work with AOL Shopping, you have to negotiate directly. |
| MSN Shopping | `eshop.msn.com` | Not quite as exclusive as AOL, but if you want to be in MSN Shopping, you still have to negotiate directly. |
| Kelkoo | `www.kelkoo.com` | Don't forget about shopping directories outside the United States. Kelkoo is one of the better-known systems in Europe. |

# Third-Party Merchant Sites

I want to quickly mention yet another type of listing you can get for your products: third-party merchant sites. I don't go into great detail here, because this is one step over the line between being in a search directory and being sold on another Web site.

You may want to consider selling your products on the major e-commerce sites, which consist of both auction and retail sites:

- ✔ With the auction sites, you sell your products, yep, at an auction and handle the transactions yourself.

- ✔ With the retail sites, the product is placed into a directory, and if anyone buys it, the retail site handles the transaction, sends you the information so you can ship the product, and then, a little while later, sends you the money (bar its commission, of course).

Many merchants use the auction sites as a way to generate traffic to their Web sites. By placing links in the ads, you can bring new customers directly to your site, and by carefully using price reserves, you can ensure that any sales you make through an auction are not at a loss.

Check out the following sites to find out more about working with third-party retail sites:

- ✔ **Amazon.com zShops:** This is a retail site where people searching at Amazon may run across your products. See www.zshops.com.

- ✔ **Amazon Marketplace:** If you sell the same products Amazon sells, you can place links to your products from the same pages on which Amazon sells its products. (You've probably seen the This Item Also Available to Buy box on Amazon product pages.) You can also find information on this at the zShops site.

- ✔ **Half.com:** Owned by eBay, this is a huge retail-products site. See halfbay.ebay.com.

- ✔ **eBay:** This is the world's most popular e-commerce site, with billions of dollars of products being sold here. See www.ebay.com.

There are also two other auction sites you might consider . . . or might not. Amazon Auctions (auctions.amazon.com) and Yahoo! Auctions (auctions.yahoo.com). The problem is, though, that few auction sites can compare with eBay. There simply aren't many items listed on these two sites, and few people even know they exist, so it may not be worth the time and energy to work with them.

# Creating Data Files

Before you sign up with the shopping directories, you probably need a data file (often called a *datafeed*) containing information about your products. This is a simple text file carefully formatted using the correct layout. A datafeed allows you to quickly upload hundreds, even thousands, of products into the directories within minutes.

Although the datafeed file can be a simple text file, creating it is a little difficult for some people. Of course, if you have geeks on your staff, they can handle it for you. The ideal situation is one in which all your product data is stored in a database that is managed by capable, knowledgeable people who know how to export to a text file in the correct format. All you do is give them the data-file specification from the shopping directory, and they know exactly what to do. If that's your situation, be happy. If not, pay attention, and I'll help you.

I'm going to explain how to format your data using a spreadsheet program, which is probably the simplest way. If you have a large number of products, you may already have your data in some kind of database format. Unfortunately, you may need to *manipulate* your data — clean it up — before you can use it. I've noticed over the last couple of decades that, for some reason, data is usually a mess, whether the data files were created by small companies or large. The files are often badly formatted — for example, the text files contain the data, but the fields are improperly *delimited* (separated).

I suggest that you use a spreadsheet program to create your data file. Creating the file in a text editor is difficult and error prone, especially if you have a lot of products. Also, remember that each shopping directory is a little different, requiring different information. The spreadsheet file is your source file, from which you can create the various text files as needed.

You may already have a spreadsheet program; Microsoft Excel is hiding on millions of computers around the world, unknown to their owners. (It's part of Microsoft Office.) Or you may have Microsoft Works, which also includes a spreadsheet program. Various other database programs are available — StarOffice and AppleWorks contain spreadsheets, too. You don't need a terribly complicated program, because the work you do with the file is pretty simple. However, you want to use a program that can have multiple sheets open at once and allows you to link from a cell in one sheet to a cell in another.

You can also use a database program to manage all this data. It's just simpler in some ways to use a spreadsheet. Of course, you may already have your data in a database, especially if you have a lot of products.

## The data you need

Take a look at the type of data you're going to need for your data file. Froogle, Google's shopping directory, requires the following data:

- ✔ **product_url:** A link to the product page on your Web site
- ✔ **name:** The name of the product
- ✔ **description:** A description of the product
- ✔ **image_url:** A link to the image file containing a picture of the product
- ✔ **price:** The cost
- ✔ **category:** The category in which you want to place the product
- ✔ **offer_id:** Some kind of product number, such as a *stock keeping unit (SKU)* or *international standard book number (ISBN)*

Those are the basic fields, but there are others you can include, such as instock, shipping, brand, upc, manufacturer_id, and so on.

Each service is different, of course. Here's the data that can be included in Yahoo! Shopping:

- ✔ **code:** A SKU or other kind of identifier
- ✔ **product_url:** A link to the product page on your Web site
- ✔ **name:** The name of the product
- ✔ **price:** The cost
- ✔ **merchant-category:** Your own product category, based on how you categorize products on your site — for instance, Electronics and Camera > Television and Video > VCR
- ✔ **shopping-category:** The Yahoo! Store category under which the product will be placed
- ✔ **description:** A description of the product
- ✔ **image_url:** A link to the image file containing a picture of the product
- ✔ **isbn:** If the product is a book, the ISBN
- ✔ **medium:** If your products are music or videos, the medium (CD, DVD, VHS, 8mm, and so on)
- ✔ **condition:** The product's condition (new, like new, very good, good, and so on)
- ✔ **classification:** A product type, such as new, overstock, damaged, returned, refurbished, and so on
- ✔ **availability:** Information about the product's availability

✔ **ean:** The *European Article Number (EAN),* a number used for barcoding products

✔ **weight:** The weight of the product

✔ **upc:** The *Universal Product Code (UPC)* number, another barcoding system

✔ **manufacturer:** The manufacturer's name

✔ **manufacturer-part-no:** The manufacturer's part number

✔ **model-no:** The product's model number

Don't worry — only five of these fields are absolutely required. As you can see, some fields are the same in both the Froogle and Yahoo! systems. (For details, you need to check the particular systems into which you want to load the data.)

Here's my suggestion. Begin by creating a spreadsheet file containing *all* the data you have about your products. At the very least, include this information:

✔ Product name

✔ Product description

✔ Product price

✔ Product category

✔ A URL pointing to the product's page on your Web site

✔ A URL pointing to the image file containing a picture of the product on your site

You also want to include any other information you have — ISBNs, SKUs, EANs, media types, and so on. And keep the file clean of all HTML coding; you just want plain text, with no carriage returns or special characters in any field.

## Formatting guidelines

Some of you may have problems with the product URL. If your site is a framed site, as I discuss in Chapter 7, you've got a problem because you can't link directly to a product page. But even if you don't have a framed site, you might have a problem or two. I discuss that in a minute.

Each shopping directory varies slightly, but datafeed files typically conform to the following criteria:

✔ They are plain text files. That is, don't save them in a spreadsheet or database format; save them in an ASCII text format. Virtually all spreadsheet programs have a way to save data in such a format.

✔ The first line in each file contains the header, with each field name — product_url, name, description, price, and so on — generally separated by tabs.

✔ Each subsequent line contains information about a single product; the fields match the headers on the first line.

✔ The last line of the file may require some kind of marker, such as END.

✔ In most cases, you can't include HTML tags, tabs within fields (tabs usually separate fields), carriage returns, new line characters within fields, and so on. Just plain text.

## Creating your spreadsheet

Take a look at Figure 16-10. This is a simple spreadsheet file containing a number of data fields; it's an example data file from Froogle. Each row in the spreadsheet is a product, and each cell in the row — each field — is a different piece of information about the product.

Although the final product will be a text file, you want to save the spreadsheet file in a normal spreadsheet file format. When you're ready to upload data to a shopping directory, *then* you save it as a text file.

| File Edit View Insert Format Tools Data Window Help | | | | | |
|---|---|---|---|---|---|
| | A | B | C | D | E |
| 1 | code | product-url | name | price | shopping-category |
| 2 | p12-x | http://www.yourstore123.com/1.html | American Pride Polo Shirt | 25 | Apparel |
| 3 | w345 | http://www.yourstore123.com/2.html | Women's Overalls | 39.95 | Apparel |
| 4 | f45 | http://www.yourstore123.com/3.html | Carrot Cake | 29.95 | Flowers, Gifts and Registry > Gourmet and F |
| 5 | f46 | http://www.yourstore123.com/4.html | Apple Pie | 19.99 | Flowers, Gifts and Registry > Gourmet and F |
| 6 | hg202 | http://www.yourstore123.com/5.html | Replacement Blade of Cof | 12.95 | Home, Garden and Garage > Appliances |
| 7 | 12kn | http://www.yourstore123.com/6.html | PowerMax Juicer | 129.95 | Home, Garden and Garage > Appliances > S |
| 8 | f235 | http://www.yourstore123.com/7.html | Soft Recliner | 399.99 | Home, Garden and Garage |
| 9 | p3002-x12 | http://www.yourstore123.com/8.html | Litter box - Gray | 14.95 | Home, Garden and Garage |
| 10 | 3exe345 | http://www.yourstore123.com/9.html | Handheld power drill | 89.95 | Home, Garden and Garage |

**Figure 16-10:** A sample datafeed spreadsheet.

## Getting those product URLs

To do this spreadsheet business right, you need the URL for each product's Web page. If you don't have many products, this is easy — just copy and paste from your browser into the spreadsheet. If you have thousands of products, though, it might be a bit of a problem! If you're lucky and you have a big IT budget or some very capable but cheap geeks working for you, you don't need to worry about this. Otherwise, here's a quick tip that might help.

TIP

Many companies have a source data file that they use to import into an e-commerce program. For this to be useful to you, figure out what page number the e-commerce program is assigning to each product. For instance, one e-commerce system creates its URLs like this:

```
http://www.yourdomain.com/customer/product.php?productid=
            18507
```

Notice that the `productid` number is included in this URL. Every product page uses more or less the same URL — all that changes is the `productid` number. So here's one simple way to deal with this situation. Suppose you have a data file that looks similar to the one in Figure 16-11, in which you have a product ID or code in one column, and an empty column waiting for the URL pointing to the product page.

| | A | B | C | D | |
|---|---|---|---|---|---|
| | File Edit View Insert Format Tools Data Window Help | | | | _ ∂ × |
| 1 | code | product-url | name | price | shopping-categ |
| 2 | 803341 | | American Pride Polo Shirt | 25 | Apparel |
| 3 | 803342 | | Women's Overalls | 39.95 | Apparel |
| 4 | 803343 | | Carrot Cake | 29.95 | Flowers, Gifts : |
| 5 | 803344 | | Apple Pie | 19.99 | Flowers, Gifts : |
| 6 | 803345 | | Replacement Blade of Cof | 12.95 | Home, Garden |
| 7 | 803346 | | PowerMax Juicer | 129.95 | Home, Garden |
| 8 | 803347 | | Soft Recliner | 399.99 | Home, Garden |
| 9 | 803348 | | Litter box - Gray | 14.95 | Home, Garden |
| 10 | 803349 | | Handheld power drill | 89.95 | Home, Garden |

**Figure 16-11:** Where do you get the URL from?

1. **Copy the blank URL into all the URL fields.**

   Copy the URL without the product ID in it, as shown in Figure 16-12. Some spreadsheet programs try to convert the URL to an active link, one you can click to launch a browser. You might want to leave the URL in that format so later you can test each link. (But working with these active links is often a nuisance because it may be hard to select a link without launching the browser.)

2. **Do one of the following to, with a single keystroke, copy the number in the code field and paste it onto the end of the matching URL:**

   • **Create a macro.**

   • **Use a programmable keyboard.**

   I love my programmable keyboard! It has saved me hundreds of hours. I use an old Gateway Anykey programmable keyboard, which you can buy at eBay.

**Figure 16-12:**
Place a
blank URL in
the column
and then
copy the
product
code from
the code
column to
the end of
the URL.

| | A | B | C | D | |
|---|---|---|---|---|---|
| | | File Edit View Insert Format Tools Data Window Help | | | _ ⵇ × |
| 1 | code | product-url | name | price | shopping-cate |
| 2 | 803341 | http://www.yourdomain.com/customer/product.php?productid= | American Pride Polo Shirt | 25 | Apparel |
| 3 | 803342 | http://www.yourdomain.com/customer/product.php?productid= | Women's Overalls | 39.95 | Apparel |
| 4 | 803343 | http://www.yourdomain.com/customer/product.php?productid= | Carrot Cake | 29.95 | Flowers, Gifts |
| 5 | 803344 | http://www.yourdomain.com/customer/product.php?productid= | Apple Pie | 19.99 | Flowers, Gifts |
| 6 | 803345 | http://www.yourdomain.com/customer/product.php?productid= | Replacement Blade of Cof | 12.95 | Home, Garden |
| 7 | 803346 | http://www.yourdomain.com/customer/product.php?productid= | PowerMax Juicer | 129.95 | Home, Garden |
| 8 | 803347 | http://www.yourdomain.com/customer/product.php?productid= | Soft Recliner | 399.99 | Home, Garden |
| 9 | 803348 | http://www.yourdomain.com/customer/product.php?productid= | Litter box - Gray | 14.95 | Home, Garden |
| 10 | 803349 | http://www.yourdomain.com/customer/product.php?productid= | Handheld power drill | 89.95 | Home, Garden |

If you don't have a programmable keyboard (and you should have one!), the spreadsheet you're using may have a built-in macro program that allows you to program actions onto a single keystroke. (MS Excel does, for instance.) Another option is to use a macro program that you download from a shareware site. If you have only 20 or 30 products, programmable keyboards and macros don't matter too much. If you have a few thousand products, it's worth figuring out how to automate keystrokes!

## Creating individual sheets

After you have all your data in one sheet of the spreadsheet file, you can create a single sheet for each system to which you plan to upload data: one for Froogle, one for Yahoo! Shopping, and so on. (A *sheet* is a spreadsheet page, and all good spreadsheet programs allow you to have multiple sheets.)

Remember, each system requires different information, under different headings, and in a different order. So you need to link information from the original sheet to each individual sheet. You don't want to actually copy this information.

Say that you have five shopping directories you're working with, and after you've finished everything, you discover that you made a few mistakes. If you *copied* the data, you have to go into each sheet and correct the cells. If you *linked* between cells, you can just make the change in the original sheet, and the other five update automatically.

Here's how this works in Excel. I will assume you have two sheets, one named Yahoo! (which contains data for Yahoo! Shopping) and one named Original (containing all your product data). And you want to place the information from the *productid* column in the Original sheet into the Yahoo! sheet, under the column named *code*. Here's how you do it in Microsoft Excel:

1. **Click the Yahoo! tab at the bottom of the window to open the Yahoo! sheet.**

2. **Click cell 2 in the *code* column.**

   In this example, this cell is A2, as shown in Figure 16-13.

**Figure 16-13:** The cursor on cell A2 in the Yahoo! sheet.

3. **Press the = (equal) key to begin placing a formula into the cell.**

4. **Click the Original tab at the bottom of the page to open the Original sheet.**

5. **Click cell 2 in the *productid* column.**

   In this example, this cell is again A2, as shown in Figure 16-14.

| | A | B | C | D | |
|---|---|---|---|---|---|
| 1 | productid | url | name | price | shopping-c |
| 2 | 803341 | http://www.yourdomain.com/customer/product.php?pro | American Pride Polo | 25 | Apparel |
| 3 | 803342 | http://www.yourdomain.com/customer/product.php?pro | Women's Overalls | 40 | Apparel |
| 4 | 803343 | http://www.yourdomain.com/customer/product.php?pro | Carrot Cake | 30 | Flowers, Gi |
| 5 | 803344 | http://www.yourdomain.com/customer/product.php?pro | Apple Pie | 20 | Flowers, Gi |
| 6 | 803345 | http://www.yourdomain.com/customer/product.php?pro | Replacement Blade o | 13 | Home, Gar |
| 7 | 803346 | http://www.yourdomain.com/customer/product.php?pro | PowerMax Juicer | 130 | Home, Gar |
| 8 | 803347 | http://www.yourdomain.com/customer/product.php?pro | Soft Recliner | 400 | Home, Gar |
| 9 | 803348 | http://www.yourdomain.com/customer/product.php?pro | Litter box - Gray | 15 | Home, Gar |
| 10 | 803349 | http://www.yourdomain.com/customer/product.php?pro | Handheld power drill | 90 | Home, Gar |
| 11 | | | | | |

**Figure 16-14:** The cursor on cell A2 in the Original sheet.

6. **Press Enter.**

The program jumps back to cell 2 in the *code* column of the Yahoo! sheet, places the data from the Original sheet into that cell, and then moves down to the cell below.

7. **Click cell 2 and then look in the formula box at the top of the window.**

You see this formula (or something similar): =Original!A2, as shown in Figure 16-15.

This means, "Use the data from cell A2 in the sheet named Original." You haven't copied the data; rather you're linking to the data, so that if the data in A2 changes, so will the data in this cell.

Here's the formula pulling data from Cell A2 in the Original sheet.

**Figure 16-15:**
Cell A2 in
the Yahoo!
sheet
contains
=Origin
al!A2.

8. **With cell 2 in the *code* column of the Yahoo! sheet selected, choose one of the following:**

   • **Press Ctrl+C.**

   • **Choose Edit⇨Copy from the main menu.**

   You've copied this data into the Clipboard.

9. **Press the down arrow (↓) to select the cell below.**

10. **Hold the Shift key and press PgDn multiple times, until the cursor has selected as many cells as there are products.**

   For instance, if you have 1,000 products, you want the last selected cell to be cell 1001. (Remember, the first cell contains the header, *code*.)

11. **Choose one of the following:**

    • **Press Ctrl+V.**

    • **Choose Edit⇨Paste from the main menu.**

    The cursor jumps to cell 2 again, and data from the Original sheet — from the appropriate cells — now appears in the cells below cell 2.

12. **Press the Esc key to stop copy mode.**

If you go to the Original sheet and change data in the *productid* column, the cells are now linked. Change data in a *productid* cell, and it changes in the appropriate *code* cell, too.

Repeat this process for all the columns you need and for all the different sheets you need, and you're ready to export your text files.

## Creating and uploading your data files

After you've created your sheets, you can export the text files you need to give to the shopping directories. Each spreadsheet program works a little differently. With some programs, you may find an Export command, and in Microsoft Excel, you use the Save As command. Here's how to export the text files from Excel:

1. **Save the spreadsheet file in its original spreadsheet file format.**

   This ensures that any changes you've made are stored in the original file.

2. **Click the tab for the sheet you want to export to a text file.**

   That sheet is selected.

3. **Choose File⇨Save As from the main menu to open the Save As dialog box.**

4. **In the Save As box, select the appropriate file type from the Save As Type drop-down menu.**

   In most cases, this option is *Text (Tab delimited)(*.txt)*, but it may be something different depending on the shopping directory you're working with; check the directory's data-file specifications.

5. **Provide a filename in the Name field.**

   For example, use Yahoo! if you're submitting to Yahoo!, and so on.

6. **Click OK.**

   You see a message box saying that you can't save the entire file; that's okay, all you want to do is save the selected sheet.

7. **Click Yes.**

   Now you see a message box telling you that some features can't be saved as text. That's okay, you don't want to save anything fancy, just text.

8. **Click Yes.**

   That's it; you've saved the file. It's still open in Excel, with the other sheets, so I suggest that you close the file. (Excel will ask again if you want to save the file — you can just say No.)

   If you want to export another text file, reopen the original spreadsheet file and repeat these steps.

If you want, you can open the file in a text editor like Notepad to see what it really looks like.

After you've created the text file, you're ready to upload it to the shopping directory. Each directory works a little differently, so refer to the directory's instructions.

These data files expire. They last only one month at Froogle, for example. Check each system carefully and remember to upload the latest data file before it expires or when you have any important changes.

# Chapter 17

# Paying Per Click

. . . . . . . . . . . . . . . . . . . . . . . . . . . . . . . . . . . . . . . . . . . . . . . . . . . . . .

*In This Chapter*

▶ Pay-per-click basics

▶ Figuring out how much a click is worth

▶ Creating ads that are acceptable

▶ Automating pay-per-click campaigns

. . . . . . . . . . . . . . . . . . . . . . . . . . . . . . . . . . . . . . . . . . . . . . . . . . . . . .

*H*ere's a quick way to generate traffic through the search engines: Pay for it. *Pay-per-click (PPC)* campaigns provide a shortcut to search engine traffic, and many companies, particularly large companies with large marketing budgets, are going directly to PPC and bypassing the search engine optimization stage totally.

In this chapter, you examine these PPC programs, discover both their advantages and disadvantages, and find out how and where to employ them. It's an overview, of course. If you decide to spend money on this form of advertising, I recommend that you read the quite splendid *Pay Per Click Search Engine Marketing For Dummies* (Wiley) by, um, me.

## Defining PPC

If you use PPC advertising, you'll pay each time someone clicks on one of your ads. Take a look at Figure 17-1, which shows search results at Google, and Figure 17-2, which shows results for the same search at Yahoo! As you can see, many of the search results on these pages are actually ads. They are placed mainly based on pricing. (*Google AdWords,* as their PPC ads are known, is a special case, as I explain in a moment.) In other words, rather than going through all the trouble of optimizing your site and getting links from other sites into your site — the things that are explained in most of the rest of this book — you can simply buy your way to the top of the search engines! Maybe.

**Figure 17-1:**
Pay-per-
click
placements
in Google.

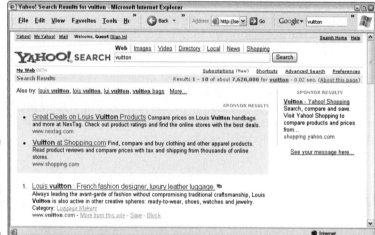

**Figure 17-2:**
Pay-per-
click
placements
in Yahoo!

Here is how it all works:

1. You register with a PPC system, provide a credit card number, and load your account.

2. You create one or more ads — providing a title, body text, and link to the page to which you want to direct visitors.

3. You associate keywords with each ad.

4. You bid on each keyword.

In general, when you bid on a keyword, you are bidding on a position. In Figure 17-3, you can see a list of keywords in the Yahoo! Search Marketing PPC system (previously known as Overture). The very first entry shows how much you are willing to bid on the keywords *web strategy*. In other words, if someone searches for *web strategy,* you're willing to pay $1.51 if that person clicks your ad. And, in this case, because the other people bidding on the term are not willing to pay that much, Yahoo! will list your ad at the top. You can see how much others are willing to bid in the Top 5 Max Bids column.

In most PPC systems, the top bid gets the top position. Google's system is a little more complicated (and because of this, Google is actually a little more difficult to use, because you can never be sure exactly in what position your ad will be placed). When Google has to position your ad for a particular search result, it chooses the ad position partly based on your bid price, but also partly on the *click rate* or *click-through rate,* the frequency with which people have clicked on your ad in the past. You may bid more than someone else, but because your ad has a low click-through rate in the past, it may still be placed below the lower bidder. As Google puts it, "The most relevant ads rise to the top . . . . Your ad can rise above someone paying more if it is highly relevant for a specific keyword."

**Figure 17-3:**
Bidding on keywords at Yahoo!

The big question, of course, is how much should you bid? Here are a few things to consider:

- ✔ You must understand how much a click is really worth to you; most companies do not know this. I discuss this issue a little later in this chapter.

- ✔ The higher your position, the more traffic you are likely to get.

- ✔ In general, if you're not in the first three positions, there's a good chance your ad won't be seen often and will get *dramatically* lower click-throughs. Google, for instance, syndicates their top three AdWords to sites such as AOL, and Yahoo! displays the top three (sometimes four) results at the top of their search results.

- ✔ Sometimes you may want to take position 3, because you want to be in the first three, yet position 1 is just too expensive. Many PPC marketers like positions 5 and 6; they still get a lot of clicks, but at a much lower price than higher positions.

- ✔ Other times, you may notice that position 1 is just $0.01 more than you're already paying; it may be worth paying the extra $0.02 to leapfrog the current bidder, just to boost your click-through.

- ✔ There's always a minimum bid level — $0.10 on Yahoo!, for instance, and $0.03 on Enhance.

Most PPC systems these days automatically adjust your bid price so that you only pay $0.01 above the lower bidder. Say, for instance, you have bid $10.00 for a keyword phrase, while the next highest bidder has only bid $2.99. You will be charged $3.00 for a click. If the next bidder raises his bid to $3.01, you'll be charged $3.02, and so on. However, note that some smaller systems don't do this, so you have to watch your bids carefully or you may pay significantly more than you need to for a position. And watch out for *jamming.* If the person in second place starts bidding $9.99, you'll be forced to pay $10.00 a click, while that person will probably still be paying $2.99 or less (a penny above the third bid).

## The two types of ads

Note that most Tier 1 and Tier 2 PPC systems (see "The three PPC tiers," later in this chapter) now have two types of ads:

- ✔ **Search engine ads.** The first are the search engine placements you've already seen.

- ✔ **Contextual or content match ads.** Ads placed on Web sites other than search engines. For instance, go to Amazon.com and search for something, and you'll likely come across ads similar to those shown in Figure 17-4.

**Figure 17-4:**
Google
AdSense
placements
at Amazon.
com.

These are ads from the Google AdWord's system.

In fact, you can sign up to run these ads on your Web site through Google's AdSense program (adsense.google.com) if you'd like to make money by running ads on your site. Sign up for this program, and Google examines your pages to see what ads are most appropriate for your page content. You place a little bit of code in your pages that pulls ads from the AdWords program, and Google automatically places ads into your page each time the page is loaded into a browser. If someone clicks the ad, you earn a little bit of the click price.

From the PPC advertiser's perspective, though, you should understand that these ads are probably not as effective as the ads placed on the search engines. Some advertisers claim that people who click these content ads are less likely to buy your product, for instance, than those who click the same ad at the search engine. You can turn off content ads if you wish, as many advertisers do.

## Pros and cons

What's good about a PPC campaign?

- ✔ **It's faster.** It's a much quicker way to begin generating traffic to your Web site — hours or days, compared to weeks or months through *natural search,* as unpaid search results are often known in the business.

- ✔ **It's much more reliable.** With a natural search, you may exert huge effort (read, expense) and not do well; with PPC you get what you pay for. If you're willing to bid high enough, you'll get the traffic.

✔ **It's more stable.** A site can do well in natural search results today, and then disappear tomorrow. With PPC, as long as you're willing to pay, your site is there.

What's bad about PPC?

✔ **You pay.** You have to pay for every click, which can add up to a great deal of money.

✔ **It's getting pricier.** Sticker shock is likely to get worse over the next year or two. Most people still don't even know what PPC is; wait and see what happens to pricing when PPC is as well known as other forms of advertising.

✔ **It's a crapshoot.** PPC doesn't always work, as you see later in this chapter — it's not possible for every company to buy clicks at a price that is low enough to be profitable.

✔ **It's not organic.** Many people prefer the free, natural search results — from 30 percent to 70 percent of all searchers (according to some research), depending on the search engine and type of search — so you're missing part of the market if you focus on PPC alone.

Ideally, PPC should be one part of an overall marketing campaign — it should be combined with the other techniques in this book. Many companies spend huge sums on PPC, yet totally ignore natural search, which could often be managed for a fraction of the sum.

## *The three PPC tiers*

The PPC companies are *networks;* that is, they place ads on multiple search sites. Yahoo!, for instance, places ads not only on the Yahoo! Web site, but also on AltaVista, CNN, InfoSpace, Juno, NetZero, Dogpile, ESPN, and many others. (Note that at the time of writing, Yahoo! also places ads on MSN's search results, but by the time you read this MSN will probably be running its own PPC system. You can reach MSN's new AdCenter at AdCenter.MSN.com.)

The other major service, Google's AdWords, appears on Google, of course, but also on AOL, Ask Jeeves, EarthLink, CompuServe, Netscape, Excite . . . even on Amazon.com. In fact, Google has a service called AdSense, which allows virtually any Web site to carry Google PPC ads.

I think of the PPC market as being split into the following three tiers:

### Tier 1

Tier 1 comprises three companies:

- ✔ Yahoo! Search Marketing at `SearchMarketing.Yahoo.com`
- ✔ Google AdWords at `www.AdWords.com`
- ✔ MSN AdCenter at `AdCenter.MSN.com`

These three systems are responsible for more PPC placements than all the rest of the networks combined. They are also the most expensive. A click that costs $0.05 on a Tier 2 or Tier 3 network may cost $2.00 on the major systems.

### Tier 2

Tier 2 comprises a handful of smaller networks that may still channel decent traffic to you, and at much lower prices:

- ✔ AskJeeves at `SponsoredListings.Ask.com`
- ✔ FindWhat at `www.findwhat.com`
- ✔ Espotting Media at `www.espotting.com`
- ✔ Enhance Interactive at `www.enhance.com`
- ✔ ePilot at `www.epilot.com`

They can't channel as much traffic as you would get by bidding for first position on Yahoo! or AdWords, but in some cases, they *can* send as much traffic as you're getting on those two behemoths, simply because you can't afford the big guys' top price per click.

ePilot, for instance, places ads on YellowPages.com, Locate.com, Search Bug, and so on. They may be small, little-known sites, but according to ePilot, the 100 or so systems they work with amount to almost 700 million searches a month. Enhance claims 1 billion searches throughout its network each month, on sites such as EarthLink and InfoSpace.

Note, however, that this situation may not last for long. The big PPC services have begun buying up the smaller fish; Sprinks.com, for instance, definitely one of the larger small fish, was bought by Google late in 2003.

### Tier 3

Finally, Tier 3. There are many other PPC networks, too; hundreds, in fact, and some are little more than a scam, encouraging the unwary to pay a setup fee with little real hope of ever getting any traffic. (You can find a huge list of PPC systems, over 500 at the time of writing, at `payperclicksearch engines.com`.)

On the other hand, there are many that can generate a little traffic for you each month; the problem, however, is that you'll spend a huge amount of time managing these Tier 3 companies. In general, it's not worth working with the Tier 3 company directly; rather, it's possible to work with a company that will sell you clicks at a fixed rate, and then gather these clicks from a wide array of Tier 3 PPC systems.

## Where do these ads go?

Figures 17-1 and 17-2 show a couple of examples of ad placements. But placement does vary quite a bit from site to site. Take the _health insurance_ search I did at Google, for instance. The first two ads were placed at the top of the search results, the first thing a searcher would see. Then ads are run down the right side of the page.

Do the same search at AOL, though, and you'll have the first four PPC ads at the top of the page, followed by a whole bunch of natural search results — that is, results that were not paid for — followed by another four Google AdWords PPC ads at the bottom of the page. At Ask Jeeves, you'll find three PPC ads at the top, and five on the bottom. So ads run in different positions on different sites, and of course all this varies periodically; the general trend over the last year has been to stuff more and more ads into search results pages. Some small sites run nothing but paid ads in their search results.

In general, it's obvious that these placements are paid ads. In most cases, the ads are preceded by the words _Sponsored Links_ or _Sponsored Web Results_ or something similar, and in fact the Federal Trade Commission mandates some kind of indication that a placement is paid. Despite that, there's a definite movement afoot to make it less and less obvious that more and more ads are appearing. Ask Jeeves used to run their _Sponsored_ label in such a light gray, on a white background, that it was almost illegible on a laptop screen, though at the time of writing the label is clearly displayed in red. On some small systems PPC ads are run without _any_ notification that they are ads. You probably won't see that happen on the large search sites, or with ads being fed by Google AdWords and Yahoo!, but some of the smaller ad networks evidently have lower standards.

By the way, the ads I've shown so far are simple text ads, but now the PPC companies are starting to allow advertisers to include, for instance, logos.

# It may not work!

*"Half the money I spend on advertising is wasted; the trouble is, I don't know which half."*

—John Wanamaker, 1838–1922

John Wanamaker's store in Philadelphia — imaginatively named *Wanamaker's* — was probably the world's first department store. He later opened one in New York, and was eventually the Postmaster General, but he's probably best remembered for the preceding quote. (Come on, be honest. Isn't that why you remember him?)

Wanamaker was almost certainly correct. Half (at least) of the money spent on advertising doesn't work in the sense that the monetary value derived from the advertising is less — often considerably less — than the cost of the advertising. Back in Wanamaker's day, there was very little way to track advertising success. Even today, it's hard to know for sure if advertising works . . . except for direct mail and online ads. Because it is possible to track viewers' reactions to ads online in various ways, it's possible to track results very carefully, which is how we know that billions of dollars were wasted on banner ads in the last few years of the last century!

And those days are being repeated, thanks to the latest online ad fad, PPC search engine advertising. The boom in banner advertising in the years 1997 or so to 2000 was based on a simple principle: There was always some other idiot who would be willing to pay ridiculous advertising rates because he didn't know any better. Now the same thing is happening with PPC ads.

Now, I'm not suggesting that you shouldn't use PPC advertising, or that some people aren't using it successfully — some definitely are. I'm just suggesting that you should be careful. In the days of the banner-ad boom, companies were paying way too much for ads, often with little regard, it seemed, for the *metrics* (that is, the measurements, the payoff). And today, many people are paying too much for their clicks, and prices are on the way up.

Do *not* assume that, just because someone else is paying $1.50 per click for the keywords in which you are also interested, you should be paying $1.51. A few things to remember:

- ✔ As weird as it may seem, many companies are losing money on their clicks. I know one company that spends almost $300,000 a month on PPC advertising that has admitted to me that it probably loses money on the clicks, but claims that "we have to keep the leads coming in." (I'm sure many of you who spend your days working in corporate America will find this easy to believe.)

✔ Some companies don't care if they make money on a click; they regard it as merely part of their branding campaign — if a company is used to spending hundreds of millions of dollars on TV ads, for instance, it may not care too much about tracking the direct benefits of a few million spent on PPC ads.

✔ Even if the company is making money on the clicks (I know another company spending $150,000 a month on very successful PPC ads), that doesn't mean *you* can make money based on the same click payment.

The last point is essential to understand. Say Company A sells books about rodent racing, making $10 per book after paying production costs. Company B sells racing rodents, and it makes $200 for every racer it sells. The book company is out of luck; there's no way it can compete for clicks against Company B. Company B could pay $50 or $100 or more on clicks for every sale it makes; clearly, Company A couldn't.

Here's a quick rule: If your average profit per sale is $10 or $20, then a PPC campaign probably won't work for you. (Probably. It just might, but it's unlikely.)

Ideally, before you begin a PPC advertising campaign, you really should know what a click is worth to your company (in reality, this isn't always possible), so take a look at the next section's points related to the value of clicks.

# Valuing Your Clicks

In order to calculate a *click value* — the maximum amount it's worth spending for a click — you have to work your way backwards from the end result, from the action taken by a visitor to your site.

## The value of the action

Every commercial site has some kind of action that the site owner wants the site visitor to carry out: buy a product, pick up the phone and call the company, enter information into a form and request a quote, sign up to receive more information, and so on. You have to understand the value of this action.

Say you're selling a product. How much would you pay me if I brought you a sale? Perhaps you have a product that sells for $50, and it costs $25 to create (or buy) and ship to a customer. Your gross profit, then, is $25, so you could afford to spend up to $25 to get the sale without losing money.

However, the value of the click may actually be higher than this. Imagine, for a moment, that if you sell a product for $50, you have a one-third chance of turning the buyer into a regular customer, and you know that regular customers spend $50 with you every 3 months for 18 months on average. Thus, the lifetime value of your new customer is actually $150, not $25 ($25 per month for 18 months, divided by 3).

Don't let some Internet geek convince you that you should take into consideration lifetime value. If you know you truly do have a lifetime customer value, that's fine, but many millions of dollars have been spent on online advertising based on the concept of an assumed lifetime value, when in fact there was little lifetime value beyond the first sale.

Of course, you may not be selling a product online. You may be gathering leads for your sales staff, or getting people to sign up for a catalog, or taking some other action that is not the end of the sales process, but in some sense the beginning. This is more difficult to project, though if you are working in an established company, it's information you (or someone in your organization) know. How much does your company pay for sales leads? Most medium-to-large companies know this number.

## *Your online conversion rate*

You have to know your online conversion rate, which you may not know when you begin your PPC campaign. If you have an established Web site that has been in business for a few months or years, then this is useful information that someone in the company should have. For every 1,000 people visiting your site, how many carry out the action you want (buy, call, sign up for more information, and so on)? How many visitors do you *convert* to customers or sales leads or subscribers (or whatever)?

Now, I said "for every 1,000 people," not "for every 100 people," for good reason. It may be a number below 1 percent. It may only be 7 or 8 out of every 1,000, for instance. I mention this because many people new to e-commerce do not realize that this is very much a numbers game, and that very low conversion rates are common. Sure, there are businesses that convert a much higher proportion of their visitors; but there are also many businesses that convert 1 percent or less. One would expect that businesses that are trying to get people to fill in a form to get a quote for insurance or mortgage rates, for instance, would have much higher conversion rates than companies selling products. (One company in this business told me its conversion rate is around 30 percent, for instance.)

Remember that e-commerce is in many ways much closer to the direct-mail business than the retail store business. Although people often talk about online stores, commerce sites are really much more like online catalogs. In particular, they share the characteristic of low conversions. The success of direct-mail campaigns is often measured in fractions of a percent, as it often is online, too.

## Figuring the click price

Back to the company selling a $50 product and making $25 per sale; you can assume that this company doesn't care about the customer's lifetime value, as indeed many small companies don't. (Either most of their sales are one-off with little repeat business, or they can't afford to invest in lifetime-value customers anyway; they have to make money on every sale.)

You can also assume that this company has figured out that its conversion rate is around 2 percent; 1 visitor out of 50 buys the product. You know that each customer is worth a maximum of $25; how much is a visitor worth, then? Fifty cents ($25 divided by 50).

That is, $0.50 is the most the company could spend for each site visitor without losing money. (The company isn't actually *making* money, of course, and I've left out consideration of the cost of running the Web operation and other company overhead.) If this company discovers that it can buy clicks for $0.75 cents or a dollar, clearly it's going to lose money. If clicks are $0.25, and if these numbers hold true, then it stands to make a gross profit of $12.50 for every sale.

## Different clicks = different values

The preceding is a simplification, of course. In fact, different visitors to your site may be more or less valuable to your company. If Visitor A goes to your site after being told by a friend that your site "sells the best rodent-racing handicap software on the Web," Visitor A is likely to be pretty valuable because he might buy several of your company's products or become a repeat customer. *Much* more valuable than Visitor B, who clicked a link or banner ad that says something like "Ever Thought About Rodent Racing?" On the one hand, Visitor A went out of his way on the recommendation of a friend, presumably because he's interested in rodent-racing handicap software. On the other hand, Visitor B may simply be wondering what these idiots are talking about.

It's likely that search engine traffic is actually more valuable than the average value of a visit to your site. Whether a click on a PPC ad or a natural search result, people who come to your site after searching for a particular keyword are likely to be more interested in your products and services than someone who simply stumbles across your site.

Some large companies spend huge amounts of money trying to analyze their traffic carefully — they want to know where every visitor comes from and exactly what each does. Unfortunately, it's difficult for small companies to do this, but at least you need to be aware of this issue when selecting keywords for your PPC campaigns. Note also that the major PPC systems provide additional services that allow you to track results — systems that will help you see what people do when they arrive at your site. You can see how many PPC visitors actually buy your products, for instance, which gives you a real solid idea of your site's click value.

# They Won't Take My Ad!

One of the most frustrating things to deal with when working with a PPC network is having your ads dropped because they don't match the network's standard. Or, as often happens, because one of the company's editors *thinks* the ad doesn't match the network's standards, or even because your Web site is not acceptable.

While some of the Tier 2 networks are much less fussy, Yahoo! and Google AdWords have very strict guidelines about what sort of Web page or Web site your ads can link to. Each network is different, but the following are the type of things that can kill your ad campaign on Yahoo! or Google:

- ✔ **Your site requires a password.** Personally, I think if you're stupid enough to point an ad to a password-protected Web site, the PPC network should take your money and run.

- ✔ **Your site's content doesn't match the ad.** Perhaps you have a very weak ad that simply doesn't provide much information about the subject area you are advertising around.

- ✔ **Your ad contains abusive, objectionable, or threatening language.**

- ✔ **Your site appears to facilitate the use or distribution of illegal drugs.** Yahoo!, for instance, won't take ads for sites that sell kits intended to help people cheat on drug tests.

- ✔ The landing page specified in your ad doesn't contain either content related to the ad or have an obvious path to the related content.

- ✔ You used a trademarked term in your ad, but there's no content related to that product on your Web site.

- ✔ Your ad doesn't explain that the product you are selling on your site can only be shipped to a very limited area.

- ✔ Your site includes multilevel marketing. Such sites are not allowed to use the terms *job* and *employment* on some PPC systems, but may use the terms *business opportunity* and *work*.

- ✔ You don't own the page you are linking to. Rules vary between systems; if you are an affiliate, you may have to link to your own page, and then direct visitors to the retailer's site, for instance.

- ✔ The ad promises information that is not on your site, but will be delivered in some manner — by e-mail or snail mail, for instance — and the ad doesn't state that fact.

- ✔ Your site doesn't function in Internet Explorer.

- ✔ You're using a term that is not allowed for your business. For instance, a finance company may not bid on the word *car* at Yahoo!

- ✔ Your auction site bids on terms related to products not currently on sale at the site.

- ✔ Your site contains content that may not be legal or is in some other way objectionable, or links to such a site.

- ✔ Your ad contains *superlatives* (biggest, best, greatest), ALL CAPS, or exclamation points!

- ✔ Your Web site disables the browser's Back button.

- ✔ Your Web site contains many broken links or is in some other way malfunctioning.

- ✔ Your ad's language doesn't match the language of the target Web site. If your ad is written in Spanish, it can't direct people to an English-language Web site.

- ✔ Your ad contains contact information, such as phone numbers and e-mail addresses.

- ✔ Your site spawns a pop-up window when the visitor arrives.

Phew! This isn't all of it, either.

---

## Super-lative

What makes it all the more difficult is that the editors enforcing the rules often don't have a full understanding of the rules themselves. One Yahoo! editor may tell you that *all* superlatives are banned; another might tell you that in some contexts they are okay. One ad I ran for a client used the term *largest warehouse,* which I was told was okay by one editor after having the ad killed by another. (It was okay, I was told, because it was a "secondary superlative" that didn't directly relate to the search term. That's one of the unwritten rules you just have to stumble across.) And in another ad, the term *our latest discounts* became a problem. "Other companies may have more recent discounts," I was told. After pointing out that the superlative referred to my clients' discounts, not everyone else's, they let it through. And when advertising a product in the city of Superior, Colorado, the ad was killed because the word *superior* is a superlative! PPC editors are a huge frustration for many PPC marketers; it seems that everyone managing large PPC campaigns has their own "stupid PPC editor" story!

---

Check your ads carefully after they've been accepted. Editors may change things without telling you, sometimes turning your finely tuned prose into something significantly different.

Why are the PPC networks so fussy? Surely, if you're paying, who cares if your site is broken or if your ad isn't relevant to the keywords you chose? It's your money, after all. Well, the networks are trying to achieve two things here:

- ✔ They want as many of the ads as possible to be clicked; they don't want to clutter up that valuable advertising space with irrelevant ads that nobody clicks because the networks only get paid when a searcher clicks.

- ✔ They want to protect the search results' relevance. PPC ads now make up a significant proportion of search results. (In many cases, in particular with the smaller PPC networks, 100 percent of the first screen of results seen by the searcher are paid ads.) So, it's as important for paid results to be relevant as it is for natural search results.

# *Automating the Task*

Working with PPC campaigns can be rather tedious. Ideally, you've got to keep your eye on the rankings each day or your ad could slip. In very competitive markets, it may be necessary to check several times a day.

You may be using half a dozen systems, too. If you are working with thousands of keywords (one client has 4,000–5,000 keywords to manage), that's a huge job.

How do you handle all this without it getting totally out of control? Here are a few ideas:

- ✔ Many companies hire a full-time person, even two or three people, just to manage their PPC campaigns.

- ✔ Programs are available that help to automate PPC management across multiple systems; GoToast (www.gotoast.com) is one of the best known, but various products are available.

- ✔ Some companies hire a third party to manage their PPC campaigns.

There's no easy answer. The automation software may be a good idea if you have a significant PPC campaign — tens or hundreds of thousands of dollars a month, with thousands of keywords over multiple PPC networks. On the other hand, having used one of the major automation systems, I have to say it was complicated, buggy, and expensive — *not* something you would want to use for a simple PPC campaign.

Sometimes it's actually cheaper to hire someone to manage the PPC campaign. One client, spending $150,000 per month on PPC, switched from having another company manage its PPC campaign to doing it itself. I estimated that the employee in charge of the PPC program probably spent 2–3 hours a day managing the program, and after my client realized that it could hire a full-time person to manage the program for 25 percent of what it was paying for another company to manage the PPC campaign, switching was easy!

One strategy some companies use is this: They manage Google, Yahoo!, and perhaps two or three of the other, more-productive Tier 2 systems themselves, in-house, perhaps using software if they have a very big keyword list. Then they use a PPC management company, or software such as GoToast or BidRank, to buy keywords from the smaller Tier 2 and Tier 3 PPC companies at a fixed price per click. For instance, you may agree to pay $0.35 per click. The management company then uses dozens, maybe hundreds, of smaller systems to get those clicks for you, keeping the difference between what they actually pay for the clicks (perhaps $0.05) and your $0.35.

# Part V
# The Part of Tens

The 5th Wave          By Rich Tennant

"Good news, honey! No one's registered our last name as a domain name yet! Helloooo Haffassoralsurgery.com!"

## In this part . . .

*A*fter you've got the basics of search engine optimization under your belt, this final part of the book gives you one last push in the right direction.

I talk about a number of myths and mistakes that are common in the search engine business. (No, most Web designers do not understand search engines, no matter what they say; and yes, you should start thinking about search engines before you build your site.)

This part also points you in the direction of some great information resources, places where you can find out more about search engine optimization or get info on a particular search engine technique. I also tell you about useful tools to help you in your endeavors, from programs that help you analyze the traffic coming to your Web site, to link checkers and search-rank tools.

# Chapter 18

# Ten-Plus Ways to Stay Updated

The naysayers said it couldn't be done, that a book about search engine optimization couldn't be written because the technology is changing so quickly. That's not entirely true — the basics really don't change, such as creating pages that the search engines can read, picking good keywords, getting lots of links into your site, and so on.

But some details *do* change. Which are the most important search engines? What tricks are the search engines really clamping down on? Why did your site suddenly drop out of Google (as many thousands did in the fall/winter of 2003, and on various occasions since)?

You may also need more detailed information than I can provide in this book. Perhaps you have a problem with dynamic pages, and you need to know the details of URL rewriting for a particular Web server, for instance. You need to know where to go to find more information. In this chapter, I provide you with resources that you can use to keep up-to-date and track down the details.

## Let Me Help Some More

Visit my Web site at www.SearchEngineBulletin.com. I point you to important resources, provide links to all the Web pages listed in this book (so you can just click instead of typing them), and provide important updates.

I also provide consulting services, including phone consultations. I can examine a company's online strategy not just from the perspective of search engines, but also from a wider view; I've been working online for 20 years now, and have experience in Web design, e-commerce and online transactions, traffic conversion, nonsearch-engine traffic generation, and so on. An hour or two of advice can often save a company from the huge expense of going down the wrong path!

# The Search Engines Themselves

One of the best ways to find information about the search engines is by using carefully crafted search terms at the search engines themselves. Say you want to find detailed information about dealing with session IDs; see Chapter 7. You could go to Google and search for *search engine session id*. Or perhaps you have a problem with dynamic URLs, and know that you need to use something called *mod_rewrite*. Go to a search engine and search for *mod_rewrite* or *mod rewrite*. (The former is the correct term, while many people talk of *mod rewrite* in the vernacular.)

It's amazing what you can find if you dig around for a little while. A few minutes' research through the search engines can save you many hours of time wasted through inefficient or ineffective SEO techniques. I suggest you read the bonus chapter posted at www.dummies.com/go/searchoptimization, which explains various techniques for searching at Google. A good understanding of how to use the search engines will pay dividends.

# Google's Webmaster Pages

Google is happy to tell you what it wants from you and what it doesn't like. No, it won't tell you exactly how it figures out page ranking, but good information is there nonetheless. It's a good idea to review the advice pages Google provides for Webmasters. You can find them at the following URLs:

- ✔ **Google Webmaster Guidelines:** www.google.com/webmasters/guidelines.html

- ✔ **Google Information for Webmasters FAQ:** www.google.com/webmasters/faq.html

# Yahoo!'s Search Help

Yahoo!'s search engine is the world's second most important, so perusing the Yahoo! Search Help area may be a good use of your time. You'll find information about how to use the system and how to work with it to get your pages indexed. See `http://help.yahoo.com/help/us/ysearch/index.html`.

The bonus chapter I mention earlier covers Google, not Yahoo!, so if you'd like to know more about how to use Yahoo!'s search engine, take a look at the Search Tips, Advanced Search, and Yahoo! Shortcuts pages. (The shortcuts allow you to search for airport information, exchange rates, gas prices, patents, U.S. Post Office, FedEx, and UPS packages, and more.)

# MSN's SEO Tips

You can find information about optimizing pages for submission to MSN at `http://search.msn.com/docs/`. You'll find a wide range of information, from how the MSNbot works, to how to handle a site move.

# Ask.com FAQ

One more for you, though not as much. Ask.com has a limited amount of information for Webmasters at `http://about.ask.com/docs/about/aj/teoma.htm`.

# Search Engine Watch

The Search Engine Watch site gives you a great way to keep up with what's going on in the search engine world. This site provides a ton of information about a very wide range of subjects related not only to search engine optimization, but also the flip side of the coin: subjects related to searching online. In fact, perhaps its greatest weakness is that it provides *so much* information; it's really intended for search engine optimization experts, rather than the average Webmaster or site manager. The site is divided into a free area and a paid-subscription area.

Danny Sullivan, who founded Search Engine Watch, has been in this business for years, and he really knows his stuff. (In fact, Search Engine Watch was one of the very first sources of information on this subject.) He's also very much plugged into the SEO community — he is perhaps one of the best-known people in the business — so he has an inside track to information that is otherwise hard to find. Visit his site at www.searchenginewatch.com.

## Google's Newsgroups

When you have a specific, detailed question about search engine optimization, where do you go? You can ask thousands of other people, many with extensive experience, by posting a question to a newsgroup devoted to search engine optimization. There are a number of great discussion groups where you may find the answer to your question already posted somewhere in an existing conversation, or you can post a question to start a conversation of your own.

Google hosts a newsgroup that is widely distributed across the Internet through many newsgroup services. If you know how to use newsgroups — if you already have a newsreader — check to see if your provider subscribes to google.public.support.general. If not, ask if they will. Or read the newsgroup through Google Groups, a free, Web-based newsgroup distribution service provided by Google itself: groups.google.com/groups?hl=en& group=google.public.support.general.

A quick word of warning about this newsgroup, and any other discussion group about search engine optimization. Not all the information you read will be correct or even close to the truth. The search engine optimization business is rife with rumor, hype, and conjecture. Some of the information in the discussion groups is just plain wrong. How can you tell? The greater your knowledge of search engine optimization, the more likely you are to have a feel for whether the advice makes sense. And one good thing about the discussion groups is that they are, to some degree, peer reviewed. Do other people agree with the advice? Do many people disagree, even disagree vehemently? If you're unsure how valid someone's advice or claim is, checking the reactions of other people in the discussion can help you determine the accuracy of the advice.

# WebMaster World

WebMaster World (www.webmasterworld.com) is a very good discussion group, with many knowledgeable people. It'll cost ya, though: $89 for six months, or $150 for a year.

# Pandia

Pandia Search Central (www.pandia.com) is a great resource site with information about search engines, from how to use search engines to how to rank well. The site also provides tutorials and links to all sorts of useful sites.

# 1HelpYouServices.com

A huge amount of information is available at www.ihelpyouservices.com/forums in about three dozen discussion groups, from those related to general search engine information, such as link popularity and page content, to those dedicated to specific search systems.

# HighRankings.com

Hosted by a search engine optimization consultant, HighRankings.com is a pretty busy forum (free at this time), with discussions covering a wide range of subjects. Check it out at www.highrankings.com/forum.

# Yahoo!'s Search Engine Optimization Resources Category

This is a good place to find a variety of resources related to search engine optimization: companies, online services, information resources, and so on. Check it out at dir.yahoo.com/Computers_and_Internet/Internet/World_Wide_Web/Site_Announcement_and_Promotion/Search_Engine_Optimization__SEO_/.

# The Open Directory Project Search Categories

Of course the Open Directory Project also has a number of useful search categories:

- dmoz.org/Computers/Internet/Searching
- dmoz.org/Computers/Internet/Searching/Search_Engines
- dmoz.org/Computers/Internet/Searching/Directories
- dmoz.org/Computers/Internet/Searching/Search_Engines/ Specialized

You might also visit www.resource-zone.com, where you can find forums hosted by Open Directory Project editors who may be able to help you.

# Chapter 19

# Ten Myths and Mistakes

*In This Chapter*

▶ Common mistakes made by site developers

▶ Harmful myths

▶ Problems that hurt your search engine rank

A lot of confusion exists in the search engine world; a lot of myths and a lot of mistakes. In this chapter, I quickly run through a few of the ideas and omissions that can hurt your search engine positions.

## Myth: It's All about Meta Tags and Submissions

This is the most pervasive and harmful myth of all, and one held by many Web designers and developers. All you need to do, many believe, is code your pages with the right meta tags — KEYWORDS and DESCRIPTION, and things like REVISIT-AFTER and CLASSIFICATION — and then submit your site to the search engines. I know Web designers who tell their clients that they are search engine experts, then follow nothing more than this procedure.

It's completely wrong for various reasons. Most meta tags aren't particularly important (see Chapter 6), or aren't used by the search engines at all. Without keywords in the page content, the search engines won't index what you need them to index. (See Chapters 6 and 7.) And submitting to search engines doesn't mean they will index your pages. (See Chapter 11.)

# Myth: Web Designers and Developers Understand Search Engines

I'm a geek. I've worked in software development for over 20 years; I still work closely with software developers (these days mostly Web-software developers); I build Web sites for my clients (so I work with developers and designers on these sites); my friends are developers and designers . . . and I'm telling you now that most developers and designers do *not* understand the search engines to any great degree.

Most Web-development companies these days tell their clients that they know how to handle the search engines, and even that they are experts. In most cases, that's simply not true, any more than it's true that I'm an expert in neurosurgery. This makes it very hard for business owners when they hire a Web-development team, of course, though perhaps this book will help. It will give you an idea of the sorts of questions you should ask your developers to figure out if they really *do* understand search engine requirements.

# Myth: Multiple Submissions Improve Your Search Position

As far as the major search engines go, multiple submissions, even automated submissions, don't help. Someone recently told me that he was sure it did help, because his position improved in, for instance, the Open Directory Project when he frequently resubmitted. This is completely wrong — in the case of the Open Directory Project, there's no way it could possibly help, as they don't accept automated submissions anyway, and all entries have to be reviewed by a human editor.

As you just read, *submitting* to the search engines — requesting that they index your pages — often doesn't get your page indexed anyway. Far more important is a link campaign to get plenty of links to your site; see Chapters 14 and 15. Multiple submissions to smaller search engines may help, it's true. But it won't help with the major systems.

# Mistake: You Don't Know Your Keywords

This is also a major problem — the vast majority of Web sites are created without the site owners or developers really knowing what keywords are important. (That's okay, perhaps, because most sites are built without any idea of using keywords in the content anyway.) At best, the keywords have been guessed. At worst — the majority of the cases — nobody's thought of the keywords at all.

Don't guess at your keywords. Do a proper keyword analysis. (See Chapter 5.) I can almost guarantee two things will happen. You will find that some of your guesses were wrong — people aren't often using some of the phrases you thought would be common. And you'll also discover very important phrases you had no idea about.

# Mistake: Too Many Pages with Database Parameters and Session IDs

This is a surprisingly common problem. Many, many sites (in particular sites built by big companies with large development teams) are created these days in such a manner that the search engines won't read them. Search engines don't like database parameters or session IDs in a URL. (See Chapter 7.)

My favorite example used to be CarToys.com, a large chain of electronics stores. This site had thousands of products, but fewer than 100 pages indexed by Google, and most of those were Adobe Acrobat files or pop-up ads ("Free Shipping!"), or links to dynamic pages that wouldn't appear when a searcher clicked a link in the search results. Luckily for CarToys.com, someone at the company figured it all out, and fixed the problem. Google now indexes over 27,000 pages on this site.

# Mistake: Building the Site and Then Bringing in the SEO Expert

Most companies approach search engine optimization as an afterthought. They build their Web site, and then think, "Right, time to get people to the site." You really shouldn't begin a site until you have considered all the different ways you are going to create traffic to the site. That's like starting to build a road without knowing where it needs to go; if you're not careful, you'll get halfway there and realize "there" is in another direction.

In particular, though, you shouldn't start building a Web site without an understanding of search engines. Most major Web sites these days are built by teams of developers who have little understanding of search engine issues. These sites are launched, and then someone decides to hire a search engine consultant. And the search engine consultant discovers all sorts of unnecessary problems. Good business for the consultant; expensive fixes for the site owner. In addition, Web developers usually don't enjoy working with search marketing experts. They think that all the search engine experts want to do is make the site ugly or remove the dynamism. This is furthest from the truth, and a Web developer who refuses to work with an SEO expert may just be worried for his or her job.

# Myth: $25 Can Get Your Site a #1 Position

There's a lot of background noise in the search engine business; companies claiming to be able to get your site into thousands of search engines, and rank your site well, for $25 a month . . . or a $50 flat fee . . . or $75 a month . . . or whatever.

The truth is that it's more complicated than that, and most people I've spoken to who have used such services have been very disappointed. They often don't get into the major search engines at all, and even if they get included in the index, they don't rank well. Search engine ranking is sometimes very easy — but other times it's complicated, time consuming, and tedious. Most of the offers you'll see streaming into your Inbox in spam e-mail messages, or displayed in banner ads on the Web, are not going to work.

# Myth: Google Partners Get You #1 Positions

If you receive a spam e-mail telling you that the sender has a "special arrangement" with Google and can get you a #1 position within hours or days, delete it . . . it's nonsense, a scam. It's true that you can buy a top position on Google through its AdWords PPC program (see Chapter 17), though you'll be bidding against your competitors. But this scam refers to something different, that Google has a special program that allows certain privileged companies to sell top positions in the organic-search results.

Don't believe it; it's nonsense.

# Myth: Bad Links to Your Site Will Hurt Its Position

Another common myth is that getting links to your site from "bad neighborhoods" such as link farms or Web sites unrelated to your site's theme will hurt your search engine position. This isn't exactly so. It won't help, but it won't hurt, either, unless it is obvious that you are actively interacting with link farms or *Free For All (FFA)* link pages.

If bad links did hurt your site, you could assassinate your competition by linking to their sites from every lousy link farm and FFA you could find. So the search engines can't use such links to downgrade your site.

# Mistake: Your Pages Are "Empty"

This one is a huge problem for many companies; the pages have nothing much for the search engines to index. In some cases, the pages have little or no text that a search engine can read because the words on the page are embedded into images. In other cases, all the words may be real text, but there are very few words . . . and what words there are, are not the right keywords.

Remember, search engines like — need — content. And to a search engine, *content* means text that it can read and index. And whenever you provide text to a search engine, it should be the text that does the most for you, text that will help you be found in the search results. And the more content, the better.

# Myth: Pay Per Click Is Where It's At

*Pay per click (PPC;* see Chapter 17) can be a very important part of a Web site's marketing strategy. It's reliable, predictable, and relatively easy to work with. But it's not the only thing you should be doing. In fact, many companies cannot use PPC because the clicks are too expensive for their particular business model (and click prices are likely to keep rising as search marketing continues to be the hot Internet marketing topic).

The growth in PPC has been partly caused by the lack of search engine optimization knowledge. Companies build a site without thinking about the search engines, and then don't hire professional expertise to help them get search engine traffic, so they fall back on PPC. Many companies are now spending hundreds of thousands of dollars on PPC; they could complement their PPC campaigns with natural search engine traffic for a small fraction of that cost.

The wonderful thing about PPC advertising and SEO is that the two work hand in hand. Want to know if a word is important enough to optimize for? Get a hundred clicks from your favorite search engine through PPC and look at the conversion rates and *return on investment (ROI)*. Want to expand your PPC keyword list? No problem, look at the words that people are already using to find you as a baseline, and grow your list from these words. (For example, if they are using *rodent racing* to find you, why don't you buy the words *mouse rodent racing, rat rodent racing,* and so on?) Many companies are using PPC profitably; just don't assume it's the only way to go.

# Chapter 20

# Ten-Plus Useful Tools

## In This Chapter

▶ Finding tools to help you check your site rank and traffic

▶ Analyzing the competition

▶ Seeing a site through a search engine's eyes

▶ Checking out some useful toolbars

*I*n this chapter, I describe a number of useful tools that you can employ in a variety of ways during a search engine optimization campaign, from finding out how well your site ranks in the search engines, to analyzing potential link partners, from seeing what a search engine sees, to seeing how people are arriving at your Web site.

## Checking Your Site Rank

How do you know how well your site ranks in the search engines? You can go to a search engine, type a keyword phrase, and see just what happens. If you're not on the first page, check the second; if you're not there, check the third. Then go back and do it for 50 search terms on several search engines. It's going to take a while.

Luckily there's help. Many programs will check your search engine position for you. You tell the program which keywords you're interested in, which search engines you want to check, and the Web site you're looking for in the search results, and leave it to do its work.

Note, however, that most search engines don't like these automated tools. In fact, Google even mentions one of the most popular of these tools, WebPosition (available at `www.webposition.com` and shown in Figure 20-1), as "unauthorized software." If Google notices a computer using one of these tools excessively, it may ban search queries from that computer . . . if it can identify the computer by *Internet protocol (IP)* number, that is.

The problem for Google is that computers accessing the Internet through many *Internet service providers (ISPs)* have different IP numbers each time they log on, making it impossible for Google to know which IP number to block. On the other hand, Google now provides a special *Application Programming Interface (API)* that programs such as WebPosition can use to send queries directly to Google, bypassing the search page. Such access *is* okay. (You can find information about the Google API at `www.google.com/apis`.)

You can see a typical keyword report, showing positions for each keyword in a large variety of different search engines — in this case produced by WebPosition — in Figure 20-2. Many other programs can create site-ranking reports for you — both programs installed on your computer and Web-based services, such as WebCEO (`www.webceo.com`) and SEO Reporter (`www.seoreporter.com`).

**Figure 20-1:** WebPosition, being set up to check a page's rank in the search engines.

**Figure 20-2:**
A page-rank
report
generated
by Web-
Position.

# Checking for Broken Links

Link checkers are always handy, whether you're interested in optimizing your site for the search engines or not. After you've created a few pages, you should run a link check to make sure you didn't make any mistakes in your links.

Again, many, many link checkers are available, including paid services such as LinkAlarm (`linkalarm.com`), that will automatically check links on your site and send you a report. I'm currently using a little Windows program called Xenu's Link Sleuth, as shown in Figure 20-3 (`home.snafu.de/tilman/xenulink.html`). It's free, which is always nice! (The creator of Link Sleuth requests that if you like the program, support some of his favorite causes.) This program is very quick — it can check tens of thousands of links in a few minutes — and it's very easy to use. It produces a report, displayed in your Web browser, showing the pages containing broken links; click a link, and it opens the page so you can take a look. You can use the program to check both internal and external links on your site.

Note also that your Web design software package may include a built-in link checker.

# Google Toolbar

The Google toolbar (`toolbar.google.com`) is a great little tool. I mainly use it for two purposes:

- Searching Google without having to go to the Google site first
- Seeing if a Web page is in Google's cache, as discussed in Chapter 1. To see the cache, click the i button and then click Cached Snapshot of Page.

But it contains a number of other neat tools:

- The ability to quickly search Google Maps. Click the Autolink button; the toolbar searches the current page for a street address, and converts it to a link that will open the appropriate map on Google Maps.
- PageRank indicator. Discussed in Chapter 14, PageRank can be useful when evaluating a potential link partner

✔ Pop-up blocker.

✔ A way to search Google for pages similar to the one you're viewing.

The toolbar has all sorts of other useful things.

# Google Zeitgeist

Google Zeitgeist (`www.google.com/press/zeitgeist.html`) is worth perusing now and then, particularly if you are looking for an online business and want to know the types of things people search for or to see how current events affect searches. Google Zeitgeist is an analysis of what people are searching for, when, and where. You can find the most popular brand-name searches, charts showing how searches peak for particular keywords during news events or in response to TV shows (Iraq, SARS, and so on), the most popular searches for particular men, women, and fictional characters, the most popular movie searches in Australia, the most popular brands in Italy, and so on; see Figure 20-4. This is a wealth of information that can give you a feel for what people are really searching for. (Did you know the number of searches for recipes jumps dramatically in October and November? Or that in France, the TV reality show *Greg le Millionaire* got only a fraction of the searches for *Star Academy?*)

There are other, similar tools:

✔ Wordtracker, for instance, will periodically send you a free report of the top 500 searches (with or without sexually explicit terms).

✔ Ask Jeeves has a service that shows you the top *advancing* search terms — the ones that are growing most quickly (`sp.ask.com/docs/about/jeevesiq.html`).

✔ Yahoo! Buzz (`buzz.yahoo.com`) can be interesting, too.

✔ Lycos 50 is published weekly by Aaron Schatz at `50.lycos.com`. The interesting thing about the Lycos 50 is that Aaron uses it to predict what will be hot or not.

What I find depressing about these lists is just how obsessed people are with celebrities! Just why do people care so much about Paris Hilton, Damon Albarn, or Angelina Jolie? (And who *is* Damon Albarn, anyway?)

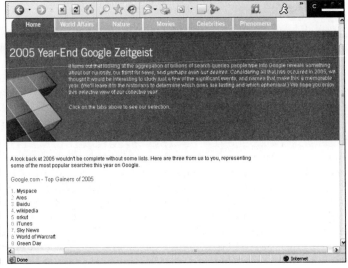

# Alexa Toolbar

The Alexa toolbar (download.alexa.com) can be handy, too. I sometimes use it to assess the traffic of Web sites I may want to work with. For instance, if someone approaches you trying to sell advertising space on their site, how do you know if it's a good deal? So many sites get almost no traffic, that it may not be worth the expense.

The Alexa toolbar can give you a very general idea of whether the site gets any traffic at all; you can view traffic details for the site, such as the traffic rank, an estimate of the number of visitors to the site out of every million Internet users, and so on. Reportedly, Alexa's numbers are pretty good for the world's most popular sites, but rather inaccurate for the average site. However, you can still get a general feel. If the site is ranked 4,000,000, you can bet it doesn't get much traffic at all. If the site is ranked 4,000, it's far more popular.

Alexa also provides a list of the most popular sites in thousands of categories, a good way to track down affiliates, for instance, or link partners. And it has an interesting search function; use the Alexa toolbar to search Google, and you'll get different results. Sites are ranked differently, though the data comes from Google, and you'll also get small images of the home page of the top few sites. And point at the Site Info link to see site information such as how long the site has been online, the number of sites linking to it, similar sites, and so on.

# Finding Links

Being able to produce a list of pages linking back to a Web site is extremely useful (and a great way to impress a boss or client). I use a link-analysis tool, SEO Elite, generally to find out how many links are pointing to a client's site in comparison with competitors' sites, and also to find out who in particular is linking to competitors — a good start in a link campaign. This tool, shown in Figure 20-5, lets me view the link pages in the program itself, though it will also export to an Excel spreadsheet for further manipulation.

**Figure 20-5:**
Link-survey
results
shown in
SEO Elite.

# Seeing What the Search Engines See

I admit I don't often use this type of tool, but it's interesting now and then. Some utilities will read a Web page and display the content of the page in the manner in which a search engine is likely to see it; see Figure 20-6. When looking at a competitor's pages, you can sometimes see things that aren't visible to the site visitor but that have been placed on the page for the benefit of the search engines. When viewing your pages, you may want to check that all the links are readable by the search engines. These tools generally provide a list of readable links.

Here are a couple of these utilities:

- ✔ **Sim Spider:** `www.searchengineworld.com/cgi-bin/sim_spider.cgi`

- ✔ **Delorie:** `www.delorie.com/web/ses.cgi`

You can also search for terms such as **search engine simulator** or **searchbot simulator**.

Another great way to check a site is to use a text-mode browser, such as Lynx, to visit your site. If your site can't be seen in Lynx, it will have problems ranking in any search engine. You can find a Lynx simulator at `www.delorie.com/web/lynxview.html`.

**Figure 20-6:** The results from Search Engine World's Sim Spider.

# Finding Your Keyword Density

As I explain in Chapter 5, you don't need to get too hung up on keyword density. You can analyze to the *n*th degree, and everyone has a different opinion as to exactly what the density should be. But it's sometimes interesting to check your pages for keyword density, and many tools are available to help you do so. WebPosition, mentioned earlier in this chapter, has a built-in density tool, and you can find various online tools, as well, such as the following:

- ✔ **Search Engine World's Keyword Density Analyzer:** www.search engineworld.com/cgi-bin/kwda.cgi

- ✔ **KeywordDensity.com:** www.keyworddensity.com

# Analyzing Your Site's Traffic

You really should track traffic going to your site. At the end of the day, your search engine position isn't terribly important — it's just a means to an end. What really counts is the amount of traffic coming to your site. And it's important to know *how* people get to your site, too.

There are two types of traffic-analysis tools: those that read server logs, and those that tag your Web pages and track traffic using a program on another server. In the first case, the tool analyzes log files created by the Web server — the server adds information each time it receives a request for a file. In order to use the tag systems, you have to add a little piece of code to your Web pages — each time a page from your site is requested, the program is, in effect, informed of the fact.

You quite likely have a traffic-analysis tool already installed on your site — ask your server administrator how to view your logs. Otherwise, you can use a tag-based traffic-analysis tool; in general, you'll have to pay a monthly fee for such a service.

Analysis tools show you all sorts of interesting and often useless information. But perhaps the most important things you can find are

- ✔ Which sites are sending visitors to your site?
- ✔ Which search engines are sending visitors to your site?
- ✔ What keywords are people using to reach your site?

You may find that people are reaching you with keywords you hadn't thought of, or perhaps unusual combinations of keywords that you hadn't imagined. This doesn't replace a real keyword analysis, though, as you'll only see the keywords used by people who found you, not the keywords used by people who *didn't* find you but were looking for products or services like yours. See Chapter 5 for more information about keywords.

Unfortunately, most traffic-analysis tools are really not very good. Some don't provide much information, but the ones that do provide a lot of information are often way too complex and confusing. One log-based system I really like is ClickTracks (`www.clicktracks.com`). ClickTracks, shown in Figure 20-7, was created by someone who worked for one of the top log tools companies, but who felt the popular tools just throw statistics at people, instead of providing useful, easy-to-understand information. This is a very cool tool that uses tables and images of your Web site to make understanding your logs very easy. ClickTracks also has a tag-based tool that you can use for a monthly fee.

The big news in traffic analysis, though, is Google Analytics. Google purchased one of the top traffic-analysis firms, Urchin, then started *giving away* traffic-analysis accounts. At the time of writing Google isn't allowing new account sign ups — they were so swamped with applications that they couldn't keep up — but by the time you read this you may be able to use the system. Visit `analytics.google.com`.

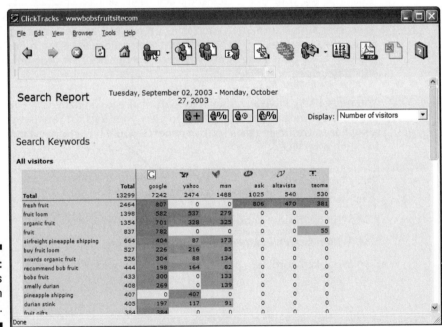

**Figure 20-7:** Log analysis from ClickTracks.

# Checking for Duplication and Theft

Copyscape (www.copyscape.com) is an interesting tool that lets you see if anyone has stolen your site content, and to see how closely your content matches other sites; for instance, if you are quoting documents or using syndicated content, the less duplication the better. The concern is that search engines may downgrade pages that they know duplicate other pages, so you don't want your pages to match others too closely.

Enter a URL into Copyscape, and it searches for pages that match the page referenced by the URL, to varying degrees. Copyscape returns the results, and when you click the links you'll see the page with the matching text colored, and, at the top, a Copyscape banner telling you how many words match: 1,803 words, 1,232 words, 83 words, and so on. An interesting little toy; experiment and see.

# More Tools

If you're looking for more tools, try these sites:

- ✔ **Search Engine World:** www.searchengineworld.com/misc/tools.htm
- ✔ **SEO Help:** www.seo-help.com/seo-reference/seo-resources.html
- ✔ **Webconfs.com:** www.webconfs.com
- ✔ **Pandia SEO:** www.pandia.com/optimization

# Don't Forget the Search Engines

Don't forget that you can find just about anything through the search engines themselves. If you have some kind of tedious procedure to work through, chances are someone has built a program to automate the procedure. So head to your favorite search engine and spend a little time tracking it down!

# Appendix

# Staying Out of Copyright Jail

● ● ● ● ● ● ● ● ● ● ● ● ● ● ● ● ● ● ● ● ● ● ● ● ● ● ● ● ● ● ● ● ● ● ● ● ● ● ● ● ● ● ● ● ● ● ● ● ● ●

*I*n Chapter 9, I describe several sources of content for your Web site. Because you can get into trouble if you take *copyrighted* materials without permission, I feel it's important to cover a few copyright basics.

Many people think that they're allowed to take and use pretty much anything they find, especially if it can be found on the Internet. Search for *usa today,* for instance, and you'll discover thousands of sites that have copied articles from that newspaper. Although you *can* do this and *may* get away with it, you should be aware that you *don't* have the right to do this. It is, to put it bluntly, plagiarism. It's illegal, and the owner of the material has the right to sue you. Whether it's text, images, sounds, or whatever — if someone else created it, you don't own it!

I summarize copyright law in Chapter 9, and this appendix goes into a little more detail about the four exceptions I describe:

- ✔ If it's really old, you can use it.
- ✔ If the guvmint created it, you can use it.
- ✔ If it's "donated," you can use it.
- ✔ It's only fair — *fair use* explained.

## If It's Really Old, You Can Use It

In some cases in which you find old works that would be appropriate for your site, you can simply take content and do what you want with it. In the old days, copyrights didn't last very long — a real contrast with the situation today.

*Copyright* is currently intended to allow the creator to profit from a work, and his worthless children to live a life of drunkenness and unmerited indolence. (Luckily for my kids, computer books have a very short life.) For works created after January 1, 1978, . . . well, you can forget the details for them because you probably won't be alive when copyright expires on such works. (I will. Having done research for a book I'm going to call *Live Forever or Die Trying*, I've learned a few tricks.) Let me just say, by way of example, that the copyright on a work created on January 1, 1978, by a 19-year-old writer who manages to live to 89, will expire in the year 2118. (No, that's not a joke.)

The situation for works created before 1978 gets complicated because the law kept changing and seems to have been intended to confuse. I'm not going to go into details — it makes my head hurt just to think about. It all depends on whether you are Uruguayan, are quick on your toes, were 28 on January 1, 1964, and have a Swiss-born mother. However . . .

Anything copyrighted — and by that I mean either published or registered with the U.S. Copyright Office — *after January 1, 1964,* is out of bounds for the foreseeable future (at least until 2059).

Works copyrighted *between 1923 (at the time of writing, in 2006) and December 31, 1963,* may have lost copyright protection, depending on whether the copyright holder renewed it. (In those days, works had to be registered with the U.S. Copyright Office and renewed to get the full term of protection; Registration, at any point, is no longer necessary.) If it was renewed, the work may still be protected. Thus *most* works published between these dates have actually lost copyright protection, renewals being relatively rare. The problem is figuring out *which* works.

If you really want to use a particular work, you can figure all this out. You need to contact the Copyright Office to see if the work was renewed, though unfortunately this means you have to do the work yourself at its offices in Washington, D.C., or pay $75 per hour for a manual search. (See www. copyright.gov for more information.)

Works copyrighted *before 1923* are not copyright protected anymore. You can take 'em and use 'em for whatever you want.

Does this help you? If you have a site selling cellphones, it almost certainly does not help you. If you have a site related to Victorian poetry, travelogues, or herbal medicine, it may be useful. (I have a friend who republishes old school books, many of which are now copyright free.)

This is a very quick rundown of copyright law, which should be sufficient for most people's purposes. However, there are many details I haven't covered — titles, short phrases, and slogans can't be copyrighted, for instance. (Be careful, though — a title can be *trademarked*. Just try publishing a book with *For Dummies* in the title and see what happens!) For the full details, visit the U.S. Copyright Office Web site: www.copyright.gov. And www.unc.edu/~unclng/public-d.htm condenses all this complexity into a simple little chart.

Before I move on, a word of warning: Be careful before you take something you think is old enough to be out of copyright. Make sure you're using a copy of the original, not a modified version, because those modifications may be protected! You can freely copy and use Charles Dickens' *Great Expectations,* but if someone has taken the original, edited it, and added notes, you can't use that. Nor can you use a version that has been translated in recent years, because the translation will be copyrighted.

# If the Guvmint Created It, You Can Use It

This is a good example of your tax dollars at work. The U.S. government spends many millions of dollars creating *content.* This content is not copyright protected. Thus you can take the full text of a government report and publish it on your Web site. Yep, that's right. As amazing as it may seem, you can take, for instance, all the tax forms and instructions you want, or videos created by the EPA, and post them on your site.

However, some rare exceptions exist. A government department may hold donated materials that were originally copyright protected, and continue to hold the copyright. It may commission a private individual or company to create a work or publish the work under another arrangement, and that person or company may hold the copyright. And works created by the National Technical Information Service or the United States Postal Service may be copyright protected.

# If It's "Donated," You Can Use It

Sometimes people simply give away their work — they "donate" it in one of two ways. In some cases, a work may be given to the *public domain,* which means the author relinquishes all rights to the work. In other cases, the author may simply allow the use of the work, but retain copyright. For instance, sometimes you see statements such as the one on the copyright chart at www.unc.edu/~unclng/public-d.htm:

> *Chart may be freely duplicated or linked to for nonprofit purposes. No permission needed. Please include Web address on all reproductions of chart so recipients know where to find any updates.*

The author has allowed anyone to use the chart under certain conditions: The use must be nonprofit (although this term is rather ambiguous, you can assume that at the very least it means you can't print the chart and sell it), and the address of the original chart should be included.

# It's Only Fair — Fair Use Explained

You can copy parts of a copyrighted work and use them on your site, under an exclusion known as *fair use*. The only problem with fair use is that one man's fair use is another man's plagiarism. In other words, there are no hard and fast rules as to what *fair use* means.

I'm not going to explain this. In fact, I'm going to take some copyright-free text directly off the U.S. Copyright Office Web site and save myself a few moments:

> *Under the fair use doctrine of the U.S. copyright statute, it is permissible to use limited portions of a work including quotes, for purposes such as commentary, criticism, news reporting, and scholarly reports. There are no legal rules permitting the use of a specific number of words, a certain number of musical notes, or percentage of a work. Whether a particular use qualifies as fair use depends on all the circumstances. See FL 102, Fair Use, and Circular 21, Reproductions of Copyrighted Works by Educators and Librarians.*

The fair use exception isn't, in most cases, terribly useful for most people, because you can't just take huge gobs of the work and drop them into your site. However, you can weave quotes from copyrighted works (make sure that you properly cite your sources) into original material you've written.

# Index

## • H •

# SINESS, CAREERS & PERSONAL FINANCE

0-7645-5307-0

0-7645-5331-3 *†

**Also available:**

- Accounting For Dummies †
  0-7645-5314-3
- Business Plans Kit For Dummies †
  0-7645-5365-8
- Cover Letters For Dummies
  0-7645-5224-4
- Frugal Living For Dummies
  0-7645-5403-4
- Leadership For Dummies
  0-7645-5176-0
- Managing For Dummies
  0-7645-1771-6

- Marketing For Dummies
  0-7645-5600-2
- Personal Finance For Dummies *
  0-7645-2590-5
- Project Management For Dummies
  0-7645-5283-X
- Resumes For Dummies †
  0-7645-5471-9
- Selling For Dummies
  0-7645-5363-1
- Small Business Kit For Dummies *†
  0-7645-5093-4

# ME & BUSINESS COMPUTER BASICS

0-7645-4074-2

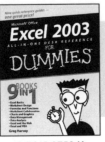

0-7645-3758-X

**Also available:**

- ACT! 6 For Dummies
  0-7645-2645-6
- iLife '04 All-in-One Desk Reference
  For Dummies
  0-7645-7347-0
- iPAQ For Dummies
  0-7645-6769-1
- Mac OS X Panther Timesaving
  Techniques For Dummies
  0-7645-5812-9
- Macs For Dummies
  0-7645-5656-8

- Microsoft Money 2004 For Dummies
  0-7645-4195-1
- Office 2003 All-in-One Desk Reference
  For Dummies
  0-7645-3883-7
- Outlook 2003 For Dummies
  0-7645-3759-8
- PCs For Dummies
  0-7645-4074-2
- TiVo For Dummies
  0-7645-6923-6
- Upgrading and Fixing PCs For Dummies
  0-7645-1665-5
- Windows XP Timesaving Techniques
  For Dummies
  0-7645-3748-2

# OD, HOME, GARDEN, HOBBIES, MUSIC & PETS

0-7645-5295-3

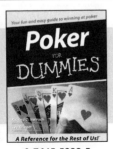

0-7645-5232-5

**Also available:**

- Bass Guitar For Dummies
  0-7645-2487-9
- Diabetes Cookbook For Dummies
  0-7645-5230-9
- Gardening For Dummies *
  0-7645-5130-2
- Guitar For Dummies
  0-7645-5106-X
- Holiday Decorating For Dummies
  0-7645-2570-0
- Home Improvement All-in-One
  For Dummies
  0-7645-5680-0

- Knitting For Dummies
  0-7645-5395-X
- Piano For Dummies
  0-7645-5105-1
- Puppies For Dummies
  0-7645-5255-4
- Scrapbooking For Dummies
  0-7645-7208-3
- Senior Dogs For Dummies
  0-7645-5818-8
- Singing For Dummies
  0-7645-2475-5
- 30-Minute Meals For Dummies
  0-7645-2589-1

# NTERNET & DIGITAL MEDIA

0-7645-1664-7

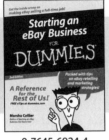

0-7645-6924-4

**Also available:**

- 2005 Online Shopping Directory
  For Dummies
  0-7645-7495-7
- CD & DVD Recording For Dummies
  0-7645-5956-7
- eBay For Dummies
  0-7645-5654-1
- Fighting Spam For Dummies
  0-7645-5965-6
- Genealogy Online For Dummies
  0-7645-5964-8
- Google For Dummies
  0-7645-4420-9

- Home Recording For Musicians
  For Dummies
  0-7645-1634-5
- The Internet For Dummies
  0-7645-4173-0
- iPod & iTunes For Dummies
  0-7645-7772-7
- Preventing Identity Theft For Dummies
  0-7645-7336-5
- Pro Tools All-in-One Desk Reference
  For Dummies
  0-7645-5714-9
- Roxio Easy Media Creator For Dummies
  0-7645-7131-1

## SPORTS, FITNESS, PARENTING, RELIGION & SPIRITUALITY

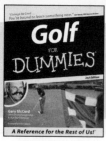

0-7645-5146-9

0-7645-5418-2

**Also available:**
- Adoption For Dummies
  0-7645-5488-3
- Basketball For Dummies
  0-7645-5248-1
- The Bible For Dummies
  0-7645-5296-1
- Buddhism For Dummies
  0-7645-5359-3
- Catholicism For Dummies
  0-7645-5391-7
- Hockey For Dummies
  0-7645-5228-7

- Judaism For Dummies
  0-7645-5299-6
- Martial Arts For Dummies
  0-7645-5358-5
- Pilates For Dummies
  0-7645-5397-6
- Religion For Dummies
  0-7645-5264-3
- Teaching Kids to Read For Dummies
  0-7645-4043-2
- Weight Training For Dummies
  0-7645-5168-X
- Yoga For Dummies
  0-7645-5117-5

## TRAVEL

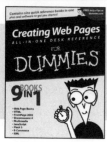

0-7645-5438-7

0-7645-5453-0

**Also available:**
- Alaska For Dummies
  0-7645-1761-9
- Arizona For Dummies
  0-7645-6938-4
- Cancún and the Yucatán For Dummies
  0-7645-2437-2
- Cruise Vacations For Dummies
  0-7645-6941-4
- Europe For Dummies
  0-7645-5456-5
- Ireland For Dummies
  0-7645-5455-7

- Las Vegas For Dummies
  0-7645-5448-4
- London For Dummies
  0-7645-4277-X
- New York City For Dummies
  0-7645-6945-7
- Paris For Dummies
  0-7645-5494-8
- RV Vacations For Dummies
  0-7645-5443-3
- Walt Disney World & Orlando For Dummies
  0-7645-6943-0

## GRAPHICS, DESIGN & WEB DEVELOPMENT

0-7645-4345-8

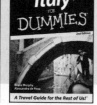

0-7645-5589-8

**Also available:**
- Adobe Acrobat 6 PDF For Dummies
  0-7645-3760-1
- Building a Web Site For Dummies
  0-7645-7144-3
- Dreamweaver MX 2004 For Dummies
  0-7645-4342-3
- FrontPage 2003 For Dummies
  0-7645-3882-9
- HTML 4 For Dummies
  0-7645-1995-6
- Illustrator CS For Dummies
  0-7645-4084-X

- Macromedia Flash MX 2004 For Dummies
  0-7645-4358-X
- Photoshop 7 All-in-One Desk Reference For Dummies
  0-7645-1667-1
- Photoshop CS Timesaving Techniques For Dummies
  0-7645-6782-9
- PHP 5 For Dummies
  0-7645-4166-8
- PowerPoint 2003 For Dummies
  0-7645-3908-6
- QuarkXPress 6 For Dummies
  0-7645-2593-X

## NETWORKING, SECURITY, PROGRAMMING & DATABASES

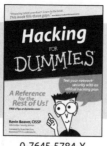

0-7645-6852-3

0-7645-5784-X

**Also available:**
- A+ Certification For Dummies
  0-7645-4187-0
- Access 2003 All-in-One Desk Reference For Dummies
  0-7645-3988-4
- Beginning Programming For Dummies
  0-7645-4997-9
- C For Dummies
  0-7645-7068-4
- Firewalls For Dummies
  0-7645-4048-3
- Home Networking For Dummies
  0-7645-42796

- Network Security For Dummies
  0-7645-1679-5
- Networking For Dummies
  0-7645-1677-9
- TCP/IP For Dummies
  0-7645-1760-0
- VBA For Dummies
  0-7645-3989-2
- Wireless All In-One Desk Reference For Dummies
  0-7645-7496-5
- Wireless Home Networking For Dummies
  0-7645-3910-8

## ALTH & SELF-HELP

0-7645-6820-5 *†

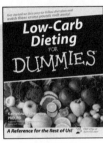

0-7645-2566-2

**Also available:**
- Alzheimer's For Dummies
  0-7645-3899-3
- Asthma For Dummies
  0-7645-4233-8
- Controlling Cholesterol For Dummies
  0-7645-5440-9
- Depression For Dummies
  0-7645-3900-0
- Dieting For Dummies
  0-7645-4149-8
- Fertility For Dummies
  0-7645-2549-2

- Fibromyalgia For Dummies
  0-7645-5441-7
- Improving Your Memory For Dummies
  0-7645-5435-2
- Pregnancy For Dummies †
  0-7645-4483-7
- Quitting Smoking For Dummies
  0-7645-2629-4
- Relationships For Dummies
  0-7645-5384-4
- Thyroid For Dummies
  0-7645-5385-2

## UCATION, HISTORY, REFERENCE & TEST PREPARATION

0-7645-5194-9

0-7645-4186-2

**Also available:**
- Algebra For Dummies
  0-7645-5325-9
- British History For Dummies
  0-7645-7021-8
- Calculus For Dummies
  0-7645-2498-4
- English Grammar For Dummies
  0-7645-5322-4
- Forensics For Dummies
  0-7645-5580-4
- The GMAT For Dummies
  0-7645-5251-1
- Inglés Para Dummies
  0-7645-5427-1

- Italian For Dummies
  0-7645-5196-5
- Latin For Dummies
  0-7645-5431-X
- Lewis & Clark For Dummies
  0-7645-2545-X
- Research Papers For Dummies
  0-7645-5426-3
- The SAT I For Dummies
  0-7645-7193-1
- Science Fair Projects For Dummies
  0-7645-5460-3
- U.S. History For Dummies
  0-7645-5249-X

# Get smart @ dummies.com®

- **Find a full list of Dummies titles**
- **Look into loads of FREE on-site articles**
- **Sign up for FREE eTips e-mailed to you weekly**
- **See what other products carry the Dummies name**
- **Shop directly from the Dummies bookstore**
- **Enter to win new prizes every month!**

Separate Canadian edition also available
Separate U.K. edition also available

available wherever books are sold. For more information or to order direct: U.S. customers visit www.dummies.com or call 1-877-762-2974.
K. customers visit www.wileyeurope.com or call 0800 243407. Canadian customers visit www.wiley.ca or call 1-800-567-4797.